Provoking the Gospel of Mark

Provoking the Gospel of Mark

A STORYTELLER'S COMMENTARY
YEAR B

Richard W. Swanson

For my mother and father,
who raised me to love stories
and taught me to ask hard questions,
Vera Swanson
and
Heimer Swanson

The Pilgrim Press
700 Prospect Avenue
Cleveland, Ohio 44115-1100
thepilgrimpress.com

Printed in the United States of America on acid-free paper

09 08 07 06 05   5 4 3 2 1

Library of Congress Cataloging-in-Publication Data

Swanson, Richard W., 1952-
Provoking the Gospel of Mark : a storyteller's commentary, year B / Richard W. Swanson.
p. cm.
Includes bibliographical references.
ISBN 0-8298-1690-9 (pbk. : alk. paper)
1. Bible. N.T. Mark – Criticism, Narrative. 2. Storytelling – Religious aspects – Christianity. 3. Common lectionary (1992). Year B. I. Title.
BS2585.52.S93 2005
226.3′077 – dc22

2005049298

Contents

Preface

WRESTLING AND RISKING

The longer I work with biblical stories, the more it is clear to me that these old stories are not drowsy old house pets that stretch themselves and then go back to sleep on your lap. These stories are lively, even wild, and they challenge anyone who encounters them to share their wild freedom. They are not tame. Not one of them is housebroken. All of them challenge us, and they respond best when we challenge them in return. In fact, the stronger the challenge, the stronger the story becomes. I have been wrestling with these stories for years, as hard as I can. My guess is that I haven't seen a quarter of their strength, not a quarter of their vigorous life. I cannot wait to learn to challenge the stories better. This book hands you some reflections, some connections, some provocations, and a translation. I hope it will help you in your wrestling.

This book grabs Mark's gospel any way it can be grabbed. Part of its wrestling is historical. The era out of which these stories come presented the challenges that shaped the stories as they developed. Study of that era and its challenges helps interpreters make sense of what the rules of engagement were when these stories were first contested.

Part of the wrestling in this book is literary. The stories grow out of oral storytelling, but they come to us as inscribed texts out of a complicated process of scripting and inscribing and rescripting.

After the whole tangled process of telling and retelling, writing and rewriting, writing and retelling and rewriting and retelling, what we have are texts, literary documents, narratives that can be read with all the tools developed for critical reading of novels. The things we have learned about wrestling with inscribed text — how an unreliable narrator shapes a story, how structural patterns determine the interactions between characters in a novel, how readers and texts struggle together in the creation of textual meaning — all these things will help us wrestle with these old stories as well. They are surely different from contemporary novels, but some of the rules of engagement are the same, or at least yield productive and provocative results.

A major part of the wrestling in this book is ethnopoetic. We have learned a great deal about the ways culture and oral "literature" shape each other. The Kumolipo, the only surviving Hawaiian origin story, was preserved and translated in an effort to resist foreign domination and to argue (beneath the radar of the colonizers) that the dynasty established by David Kalakaua shared genealogy and legitimacy with ancient traditional rulers of the nation. The story was told, the chant was performed, and the world was preserved, at least for a while. The things we have learned give us glimpses of the oral/aural world that gave birth to the gospels. The formed texts show traces of that oral/aural life and offer us hints of how these old stories made their way in ancient society. These hints suggest that these old stories ought to be explored by contemporary performance if we are to discover their full richness and life. These new performances will not exactly replicate ancient performances any more than ancient performances slavishly copied each other. The study of ethnopoetics makes it clear that improvisation is essential to the life and growth of oral/aural narratives. To that end, the reflections, connections, and provocations offered in this book are chosen and shaped to give glimpses of ancient oral performance, to share the results of contemporary performance of these stories, and to provoke your own improvisatory exploration of these old stories.

My translation of the gospel (pp. 255–333) is shaped by these intentions. It is experimental. For one thing, the story is presented in broken lines that hop back and forth on the page. This way of putting text on the page (which resembles the ethnopoetic notation used by John Miles Foley) attempts to honor the rhythms of the ancient Greek text. Greek and English are very different languages, and rhythm is only one of the differences. Greek is a language that manages foreshadowing and suspense better than does standard English, which makes for wonderful surprises even in the telling of simple stories. I have tried to render some of this agility in my English version, and the use of broken lines on the page is part of that attempt. Beyond that, Mark is a story that takes some stunning risks in the way it presents itself. I have tried to honor those risks by taking chances also in my translation. I repeat: the translation is experimental. I have not aimed to run my translation right down the center of the highway. Sometimes there are good things to be found in the ditch.

In my translation, I have attempted to honor the rhythms, the surprises, and the risks that make the gospel of Mark such a fascinating story. Have I succeeded? Sometimes. I work with a team of storytellers. Together we explore and perform biblical stories. But before we perform, we work together to remove what we call "translational abominations" from every script we develop. The translation later in this book has gone through several processes of "de-abominizing," but that does not mean that you will not find things that you will want to change. Change them! Try to figure out why the oddities exist, but make any alterations you find necessary. But remember, Mark takes risks. This is a model for interpreters to follow. Please do not simply make the words behave themselves. Please do not attempt to housebreak these stories. They are more interesting in the wild.

This book will support you if you want to study the gospel of Mark, or teach it, or preach on it; it will help you even more if you want to learn to perform Mark's story. Perhaps you will tell single episodes from Mark by yourself; the book will help. Or maybe you will tell single episodes with an ensemble; there too the book will help. And if you want to weave several episodes together and perform them, either in an ensemble or alone, or even if you will perform the entire story, this book will also help you as you study this old and fascinating story.

This is a storyteller's commentary, and as such it attempts always to weave story with story, text with context, and interpreter with performer with audience. Such weaving involves some risks, and this commentary takes them, but the risks taken in this book are nothing next to the risks taken by the storytellers whose work created the story that Mark tells. Those risks are so much greater than interpreters normally take that it takes your breath away. This book and this approach to Mark's story honor those ancient risks and aim to discover them anew.

Physical embodiment of the story is the best tool I've found for honoring these old stories. Working with an ensemble gives you perspectives you would not have otherwise, and creates an environment of responsibility. When you work with text this way, people see things, or hear them, sometimes things that no one has seen or heard before. I think this happens because space is governed by physics, not ideology. A smooth baritone voice will not cover a physical offense. An audience will not miss an embodied lie.

These are the stories of Israel. Anything that provokes honest wrestling will introduce you to the heart of the story, the heart of Scripture, the heart of the faith. Perhaps even more important: anything that provokes honest wrestling will introduce you to a public audience who will help you read these good old stories. You should not imagine that you will read these stories the same old way, or that you will be delivering a truckload of evangelism when you play these old stories for a public audience. The experience will change you and the audience. It is my conviction that the exercise of public performance will reveal the true character of the stories. They are not tools in anybody's hands. These old stories are not things that can be picked up or put down. The image is simply wrong from the start. These old stories are provocations to wrestling. They do not deliver packaged answers to questions so much as they encourage performers and audiences to ask better questions. They do not settle arguments so much as they draw performers and audiences into the arguments that are really worth having. And in those arguments they do not allow anyone to assert the single correct answer. These old stories, when engaged with integrity, equip their readers, performers, and hearers to wrestle afresh with issues that people of faith (Christian and otherwise) must engage today.

It is my settled conviction that these old stories present to us intimations of the labor that gave birth to the Christian faith. Even more important, these old stories model for us the wrestling that has always been at the heart of the people of God. For Gentile Christians living in a moment that requires honest struggle against imposed ideology, this is a great gift. The gift is given us by the Jewish grandmothers and grandfathers, by the old ones who knew the most stories and thus had the solidity needed to preserve the people in the midst of disaster. Jewish storytellers argued with each other, argued with their stories, argued with their tradition, argued with people in power (inside the faith and outside), argued even (and most ferociously) with their God. To receive their gift with proper gratitude, we must honor the stories, learn the stories, embody the stories, and practice taking the risks that these old storytellers took. This book, and the practice of provocative interpretation it grows out of, are offered in gratitude and hope: in gratitude to those old fearless storytellers who struggled for life and humanity on the field of these old stories, and in hope that contemporary people of faith will apprentice themselves to this same struggle. May you learn to wrestle like Israel.

•

In my own apprenticeship I have had many companions and teachers. I have had the privilege of working for many years with a growing team of storytellers: Melissa Larsen, Erika Iverson, Michael T. Smith, Brooke Baker, Kristin Barnett, Kira Christensen, Jason Dybsetter, Katie Fick, Jennie Graves, Sandra Looney, Amanda

Mitchell, Desiré Kelly, Kerri Smith, Meghan Swanson, Mandy Youngers, Kristin Zingler. These have been my students and my teachers throughout our shared work. They have been a gift from God. I would like also to thank the trustees of the Clara Lea Olson Endowment who provided funding that has made some of our experiments possible.

Above all, I would like to thank my parents, Heimer and Vera Swanson. They fed me on stories as surely as they fed me food. With them I discovered how easy it is to love stories, and what a delight it is to ask hard questions about them. I thank them for the stories, for the questions, and for their patience as I asked the questions.

Introduction

WHAT DOES A STORYTELLER NEED?

> *"Any story worth its salt can stand a little shaking up."*
>
> —Butt the Hoopoe, in *Haroun and the Sea of Stories* by Salman Rushdie

What does a storyteller need?

A story, surely. An audience, obviously, and time to spend with them. An occasion, at least mostly, since most storytelling springs from specific situations and not simply out of the blue.

But you can have all of that and still not have a story that lives and breathes and walks around. What could make a story do that? I have been reading the work of John D. Niles, a scholar who studies Scottish storytellers and singers. Lizzie Higgins, a singer and a storyteller, was particularly fascinating. The extra thing that was necessary, she said, was the "maysie," that power (she linked it with the notion of a muse) that allows singers and storytellers to a-muse and a-maze audiences. The maysie sparks songs and stories, spins their performance out of the ordinary into something that, as Niles describes it, "takes the form of a sort of chill. There are shivers at the spine, and the small hairs on your body start to rise and move."[1]

When I read Niles's words about the effect of the maysie, I hear something that I recognize. I hear something that I have encountered with my troupe of storytellers: the shiver, the chill, the sense that something big just came into the room. Such moments are beyond easy description, which makes me grateful to Ms. Higgins for the gift of a word to name something I need to tell you about, but otherwise could not. Muses and maysies are notoriously uncontrollable, but if there is such a thing as the maysie, in our work it arrives in response to provocation.

That is what this book seeks to offer: not the maysie itself, but a glimpse of the provocations that might just bring the maysie into the room when you work with a biblical story. These provocations are sometimes exceedingly ordinary, in and of themselves: an exercise, a rag of a backstory, a disruptive story to cross-read with the biblical episode at hand. What is not ordinary is the result of bringing these provocations together with old, familiar biblical stories. It might just be the maysie.

But I am getting ahead of myself. The question before us asks what a storyteller needs.

A Storyteller Needs a Story

The first thing a storyteller needs is a story. There are plenty to be had since human beings are unstoppable storytellers. Some of the stories we tell are simple everyday stories, and some are stories that do not fit into any known world. We tell all kinds. And then there are the stories in the Bible, particularly the gospels, particularly the gospel of Mark, the focus of this book. This very old, very strong story has been told and ignored for centuries.

Mark's story was ignored because it was perceived in the ancient world to be fragmented and ill-formed. You can hear this judgment already in Papias, that ancient describer of the gospels who judged that the gospel was so disorderly because Peter was so impetuous.[2] Other, smoother texts were preferred, and the preference endured. Lectionaries in use even during my childhood (some years after Papias, no matter what my children think) concentrated on Matthew and ignored Mark mightily.

But all of this is based on the gospel as a written text. Before the written text came the storyteller, the oral performer who embodied the story. Joanna Dewey suggests that Mark's gospel survived because when it was told (rather than read off a page) it was a rousing good story, far too compelling to get rid of.[3] And so Mark became one of the canonical gospels, one of the four (out of a mass of other stories about Jesus) that landed in the Bible, where it was ignored. If Dewey is correct, it will have been the oral performance of Mark's story that has made it indispensable, both in the ancient world and in our world.

The gospel of Mark was surely not the first story ever told about Jesus. Such stories will surely have swirled around him from early in his career onward, and the swirl of stories will have become more intense, more insistent, after his death and resurrection. As the movement around Jesus exploded around the Mediterranean basin, the stories about him will have exploded along with the movement. And all this will have happened before Mark in its current form was ever written down.

Mark's written text emerges out of a dense and complex history. Oral originals spun into subsequent improvisations. This rich mix of improvisations solidified into texts that precipitated out. These texts catalyzed new developments in oral performance, which swirled into new improvisation, new development, new texts, new performances, on and on, around and around.[4] The process will have been complicated. Mark's story could have been the base story (oral) from which Matthew and Luke expanded (orally). Mark's story in the form we have it could have been a written development from an oral original that Matthew and Luke also knew. Or Mark's written story could have been the exemplar from which Matthew and Luke worked as they (orally) supplemented the basic story. Or it could be that Matthew and Luke (as representatives of other oral storytelling communities) read Mark's text, disliked it, and set out to write a story to supplant it. There are other possibilities as well. What we know is that when the dust settled, four written texts stood next to each other in the canon.

Most scholars guess that these four gospels were written down sometime after 70 CE and before 100 CE, and most still guess that of these gospels, Mark was most likely somehow written first. What matters is that the text of Mark emerged out of a complex living practice of oral storytelling. This complexity impels the improvisatory interpretive practice out of which this book grows. My troupe of storytellers and I have been playing Mark's story for years now, exploring it by provoking it, winding it in a process of improvisation and crystallization, with each performance script catalyzing a fresh engagement with Mark's original inscribed text. The aim in each new improvisation is to build something new that cracks open something old so that it can create yet another new living performance. In this study of Mark's story, I will treat the text as the beginning point for contemporary embodied performance, as sheet music that must be explored through performance to be truly comprehended.

In this book, I will not examine every scene out of Mark's story. The scenes that are omitted are not judged somehow unworthy. By no means. Instead, this book focuses on the scenes that appear in the Revised Common Lectionary (RCL), which is used by many Christian congregations as the guide to readings, preaching texts, and Sunday school lessons through the year. I also include several scenes the RCL omits. These scenes I judge to be essential to any adequate exploration of Mark's story. But for the most part, this book confines itself to the RCL. There are plenty of good stories to be had there.

A Storyteller Needs an Audience

The next thing a storyteller needs is an audience. The gospel of Mark has always had one (even when it was ignored), though the argument continues over exactly what audience that might have been. Did the audience live in Rome, or Alexandria, or Asia Minor? Interpreters in earlier generations specified various geographical locations as the story's place of origin. Was the audience a single Christian community, or was the story intended to be THE story of Jesus for ALL Christian communities? Interpreters disagree. Was

Mark's story told to enrich or restrict storytelling practice? Was it told because audiences always need another story, or because a particular audience insisted that there should be only one authoritative story? In part, this is an argument about how interconnected the early Christian communities might have been, and about the place of Mark's community of origin in that web of interconnection. Did the communities that nurtured storytelling around the character Jesus turn toward each other or away from each other?

In addition, interpreters continue to argue over whether these stories developed as private stories or public. Were they told inside Christian communities in the setting of worship, or study, or meditation, or as part of community rituals of transformation and nurturance? Or were they told as public stories to audiences beyond the boundaries of the Christian communities? And if they were told publicly, why were they performed in public? Were they performed as a tool in evangelism? Or were they performed because they were simply good stories? This makes a real difference, and shapes the way contemporary interpreters and performers pick up the text.

I will not settle these historical questions, but I will benefit from the ongoing discussion that surrounds them. Each possibility offers a particular provocation, and out of provocation comes strong and vigorous interpretation. Above all, it is important to remember that a storyteller does indeed need an audience and that the audience that matters most is the one that is sitting in front of you waiting for the story to begin. As you will discover in chapter 1, I am most interested in what happens when these stories are performed for a public audience as good stories. My storytellers and I aim to perform public stories to insiders and outsiders, and we take it as a sign of success when the outsiders sometimes have to explain things to the insiders. More on that later.

A Storyteller Needs an Occasion

The next thing a storyteller needs is an occasion. Stories and performances do not simply erupt out of nowhere. This is true even for the raggediest forms of street theatre. Always there is an occasion, a reason for the performance of this story in this place at this time. Even if the audience is surprised by the sudden performance on the street or in the subway or wherever guerilla theatre has struck, the surprise is crucial to the occasion of the story. This needs more consideration than is often given. Certain occasions call for certain stories, and different occasions call different things out of stories. Biblical stories come to Sunday school all the time, and to church, and such in-house performances have their own occasions and their own integrity. In my work with these stories, however, I find it extremely helpful to pay attention to what happens to these old stories when they get out of the house, when they are played outside of their usual ideological environment.

I find that these old stories do, in fact, get out more than most people imagine, though too often people telling biblical stories in their usual settings and occasions don't see them when they are out and about. The characters show up in popular music; the plotlines and patterns of tension and release show up in popular movies. I find two things about this to be fascinating. First, I am reminded, when I encounter one of our stories on the street, how interesting these old stories, in fact, are. These are good stories indeed, and public audiences are already thoroughly engaged in hearing and telling these stories (in some form or other).

Second, I am intrigued by what I learn about our stories when I meet them on the street. Outsiders often hear the most remarkable things in our stories, and when they tell them back to me I learn something new. For instance, Lou Reed (a dark and dangerous and ever-so-urban songwriter from New York who offered an alternative to the folk music that was winning the hearts of middle America) wrote a song called "Dime Store Mystery." The song focuses on Jesus' death on the cross, in terms very like those laid out in Mark's story. The song is sensitive and aware, and it probes fascinating corners of this old story that I know thoroughly and well. Reed presents a crucified character:

He was lying banged and battered, skewered and bleeding
Talking crippled on the cross
Was his mind reeling and heaving hallucinating
Fleeing what a loss

Reed then proceeds to reflect on the duality of divine and human nature. This sounds exceedingly familiar.

And the song is written for Andy Warhol. What a strange application of the story of Jesus' death (in Mark) to that odd icon of the 60s and 70s in American culture: Campbell's soup cans, Marilyn Monroe. Warhol either transformed contemporary art or trivialized it. Or maybe he did both. What odd tensions spring out of the story when it is played with Warhol's self-absorbed persona on the screen with Jesus. "I find it easy to believe/That he might question his beliefs," writes Reed, only now the visions of Jesus (whatever they might have been, exactly) are wound around the visions that led Warhol on.

Some of the reflections that come out of this interweaving of visions are rather disturbing. I find the disturbance enlightening. What was it that drew Reed to stories about Jesus when he wanted to think about Warhol? What is it about Warhol that makes him (or anyone!) like Jesus? What has happened to crucifixion that it has become a metaphor for facing opposition? How does this square with ancient understandings of crucifixion as a desperate obscenity? Is the obscenity the link between Warhol and Jesus? I finish listening to the song, one more time, and find myself wishing that our stories got out even more than they do now. This odd occasion for telling the story of Jesus' death adds notes that my ear did not hear before. This is a gift to any performer. Every storyteller needs an occasion. The more challenging the occasion, the better the story.

What a Story Wants Is Provoking

But we need to begin our discussion even earlier: before there is an occasion, before there can be an audience, when there is only a story and a storyteller. This is when it all begins, if it is to begin at all. A storyteller needs a story, and a story needs a storyteller. The whole process of performing and interpreting these old stories begins in a moment of odd isolation.

When I sit in such situations, alone with a text that I will interpret, sometime, somewhere, somehow, I find that what a story wants is a little provoking. Without a little provoking, a story can just sit there, inert and agreeable, tame and safe. But once you poke it a little, sparks start to fly. Where there are sparks, lively interpretation can catch fire. I imagine that you are reading this book because you are sitting with Mark's story, knowing that you will interpret this story sometime soon, tell this story sometime, somewhere, somehow. I imagine that you are hoping for something more than one more tame, ideologically safe interpretation. I aim to help you poke the story and provoke it.

What a story wants is a little provoking. But you can read that sentence at least two ways. Sometimes it means that the story needs to be prodded into motion. But sometimes it means that what telling the story demands irritates and provokes me. I do not always like to be provoked. What if the character Jesus in the stories emerges as looking different from the Jesus everyone meets in Sunday school? What if the story we are looking at does not confirm our own deeply held ideologies? What if the demands of playing these stories and honoring their physical integrity requires that we take risks that we would rather not take?

These are real questions. If you commit yourself to performing these good stories publicly, you will find yourself more than occasionally provoked by the process and its demands, and you will find yourself wishing that you could just back off and play the Sunday school circuit. But even there it is true: what these stories want is a little provoking. No matter where and on what occasion you play the story of the gospel of Mark, you will need to provoke the story, and the story will provoke you. There are audiences that will cheer for anything with Jesus in it, as long as Jesus agrees with everything they ever thought and wished for. There is applause to be had from pandering to such audiences, and probably money to be made. But there is little integrity there, and little respect for these stunning old stories that poke back when you poke them. The longer I work with these stories, the more I am convinced that these stories have survived and thrived for so very long because they have always poked back at their performers. What a story wants is a little provoking, and maybe especially when that story is the gospel of Mark.

Getting Started

How do you begin to poke the story? First, you read the story. All of it, and preferably at one sitting. (See my translation on pages 255–333.) Read it and imagine it. Notice what you notice, wonder about what puzzles you. Do this if you are reading the story for the first time. Do this even if you have read the story hundreds of times before. Do this even if you are teaching or preaching on the gospel of Mark yet again this year after doing the same thing three years ago, and three years before that, and three years before that, and three years before that. You are reading and hearing in an entirely new world this time around. You are older. You know more. You've experienced more. You maybe ache more, and not just from arthritis. Experience often brings new aches, even for very young storytellers. First you read.

This book is designed to help you as you read. Chapter 2 explores Mark's narrative arc. Where does the story start? Where does it end? How does it get there? And, most important, how does it all hold together? The chapter tries out several possible schemes that might give the story wholeness and integrity. I do not suppose that these are the only schemes that a reader and a storyteller might try, but I find them to be helpful in making sense of (and with) the puzzles that Mark's story poses. That seems to me to be always the first step: figuring out what puzzle is being posed. I suppose that it would be possible that one of the gospels aspired to do nothing more than list information. I suppose such a thing to be possible, but I do not find it to be true. Especially not with Mark. This old story has puzzled and confounded readers and storytellers from its earliest days up until the day before yesterday. Chapter 2 will help you figure out what puzzles might be solved in Mark's story.

In chapter 3 I dig around in various scenes from Mark's story. The scenes are arranged in the order they appear in the Revised Common Lectionary, which means that things hop around a little bit. You'll want to consult the appendix at the back of this book for help in studying the scenes from Mark in story order rather than lectionary order.

For each scene, I have played with the text four different ways. First, I explore how the scene sounds in the context of the ritual year of the Revised Common Lectionary. What happens to Mark's resurrection story (with Jesus as a no-show) when you play it at Easter time? If Epiphany is the season of revelations, what gets revealed in Mark's story when it is played during that season? What do our patterns, our rituals, our traditional dances (religious or otherwise) contribute to the way we hear, see, tell, and play Mark's story?

Second, I explore the scene as it fits and flows in Mark's whole story. Sometimes the exploration digs at particular words that contribute an intriguing bite to the story. Sometimes I wonder about how this scene is shaped by where it lands along Mark's narrative arc. Always I look for ways to consider the scene not as an isolated "Bible story" but as a working part of a much larger and very good story.

Third, I poke at the story with other texts. Sometimes the other texts come from Jewish Scripture, sometimes from apocryphal works. Sometimes the other texts that poke at Mark's story come from novels or lyrics or history or any other source that promises to provoke the scene helpfully. Sometimes the other texts are not texts at all, but always these "inter-texts" create interpretive tension by providing a sometimes surprising context in which to read and play the scene.

And finally, I devote some time to provoking the story. In fact, each of the four reading perspectives aims to provoke the story. Each aims to poke at the text and to be poked in return. But in the final section I poke harder. In this section I also often include suggestions for how you might consider playing the scene for maximum provocation. All of this aims to help you read.

So, as a first step, just read.

Next, gather a community of readers and players and performers to help you. It does not need to be a big community. In fact, it is best if the group you read and play and perform with has no more than seven or eight people in it. You can do it with two or three people. But gather a group; even if you only read with them and never pick up the stories and play them, still gather a group. Gather people who will read the whole story and notice what they notice, wonder about what puzzles them. Pick these people carefully. You want people of integrity, people who see clearly and who will tell you what they see. You want people who see things from different angles. You want perceptive people who will see what you cannot see. Gather women and men, younger people and older people, people with backgrounds and languages that are not native to you. This is sometimes easier and sometimes harder to do, but try. It will not always make reading and playing and performing easier, but it will make these activities more provocative, and that is the goal of this approach to these old stories. No matter who you gather, you want collaborators who will challenge you, challenge the story, and challenge themselves.

This is especially true if you (like me) imagine that these old stories ought to get out in public more than they do. Even if all you do is read together, try to find some outsiders, some people who do not know Mark's story like the back of every Sunday school kid's hand, to enrich your group.

Gather a group; read together, but don't stop with reading. Something big happens when you start playing the stories together. These stories grew out of performance, out of live playing, live telling, and they reveal some of their secrets only when they are played again. Maybe you are aiming at a full performance of Mark's gospel, with costumes and light cues, with live animals and a cast of thousands. More power to you. Go for it. But maybe all you are doing is studying the gospel of Mark (for a class, for a sermon, or for fun). Gather a group and play the scenes together anyway. You will discover things about Mark's story that you didn't even know were things. You will get to look into the story through windows in what you had always thought were only blank walls. Always this way of working pokes something into motion and surprises everyone in the room. So play the stories, even if you never perform for any audience on the face of the earth. Play the stories. (Did I mention you should play the stories?)

But how? I include suggestions in many of the "Provoking the Story" sections in chapter 3. Those suggestions grow out of many years of exploring these scenes with all kinds of groups. The suggestions are not the only ones that might be productive, or even the only ones that I might have included. (My editor made it clear that this book had to be small enough to pick up without a forklift.) Feel very free to try things that go well beyond what I have included here. Use the discussion about holding an audience in chapter 1 to help you as you experiment with ways to play these scenes. Look for ways to play the texts that would hook an audience and draw them into the story. Remember that hooking an audience requires taking some risks. Take some risks. If what you try doesn't work, you don't have to show it to anybody. Not ever. To help with this process you might want to consult my earlier book, *Provoking the Gospel: Methods to Embody Biblical Storytelling through Drama*. There I provide a detailed guided tour of ways you might play with these texts productively and provocatively. You might also explore with books of exercises for beginning (and experienced) actors. Theatre games can be very helpful in cracking open these old stories.

And finally, after you have read the story, gathered a team of collaborators, and played with the stories, find a way to perform something for an actual audience. Any audience will do, at least to start with. If your experience is anything like mine, you will discover what actors and musicians, artists of all sorts, discover over and over: the audience adds something crucial. Their reactions, their silences, their warmth, and the effort it takes to connect with them will open whole new vistas on the story that you have studied, read, played, and prepared so thoroughly and so well.

It's Not Just Bible Stories Anymore: The Maysie

In this whole process, you provide for yourself what you will later provide for your audiences. You move the text off the page into the space between human bodies, the space that allows the theatre to explore the disasters and delights of the real world. You open the text and your ensemble to the risk of new discoveries. You will risk new connections between these old stories and a world that has always shifted and changed and surprised us. These old stories come to us out of a lively and durable tradition of storytelling, and storytelling has never been simply a diversion that communities engage in to pass an otherwise boring evening. Stories are how we cope with the inexorable, the unmanageable, the incomprehensible. Telling stories, including these old stories, is something we do to survive, something that teaches us how to thrive.

I think that is part of what Lizzie Higgins means by the "maysie." It may bring with it a chill, or a sense of vertigo when you look over the edge of a precipitous story. It may erupt in the shocked humility that actors and other insiders discover when an audience of outsiders helps them comprehend what they have given themselves to perform. But I think that the maysie is the discovery of the shared depths of human being, of life in God's creation. Whatever it is, exactly, I offer this book to you in an attempt to help you discover it, too. Whatever you do, open Mark's story and see what happens. Provoke the story and expect it to provoke you. This is the beginning of an adventure.

Chapter One

THE AUTHORITY OF BIBLICAL STORIES

We were dug in along this little thicket, all of us in foxholes. I had this trouble with my knees so I didn't dig a regular foxhole. What I dug was like a slit trench, and I could lie down in it and shoot. We were all dug in and then they brought up these big railroad guns. Great big things, the ground would just shake. In my trench I had this root from a tree running through it, and I was holding onto it so that I wouldn't get bounced out when the shells hit, because they would just shake the ground. Like I said, they had these big railroad guns and they were firing them, and this shell hit so close it just popped me right out of the hole and out into the open. Next day I went back there and saw the shell crater. It was about fifteen feet from my trench, and you could have buried a car in it.

What is the authority of a story? I will eventually ask the question of biblical stories, but for now I am simply asking about any story. Any story at all. Like, for instance, the one I just told you, the one I heard from a man, now eighty-some years old, who served with my father in the 82nd Airborne during the Second World War.

A First Glimpse: The Authority of a Story

What is the authority of a story? There are many good answers. Some answers will inquire after the accuracy of the story. Some will ask after the forcefulness of the storyteller. Some will investigate the significance of the story in the overall scheme of things. And most of this will miss the authority of the story I just told you.

The story riveted me. If we are to investigate effectively the authority of a story (biblical or otherwise), this is the effect with which we must begin. There was an authority to the man's story. Though I had no way to assess its accuracy, though he told the story haltingly and in a shaky voice made quieter by age and disability, though he did not make any large claims of any sort about the story, still it riveted my attention. And I was not the only one. By the time he finished this little scrap of a story, people in the gate area of the airport were crowding around him to hear more. The story had power and real authority. What accounts for this power? What creates this authority? At first I thought it could be the explosions and the warfare, but the story had none of the cinematic qualities that usually dress up such exhibitions. If the power of a story were measured by its bombastic special effects, this one should have failed miserably. The story was broken and halting and short and didn't lead to a next story. It just riveted its audience is all.

Why?

For one thing, the story needed to be told. As I listened to this man, this old man who had been a paratrooper as a boy, it was clear that he would have been telling the story whether I was listening or not. He checked once in a while to see if I were following him, but I had the impression that he was not so much delivering the story to me as raising the overhead door on his garage and letting me see what was continually playing out inside. The story was going to be told of its own necessity.

It was also clear that this was a story that shaped the teller's identity. He had lived a full life and had worked his way through a career full of accomplishments and setbacks. He had come home from the war and had gone back to whatever was left of normal and had helped to raise a family. (I heard those stories, too.) He had lived a regular life like so many men of his generation, surrounded as they were by families and communities who had no idea what they had seen and done. And now in an airport on his way to a reunion of his old outfit from the army, a group of men who understood every part of every story, he opened the door and showed me what had always been going on inside. "I didn't hear these stories for many years," said his wife, when he finished. "But I could tell there was something he wasn't saying."

Both of these characteristics lent authority to this story, but the thing that struck me most of all was that this story overwhelmed its teller. There are stories that we can control, stories that have been housebroken and taught to behave around company. A housebroken story is one that we can tell the same way one hundred times if we wanted to, or that we could change any time we chose. A story that has been taught to behave is one that teaches a lesson that we want to teach. This was not one of those stories. It did not come down to a concise (but maudlin) maxim. It did not even end with a sense of completeness. When he finished telling the story, all he said was, "It just makes you wonder why, that's all, you just wonder." This is not an ending to the story. It does not even obviously follow from the story. It shows no tight connection to the substance of what was told. And it may be what gave the story its authority. What is clear is that this fragmented half-telling of a story had the authority to hold an audience.

I would like to suggest that reflections about the authority of biblical stories ought to start with careful analysis of how a story like this holds its audience. Before we ever ask about truth and authority and other high-octane words, we should wait and wonder about what it takes for any old story to gather and hold an audience. Too often it is simply assumed that biblical stories will hold an audience. They're Scripture, after all. They're the word of God. Of course they hold an audience. And so we skip this first step and leap ahead to more important matters. But by skipping this first crucial step, and especially by skipping it for the sake of presupposed ideology, we set ourselves up to misunderstand the authority of biblical stories at a fundamental level. I think we set ourselves up to misunderstand the stories themselves.

The stories of the gospels were stories before they became BIBLE STORIES. We forget that at our own peril. We forget that to the detriment of the stories that shape us as people of faith and responsibility in God's creation.

A Second Glimpse: Authority That Does (and Does Not) Hold an Audience

So how do stories hold an audience? John Miles Foley, a prominent student of oral narrative, tells of tuning in a Belgrade television program that promised an oral epic performance, only to encounter "four solemn academics in baccalaureate robes droning ostentatiously from hymnal-shaped prompt-books."[5] Foley does not say whether he watched the entire sorry performance or not, but it seems a safe bet that few other people even bothered to tune in. Most of us have been subjected to such "educational" events often enough to know to avoid them.

This televised performance he contrasts with his encounter with a South Slav *guslar* who performed an epic song live.[6] The first performance, he notes, was coded to establish distance between the text, the performers, and the audience. The academic costume set up a relationship between performer and audience, and between performer and text, and in each case the relationship is characterized by distance. The authority of the text and the performers killed the authority of the story. How odd. The second performance was coded to draw the audience and the text together by winding them both in deep tradition, in shared cultural memory. Everything from costume to music to the ways that language was used reached out to an audience that knew how to read the code.

The first performance (by authorities) lacked authority; the second riveted the audience. The code of the performances made the difference, as Foley sees it.

I would like to suggest that reflections about the authority of biblical stories ought to spend considerable time reflecting on the way our typical performances encode the story. What expectations are created by the code we weave into our performances? What doors are opened and what doors are slammed shut by the code we use? In particular, if we have coded the story as private (not public), uplifting (not provocative), and well-behaved (not wild), then we will have radically limited the ways an audience can engage (and be engaged by) biblical story.

A Third Glimpse: Authority That Really Works, or Storytelling and Magic

The novelist Tim O'Brien writes about his passage from magician to novelist.[7] As a child, O'Brien performed magic tricks. What drew him to magic was the mystery, the drama, the effect on the audience when the magician's guillotine cuts the carrot clean in two and then the volunteer from the audience puts his hand into the same guillotine. "This is drama," says O'Brien. "This is magic."

He became a novelist, which requires him to create the same mystery, to concoct the same magic, only now it is done with plot structures, and with patterns of tension and release. The art of magic, like the art of writing stories, requires a "sense of theater and drama and continuity and beauty and wholeness."[8]

Now, to be sure, a contemporary novel is different from an ancient oral story. Even when the old story is inscribed (becoming what John Miles Foley calls a "Voice from the Past"[9]), still it is not much like a contemporary novel. But for all their differences, they both resemble magic, real magic. Real magic is not a string of tricks learned by an amateur. Real magic has the power to work transformation in the audience. As O'Brien notes, rabbits become doves who fly off to the balcony to retrieve the marked card chosen out of the deck by someone from the audience. But these transformations must not simply occur randomly or too quickly or too easily. A real magician takes risks with the audience's hopes and fears, thus drawing them into the tension and the transformation it brings. So too, stories with authority (whether the stories are oral or inscribed) draw audiences into risk and reconciliation. They create change that takes real time, real effort, and real risk. Aristotle knew this millennia ago. When he sketched the working of tragic drama in ancient Greece, he understood it to do its work by stirring the passions of the audience in order to accomplish catharsis.[10] I would like to suggest that the magic of tumultuous transformation creates the change that audiences will call the authority of a story.

From Mining to Reading: A Glimpse of Biblical Authority

Since at least the nineteenth century, biblical texts have been studied historically. Interpreters dig deep into texts, hoping to uncover ancient communities and cultural practices. Sifting and sorting, they work to identify actual situations in which human beings began to use the words, ideas, and practices that eventually were woven into biblical narrative. This is an extremely valuable interpretive method. It focuses on the way the Bible actually grew out of the real historical world out of which all of life grows. Prospecting for history yielded useful results, but like any productive method it has had troublesome consequences. Mining is an extractive industry, and the value of what is found increases as the extracted bits are further and further separated from the earth from which they were taken. When such interpretive methods are the norm, authority will adhere to the highly refined products that were dug out of the Bible, and "authority" will be a small thing, limited to determinations of historical accuracy and verifiability.

In the 1960s interpreters began to explore the gospels as stories. Texts long mined for historical nuggets were read as narratives. Instead of hunting for gaps and seams in texts, interpreters analyzed biblical literature using interpretive techniques developed for literary criticism. Questions about characterization and plot shaped the way gospels were interpreted. Patterns of tension and release revealed things about the texture of the texts that stirred imaginations. Texts were experienced as living, vibrant, and valuable.

In all of this, however, there were questions that were deferred. Though both the gospels and contemporary novels were narratives, were they sufficiently comparable to allow the application of the same interpretive techniques to each? Did the modes of reading developed for contemporary novels apply to narratives generated two millennia ago in a culture far separated from contemporary Western culture? And back behind all of these questions was another question that waited for renewed attention: what ought to be made of the relationship of the gospels to oral narrative?

This last question was difficult to ask and answer. It was difficult because the practice of reading gospels as novels was producing useful results, and so questions about original orality could naturally be deferred for the moment. It was difficult, more importantly, because the matter of oral tradition had been considered before, and had been set aside along with the historical-critical methods of the previous generation. The quest for oral tradition was part of earlier reading strategies and retained its connection with older methods that had been (in their turn) wonderfully productive. But "oral tradition" in the earlier paradigm had been the name given to the incoherent basket of atomized sayings that was presumed to have been passed down in fragmentary form from the earliest times. On this model, the gospels were pasted together out of scraps and fragments that were stuck on a basic narrative framework. To seek after "oral tradition," therefore, meant (to literary critics in the last few decades) to resume the hunt for ragged relics and discontinuous bits, tatters and scraps of an incoherent past. For interpreters experimenting with reading the gospels as coherent stories, this made the question of how the gospels related to oral narrative exceedingly difficult to address, and probably made it impossible to answer, and therefore also easy to ignore.

From Reading to Telling: Another Glimpse of Biblical Authority

But the question of original orality would not go away. Studies of ancient literacy made it clear that the gospels must have had some sort of life embodied in oral storytelling. The low rate of literacy in the ancient world[11] meant that only a small minority of people in the Christian movement could have read the gospels for themselves. Either the gospels lived in storytelling or very few Christians would have had any connection at all with the gospels in any form. In addition, studies of the gospels themselves made it clear that these narratives showed signs that one would expect in oral narratives: type scenes, strategic repetitions, and the like. If these stories weren't originally oral, why did they look like oral stories? And under all of this was the simmering realization that contemporary literary theory was built on the presupposition that reading happened silently and privately while in the ancient world "reading" would have likely included hearing and would most often have been conducted in front of an audience.

And so interpretive practice shifted again, and interpreters began to look at gospels as storytelling texts. Perhaps the inscribed gospels were condensations made from oral performances. Perhaps they were written down as prompt books for oral performers. Whatever the origin of the writing, interpreters increasingly explored the oral dimension of the gospel stories.

This shift had consequences. Literary methods, too dependent on modern understandings of printed texts, were displaced by studies of oral poetics. Performance theory became important as an interpretive tool. And, of course, there were deferred questions yet again. If Mark's story can be read (!) as the precipitate of oral storytelling,[12] can Luke's gospel? And whatever will we do with John? And if the gospels (or some of them) are originally oral compositions (with all the possible permutations that implies), then what is the status of the inscribed texts that we have? Are they poor photographs, blurred because they fail to capture the lively motion of the original oral stories? If so, when will it be legitimate (even necessary) to defer to assumptions about the nature of the oral original when trying to solve interpretive problems encountered in the inscribed texts? For instance, what becomes of the troublesome ending of the gospel of Mark? Will all tension be drained out of ancient problems by appealing to hypothetical storytelling practice?[13]

So now we find ourselves with old biblical stories that have been mined for nuggets, analyzed for plot tensions, and told as oral stories. Which interpretive method is the correct one to use?

I would like to suggest that the correct answer to many either/or questions is yes. The list of deferred questions surely implies that we are not done with shifts in interpretive paradigms, but such shifts ought not entail the abandonment of productive methods. The aim, after all, is not to generate the only true interpretive method but to benefit from the methods that you use. Methods must actually serve the work of interpretation, not the other way around. In this study of Mark's story, I will use multiple methods: historical, literary, ethnopoetic. Always, however, I will concentrate on what can be learned by reading the text as a script from an ancient performance that calls for contemporary performance.

Performing and the Authority of the Audience

If the authority of biblical stories is rooted in their ability to catch and hold an audience, and if this audience is properly a mixed gathering of insiders and outsiders, then there is another aspect of this authority that must still be considered.

Hans-Georg Gadamer, back before the rise of literary critical interpretive methods for biblical narratives, argued that a play is not a play until it is played.[14] While his work was crucial for those interpreters who developed the practice of literary critical interpretation, his understandings of play are even more aptly applied to emerging forms of interpretation through performance. If play is the structure of being, then the uncontrollable interaction between script and audience is an instance of the mutual exchange and modification that is the game of all interpretive existence for Gadamer. But notice that this implies that it is not sufficient to simply perform the sheet music of the gospels as a kind of private chamber music available only to selected aficionados and other such cranks. Performance for a public audience is not, under such an understanding, a nice extra, an additional bonus; it is an absolute requirement. If a play *must* be played, there must be an audience there to catch it and to throw something back.

This is always where the rub comes. As any actor knows, the audience can throw back anything it wants to throw. It is rare indeed that actual physical objects are thrown, except in forms like melodramas that actively encourage such egregious behavior in the audience.[15] But audiences throw things back at the performers all the time. They applaud or they do not. They laugh or they do not. They hang tight with the performers or they do not. They are warm or they are cold, responsive or dead, riveted or watching the clock.

Performers can feel all these things and much more. This life-and-death game of catch is essential to the life of a performer. Talk to any actor, any musician, any performer. She will tell you about the terror and ecstasy of performing for a live audience. There is nothing like it in the world. A play that is sitting still and becoming dull and regular as rehearsals grind on will pop into life when the audience comes in, sits down, and starts to throw its attention back at the actors. What had become a matter of memorization suddenly has a sharp edge.

Gadamer's understanding of the existence of aesthetic objects (like stories) makes it clear that stories require audiences that throw things back. But now this gets complicated. I have already introduced the melodrama into the discussion. Melodramas are fascinating theatrical forms. This loosest of theatrical genres proceeds according to rigidly defined plot structures. Melodramas carefully break every rule of ordinary theatre, but they cannot break the rules that govern the stories they are allowed to tell. In the end, the villain must lose and virtue must triumph. On the way, innocence (usually embodied in a woman) must be threatened and must find a defender (usually embodied in a man). Throughout the play, good and evil must always be clear to the audience. The audience will have it no other way.

But what do you do when your script is not a melodrama? Audiences love such plot structures and sometimes demand them even in genres that are ill-suited to such formulaic rigidity. What does a troupe of performers do when the audience authoritatively demands the performance of a clear melodrama with good and evil clearly marked, but the script they have to work with constrains them to perform some other form of story?

This is a real problem. Why do so many American movies feature smashing car chases? The audience will pay to see a car chase. Why do so many movies stage romances between middle-aged men and young nubile women? The audience will pay to watch such fantasies, particularly when the young woman is classically cute. Why do some movies and some plays close after losing big money and playing to half-empty theatres? The audience found itself locked out of the story. You do not need to see very many plays, or read very many reviews, before you discover the compromises created by audiences that demand easy clarity, or before you encounter the blind disasters that occur when performers refuse to allow the audience inside the play. Stories are either dumbed down or played as "art for art's sake." The audience is either dominant or ignored. And either way performers are left to wonder about the authority of the audience.

I would like to suggest that this leaves performers of biblical stories in a wonderful place, a difficult place, a place that encourages truthful creativity. I would like to suggest that the terror that goes with this fruitful tension is precisely what is needed if a storyteller would tell a true story. Out of this tension grows an awareness of the importance of attending to the basics in telling a story to an audience. Read again the first explorations of what it takes to hold an audience. These are the basics that must be honored if you are going to tell an audience a story that is not a melodrama.

Or you could decide simply always to tell melodramas. They have simple plots. They are awash in clarity. They allow you to overact, chew on the scenery, paint characters with broad brushstrokes, reinforce common gender stereotypes, talk to the audience directly while breaking character. They allow you to sacrifice subtlety for simplicity. And, of course, they require you to give up telling the kind of true story with which this chapter began, the kind of true story that is so abundant in the Bible. Oh well.

I would like to suggest that you decide not to tell melodramas. But in order to honor the authority of the audience, I would suggest that you learn to offer your stories humbly to the audience, with full awareness that they may throw something back that you had not hoped for. Humility is crucial. Actors know this. This is why actors bow to the audience at the end of the show. It is not to curry favor and applause; it is to thank the audience for the privilege of performing, to thank the audience for the privilege of sharing a story that provokes us all. There is risk in such performances, but only through such risk do we discover the proper authority of the story and the proper authority of the audience. Only in this risky interaction is the authority of biblical stories encountered.

Creation and Risk: Performing the Stories of the Bible

We have been exploring performance for quite a while now. "Performance," however, includes more things than you might initially expect—for instance, writing. It strikes me as I read Tim O'Brien's reflections on the art of writing stories that he calls his practice "storytelling." Reading is surely different from hearing, but what if writing a story were somehow akin to telling a story?

Surely, both writers and tellers share (with magicians) the responsibility to create "drama and continuity and beauty and wholeness."[16] And if a novel is not a novel until it is written, and if a play is not a play until it is played,[17] then the kinship between story-writers and storytellers might be real. In any case, both create the story. What does creation entail? Many things, surely, but in O'Brien's understanding, creation involves mystery and magic. Above all, creation requires risk.

This has implications for the authority of biblical stories. When the interpreter must become a creator, when she reads the inscribed text as sheet music, a script for public performance, it imposes a new and powerful responsibility on her. Every line must be embodied, and the embodiment must be believable and true. Audiences catch lies very quickly, and a single line delivered without awareness can puncture a performance. Performers must ask a basic, awkward question: what if this line does not mean what I always thought everyone thought that it meant?[18] Every line must develop truthfully out of the demands of performance, no matter what anyone thought it meant in the past.

Performance of a biblical narrative, even in small fragments, will acquaint you with something essential about the authority of the story: authority requires risk, requires that you not simply repeat ideology. "Same old" readings simply will not do.

The Authority of the Bible

So far, I have talked about authority in every form except the form you might expect in a commentary on Scripture. That is, of course, not an accident, but neither is it an avoidance. The matter of the authority of Scripture is at the heart of all biblical interpretation.

The problem is that everyone disagrees about what it means.

What is the authority of the Bible? The issue usually comes up when there is a border dispute between groups that disagree with each other. The differences are generally absolute, as religious differences usually are, and it all comes down to the authority of the Bible.

I have watched such disputes carefully for a few decades now, and I have noticed some regularities. I have noticed that when the authority card is played, it usually is a signal that the game is finished, except for the shooting. Most often, the shooting is theological, with each side finishing the other off quickly and simultaneously. And each side is sure that it has won.

I have noticed that each side is convinced that the other has a weak view of the authority of the Bible. This surprised me. It is not that one side thinks that the other has too high a view, while the other has too low a view. Sometimes the view is judged to be weak because it is not rigid enough. Sometimes the view is judged weak because it is too rigid, even superstitious. But whatever the situation, still each side attributes a weak view of Scripture to the other side.

Even more distressing, I have noticed that both sides, all sides, any conceivable sides, tend to operate with notions of the Bible that guarantee weak views of the authority of Scripture. Both sides and all sides tend to bring the Bible into the dispute far too late for it to do any conceivable good. Ideology has generally already dug its trenches on both sides of no-man's-land. Bayonets have been brandished, and helmets have been buckled, insults have been hurled. And only then is the "Authority of the Bible" wheeled out. From the timing of all of this, you would guess that the "Authority of the Bible" was some kind of ultimate weapon. But notice that both sides assume that ideology and anger should be allowed to arrange the field of battle, to inflame the argument, to harden the sides — in fact, to do whatever they want first. Notice also that the "Authority of the Bible" is sent for and given specific orders, like any slave or flunky incapable of self-directed action. How odd. In fact, by the time Authority is wheeled out, it might as well be on a hospital gurney for all the good it can do. The Bible is wheeled in (the poor old thing can no longer stand on its own), but only to provide ammunition for one particular side, for one particular point. And then it is wheeled back to the infirmary.

This is no way to read the Bible. The authority of the Bible is not a weapon to be used to beat the other side into submission. Biblical stories are not flunkies, and they must not be the slaves of anger and ideology. Any notion of biblical authority that grows out of such ground will be toxic.

I would like to suggest that it is time to take things back closer to the beginning, to reconsider what the authority of the Bible might be, what it might become, and what it might always have been.

The Stories of Israel

The first thing that an interpreter of biblical stories needs to remember is that the stories of the Bible are the stories of Israel. This is true for all of the stories, whether from Jewish Scripture or from the Christian Testament. All of these stories are told by Jewish storytellers in a Jewish voice out of a Jewish storehouse of hopes and demands and loves.[19] That means, first of all, that these old stories are the creation of Jewish grandmothers telling and retelling the oldest stories they know, weaving and reweaving the fabric that winds them and their families into their identity and their responsibilities before God and the whole creation.

Whenever you pick up these old stories, you will feel in the texture of the woven text something of the disasters and delights that have called for the story to be told and retold, over and over, grandmother to grandchild, from the most ancient world to the world of the day before yesterday. As you learn to tell these old stories, no matter which Testament and community you come from, something of the authority of those old grandmothers will impress itself on you, and you will discover something of the twists and pains and soaring joys that go with becoming the people of God.

The other first thing an interpreter needs to remember is that these twists and pains and joys have given birth to a peculiar and powerful kind of reading and rereading, telling and retelling. It is not accidental that the people of God are named in their own stories as "Israel." The name is given to them by God, both as a description and as a task. The name means "he wrestles with God," and throughout history this has been the heart of Jewish faith and life. Most important for my current investigation, this has been the heart of Jewish reading of Scripture.

Gerson D. Cohen describes the process this way: "In Aggadic Midrash the imagination ranged freely, . . . converting law to love and ritual to caress. The Bible was no longer only the guide and master to the Jew; it was his intimate companion, his alter ego."[20] Notice the tenderness, the sense of intimacy. When you read the rabbis, notice how wrestling and caressing are woven together. The wrestling that gives Israel its name is loving rather than violent, but that does not in any measure make it less passionate. Family legends are full of stories about children who discover their parents making love and think they are fighting. They are wrong about the violence, but they are right about the way passion takes us beyond normal self-control. It is the same with the biblical interpretation proper to Israel, proper to a people trained to wrestle with God. Gentile Christians would do well to apprentice themselves to this practice.

Biblical stories are not weapons to use in a dispute. The image is simply wrong. Biblical stories are the fields on which we discover what issues must be disputed, what wrestling will be required for faithful, passionate people of God.

Spiraling into Stories

So there are two "first things" for interpreters to remember: biblical stories are the stories of Israel, and this reading requires wrestling. The first winds the community into its identity. The second wrestles with, even fights with that identity and with the texts that shape that identity. These two kinds of reading are often imagined, at least by American Christians, to contradict each other. It is imagined that one either accepts the ideology of the faith or one questions it. This dichotomy is too simple, and quite dangerous. Remember that the stories of the Bible are the stories of Israel. They are the stories that create and re-create God's people as faithful wrestlers. Remember that passion is involved.

These two modes of reading are not separate at all. In fact, they spiral into each other, each spurring the other and driving it on. And when these two modes of reading drive each other on, together they draw the community deeper into the story, deeper into its identity as a wrestler with God and all forms of authority.

This spiraling into identity will be familiar to any student of traditional cultures. A friend and colleague of mine, Martin Brokenleg, explains Lakota tradition by drawing just such a spiral. On the outside of the spiral are young people who do not yet know enough stories to have much substance. Deeper in the spiral are older people who know more stories and live weightier lives. Deeper still are the elders who know all the stories that can be known. They have the most gravity of all, and the most reality, all because they know the stories. But the spiral does not stop with the elders. Deeper into the spiral are the stories themselves, getting older and older as you spin deeper into reality.

I was reading *Ceremony* by Leslie Marmon Silko. I was reading it because Martin recommended it to me and I had learned to trust his recommendations. He asked me if I was understanding the book. I told the truth (always a good idea with Martin). I was understanding some of it, and was confused by much of it. "That's because," he said, "you think that you are real and the stories are fictitious." He was right. "That's backward," he said. "To understand native culture you have to realize that the stories are real and that you might someday become real."

The more I read the Bible and the rabbis, the more it seems to me that what my Lakota colleague has taught me applies also to me in relationship to those texts. As the Jewish community wrestles its way deeper into the text, the members of the community become more fully who they are. As they become more fully Israel, they become able to ask more powerful questions, to wrestle with more passion. And this is true because the stories themselves embody a wrestling that takes bigger risks than any living human being would ever have enough solidity to take. Jacob himself, the first to bear the name "Israel," wrestles in the story so strenuously that he limps away from the contest.

I would like to suggest that Gentile Christians have much to learn about faithful wrestling with the Bible. What may look like violence is more often passionate faith. To learn this, we may have to refigure our understanding of the place of questions in the midst of faith. While questions may be figured as a sign of disrespect in our enveloping culture, in a culture of wrestling they are the sign of the highest possible respect. This will take some getting used to.

The Authority of Public Wrestling

Earlier in this chapter, I made a passing reference to the matter of coding the stories we tell as private and not public. I would like to return to that matter now for further consideration.

Every story we tell is wrapped in code, and every audience that watches us tell a story reads the code (as best they can) as they read our performance of the stories we tell. If when we tell our stories we do it in places we (and we alone) control, this codes the stories as private stories. An outsider (a member of the public) might peek in through the window, but such behavior leads to a visit from the police. If when we tell our stories, we tell them in language that rings with rhythms and word choices that belong to our own arcane rituals, the stories will sound like secret clan handshakes, at least to members of the public. Above all, if when we tell our stories we imagine that we control the stories and perform them for "the public" in order to have a desired and understood effect on "the public," then we have encoded our stories as permanently private stories. If "the public" (for some reason) should wish to gain admission to these stories, they will have to apply to us in triplicate and undergo an extensive security clearance.[21] If we will not allow the security risk, our stories will fall short of public reality.

This last bit of private coding must be examined carefully. The problem with the assumption that we control our stories and their messages is not just the colonial presuppositions that are revealed in this odd notion. The real problem is that these assumptions actively misunderstand our stories and our relationship with them from the DNA outward.

These stories are, as I have earlier argued, the stories of Israel. For Gentile Christians they are not in the first place "our" stories at all. It would be exceedingly odd for us to imagine that we control stories that are not ours in the first place. These stories are, at their deepest level, stories about desperate wrestling. No one controls how that wrestling will turn out. No one. If you read the rabbis, you will see how true this is. No one controls the outcome, not even God.[22] Look closely at the Bible itself. This same wrestling characterizes story after story. The book of Job may be the best laboratory example of this. Throughout the story, Job wrestles with God, which is just what you should expect in the stories of Israel. But what you might miss is that through the story the audience is also drawn into the wrestling match. Surely this happens when the "comforting friends" say things that everyone has said, only in this case the effect is disastrous. Pay careful attention to the way Job's story ends. After the testing is done, Job is restored. He is returned to health. He gets new camels. He gets new sheep. He gets new children.

He gets new children. Certainly this solves the problem of providing for his old age, but Job has not been portrayed as a distant and calculating father who saw his children as nothing more than a kind of pension fund. He is shown offering sacrifices for his children and praying for them. And he is shown mourning for them. And now the audience is told that all things are back to normal and Job is restored. And he gets new children.

Would any attentive person in any imaginable audience think that this solves the problem posed by the beginning of the story? God is shown making bets on Job's endurance and faithfulness. The betting gets out of hand, and the children are killed in the bargain. And now the story blandly implies that the provision of new children will balance accounts. I think that the story draws the audience into the wrestling most deeply at this point. I am guessing that very few audience members go home without arguing about this strange story. I imagine that the arguments are intense, all because the story has worked to perfection.

But the stories do their work by provoking arguments. It's not just the interpreters; it's the stories themselves.

How do the arguments turn out? That's the way it is with real wrestling matches: you can never tell ahead of time. What really matters is that this story is presented to the public to provoke it to wrestle. Surely Jewish audiences will hear things that sharpen their wrestling even further, but any audience of insiders and outsiders is drawn into the same scrap. This is important.

I would like to suggest that authentic provocation is part of the public authority of biblical stories. One could state this negatively: if we tell our stories while imagining that we control both the stories and their proper interpretation, we code the stories as our private preserve and close them to the public. But I am more struck by the effect of stating this matter positively. Our stories (in their very DNA) are coded to provoke any audience to wrestle passionately, even desperately sometimes. The real authority of these stories consists in their power to provoke exactly such wrangles, fights in which truth and life are always at stake. This power to provoke is what catches and holds an audience. Oddly enough, this is accomplished by driving insiders out of their position of dominance and control.[23]

Authority and How to Tell a True Story

Everything in this chapter has been complicated, and every word in this section title has its own tangles. "Authority" has consistently been more complicated than it first appeared. "Telling" has morphed into desperate and humble risk. And "story" has been blown up from simple forms into forms even more simple that are unfinished and therefore complete.

Now I take up the simple matter of truth.

From what I said about the negative effects of imagining that you control the effects and force of stories, you might guess — correctly — that I do not imagine that truth is a commodity that any storyteller dispenses on her own terms to a selected target audience. If truth were somehow a hothouse flower that can only be grown inside a sealed community, then it would not deserve such a powerful name. You could call it opinion or call it a hobby, but don't call it truth. Truth ought to name something that lives in jagged heat and frigid winds; truth ought to name something that is bent and warped and twisted by real life, but still lives and grows, though no one knows how. It just makes you wonder why, that's all; you just wonder.

My father was in the 82nd Airborne in World War II. He was in the 508th Parachute Infantry Regiment, an outfit that saw action on D-Day, in the jump into Holland, and in the Battle of the Bulge. Members of the 508th received every medal and commendation that can be awarded by the United States, and several awards from European nations.

My father did not serve in combat. He was a rigger, a parachute packer. Many riggers jumped into combat, but my father was never sent to do that. He packed the parachutes that his friends and comrades rode down into tracer fire and flak. The 508th lost more than a thousand men who died in combat and from combat-related injuries during the war. My father did not see those casualties. He saw the men who returned, and learned of those who did not. And he did his job and packed the parachutes so that his friends and comrades could trust them.

My father did not serve in combat, but he did see casualties. It was during a regimental jump, a training jump during the war. It was at Sissonne in France. My father had packed the chutes, he and his company. They were packing the chutes for the next jump, and they took a break and went out to watch the jump. They saw the airplanes. C-47s. They saw the men step out of the door into nothing. Left foot, right foot, out into the prop blast. They counted with each man: one thousand, two thousand, three thousand, four. They saw the chutes open, the chutes they had packed. They saw them all open. Someone probably nodded. Nobody needed to smile. These riggers all had their jump wings, they knew what it felt like to step out of the plane and fall and count and wait to feel the chute open, the parachute they had packed.

And then they saw a plane lose power. The troopers in the plane had just jumped, all of them, and this plane lost power. Someone said it lost a propeller. Someone said that no one knew what had happened. It just lost power and turned and curved and arced its way to the ground, right through a group of troopers that had just jumped out of the next plane ahead. Thirteen men were killed. On a training jump when the war was almost over. On a nice sunny day while my father and his company were taking a break and watching the parachutes open just the way they were supposed to open.

Another man in my father's company was there, and he was sent to pick up the men who were killed. "One guy was cut off, just right at the knees, probably from the propeller," he says, "just cut right off. Clean." Then this guy looks away from me, looks at the ground, looks at my father, and they both get quiet. The guy sort of shakes for a second. And then he looks back at me and smiles real quick before he glances away.

My father and the riggers in his company went back to work. They had chutes to pack for the next jump.

My father says, "It wasn't even the troopers in that plane that got killed. It was the guys in the next one ahead." Then he looks at the guy from his company, and they're both quiet for a while. Then he shows me how they stepped out of the C-47s when they jumped. Left foot, right foot, out into the prop blast, then you count. Airborne all the way.

Tim O'Brien writes about telling the truth. In particular (and truth is always particular), he writes about telling a true war story.[24] He tells some scraps of stories. He tries again. He draws some conclusions. He draws some more conclusions, and then he draws some different ones. "A war story is never moral," he says. "If a story seems moral, do not believe it." "In any war story, but especially a true one," he says, "it's difficult to separate what happened from what seemed to happen." Another time he says, "In many cases a true war story cannot be believed." Later he says, "In other cases you can't even tell a true war story." Then he says, "True war stories do not generalize."

After many tries O'Brien comes down to this:

> Mitchell Sanders was right. For the common soldier, at least, war has the feel — the spiritual texture — of a great ghostly fog, thick and permanent. There is no clarity. Everything swirls. The old rules are no longer binding, the old truths no longer true. Right spills over into wrong. Order blends into chaos, love into hate, ugliness into beauty, law into anarchy, civility into savagery. The vapors suck you in. You can't tell where you are, or why you're there, and the only certainty is overwhelming ambiguity.
>
> In war you lose your sense of the definite, hence your sense of truth itself. And therefore it's safe to say that in a true war story nothing is ever absolutely true.[25]

It matters who Mitchell Sanders is. Read O'Brien to find out why.

I would like to suggest that the criteria O'Brien haltingly develops for how to tell a true war story might apply to the gospels as well. As always, the forms are different: war stories are not gospel stories, ancient stories are not contemporary stories.

But maybe they are. Storytellers, by definition and by mandatory practice, only tell their stories in the present moment. Texts may come to us (and to them) out of a distant past, but (as Foley notes) even these texts are properly treated as the traces of voices, not as simple inscriptions. Texts may come to storytellers out of any century, any culture, but they come out of the storyteller's mouth in this moment and in this culture. When storytellers work, ancient stories become contemporary. Somehow. At least for the duration.

And maybe war stories are gospel stories, or maybe at least gospel stories are war stories. It surely is the case that all of the gospel stories emerge out of a world still smoldering after the crushing of the First Jewish Revolt. Read other texts from this painful period. Read 2 Esdras; read 2 Baruch. You may well see what I see: "There is no clarity. Everything swirls. The old rules are no longer binding, the old truths no longer true."[26] Indeed. Read even the Mishnah, the Jewish codification of binding rules and faithful practices. As Jacob Neusner notes, substantial effort is exerted on specifying rules and behaviors appropriate in the Temple, even though the Temple had been destroyed fully 130 years before the Mishnah was published. How strange. The Mishnah emerges out of the smoke of the Second Jewish Revolt against Rome, also crushed. The Temple was still a smoldering memory, a ruin that would never be rebuilt. Everything swirls. Sometimes you just wonder. Look at the gospel of Mark, a story full of jagged jumps and bumps. Look at its sheer refusal to make easy sense. Look at its insistence on stopping without ending. There is no clarity. You just wonder is all.

If gospel stories are war stories and if storytelling makes all stories somehow contemporary, then any proper consideration of the authority of stories, especially biblical stories, ought to spend time watching and listening to how such stories are told. How can you tell a true story?

True Stories Are Broken Stories

Here's what I see and hear, from O'Brien and from the Bible. True stories, and not just true war stories, are always broken. This is true even when they are complete and well-rounded. Maybe especially when they are complete and well-rounded. You can hear the brokenness when the story reaches for wholeness and doesn't quite get there. You can see the brokenness, if you are looking, when storytellers smile real quick, looking for something that they don't quite find. You can see the brokenness when storytellers look away, hoping to see in the distance what they couldn't find in your face.

True stories are always broken. You can hear the brokenness when a storyteller tells you of horrible things with a smooth and flowing voice and then stumbles while trying to tell you about something simple and beautiful and true. A friend of my father's from those days said, "I think they're looking for healing, even after all these years." And then he smiled real quick and looked away. And I realized that I hadn't understood him at all. That is true.

True stories are always broken. A story out of the Battle of the Bulge:

> I was pulling guard duty on this shed where we had stored some equipment, and when the sun started to come up, the fog started to lift and the clouds went away. Then just like that right away you could hear the drone. The con trails covered the sky. It was bombers. They were going to give 'em hell. It was beautiful and it was Christmas morning. Every year at Christmas I remember those bombers.

True Stories Are Told by Bodies

Here's what I see and hear. You can tell a true story by the body. The truth is always in the body. The lift of the shoulders, the sudden glance away, the tremor that shakes everything except the voice, the sag when the story is finished: you can tell a true story by the body. That means that storytellers must chart the physical course of a story as much as they must chart its verbal course. Storytellers who are telling a story that is not their own story (and it's always that way with ancient stories, biblical stories) must experiment with the physical flow of the story to see what happens when they move their bodies differently, when they shift the glances and shudders and jerks of the chin to other places in the story. That means that storytellers need audiences, bodies in the seats, to help them learn how to tell a true story. When a true story is told, bodies move and bodies respond. Bodies throw things back and forth. Storytellers need to learn from audiences what is true and what is not. The authority of the audience may demand melodramas, but it will also demand bodily truth.

"True" Is a Verb

Here's what I see and hear. The word "true" is not an adjective, not an attribute of some more substantial thing. "True" is a verb, and an active verb at that. Let me tell you why.

I am trained as a meatcutter, only the man who taught me never used that job title. He was an old-fashioned butcher, and he taught me to be a butcher, too. A butcher uses knives. Obviously. So a butcher sharpens knives. Obviously. Dull knives make hard work. Worse: dull knives are dangerous. So butchers sharpen knives. But more often than a butcher sharpens a knife, a butcher trues the edge of the knife. Every time you pick up a knife, you check the edge and true it. You do this with a steel, a metal rod with tiny ridges running down its length, and you hold the steel up in the air and stroke the knife down the steel, one side and the other, over and over, over and over. Then you check the edge. You use your thumb, you drag it across the edge of the knife, first this way and then that, back and forth. When a knife is sharpened, it has a thin edge, a very thin edge, so thin that you can't see whether it is there or not. But you can feel it with your thumb. Back and forth, your thumb feels the edge catch and pull as you drag your thumb across it. When a knife is sharpened and when a knife is used, this thin edge gets turned, bent one way or the other. You can feel the bend. You drag your thumb and it catches more going this way than that: the edge is turned. It needs to be trued. The knife is still sharp, but it is not true and it won't cut. You true a knife on a steel, this side and that side, back and forth, over and over. You can tell a knife that has been trued: your thumb catches evenly both ways. You can tell a knife that has been trued: it cuts deep and clean and right to the bone and you can feel it catch and drag cleanly in the meat, just like it catches on your thumb, back and forth. For a butcher, "true" is a verb.

I would like to suggest that "true" is a verb also for a storyteller. You maybe can hear the benefit of the metaphor in the notion of cutting deep and clean, right to the bone. For a long time that is what I heard the metaphor doing, too. These days I hear it in the truing itself, in the back and forth, the pulling and pushing. I am also an old wrestler (not a very good one, I'm afraid). I remember wrestling as pulling and pushing, holding and balancing, tipping and twisting back and forth. When I watch wrestlers, I see something that looks like a butcher truing a knife. It is not a contest simply of strength or technique. It is a contest of back and forth, of balance and quickness. What is true in wrestling is the moving, the pushing, the truing of the action until on a knife's edge the match comes down to a hold, a strain, a shift, and it's over.

I am a storyteller. I read biblical stories and they read me. I tell them and they tell me. The longer I work with biblical stories, the more I see the process as a process of truing. Back and forth, wrestling and straining, the stories move me and bend me and straighten me, and I wrestle with them, moving and bending them in turn. The stories we tell are indeed the stories of Israel, who wrestles with God. The wrestling trues the stories, and it trues the storyteller. The wrestling trues the audience, too. But most important, the wrestling trues the truth. You can tell a true story because it bends and straightens truth itself. It subverts old truths that have been tamed and housebroken. It sharpens old truths that have turned dull. You can tell a true story because it refuses to imagine that truth is a noun, a person, place, or thing that could be conquered or possessed. You can tell a true story because it knows that true is a verb.

And so you wrestle on, back and forth, back and forth, over and over, truing the blade so it cuts deep and clean and you can feel the drag.

> In a true war story, if there's a moral at all, it's like the thread that makes the cloth. You can't tease it out. You can't extract the meaning without unraveling the deeper meaning. And in the end, really, there's nothing much to say about a true war story, except maybe "Oh."[27]

It just makes you wonder why, that's all, you just wonder. This is the authority of a biblical story that trues the truth and trues you. You just wonder. Otherwise it wouldn't be true.

Chapter Two

HOW DO YOU HOLD MARK'S STORY TOGETHER?

> It is the dull man who is always sure, and the sure man who is always dull. . . . A great literature is thus chiefly the product of doubting and inquiring minds. —H. L. Mencken

The two greatest problems in Mark's story are linked to each other. The first of these problems Mark shares with each of the other gospels: How do you tell a true story about resurrection from death? This problem is not to be minimized. From the beginning each of the gospels spirals toward the moment when the dead Jesus is raised to life. It is not a separable part of the story. Every moment in the story feels the tug of the end of the story. But the end is impossible. Adults know this, and pretend to forget it at their own peril. Dead people stay dead. Whatever else may be treated as a two-way street, death is a one-way, one-time event. To be sure, people are resuscitated every day in hospitals all around the world. People who would have been dead a century ago, people who have stopped breathing, people whose hearts have stopped beating, such people are brought back to life all the time these days. Just to be clear, however, this is not what we are dealing with in the case of Jesus. Jesus is publicly tortured to death by professionals. Once he is certifiably dead, he is buried and left in the tomb into the third day, for something approaching forty hours, more or less. The number of hours is less significant than the notion that he is dead into the third day since ancient Jewish understandings in the first century held that life departed irrevocably in the third day. Jesus is certifiably dead. And then he rises to life. Children typically believe that such things are possible, and pious adults often demand of each other that they affect the same credulity in the face of the knowledge that made them into adults. Sometimes pious adults even make such matters into contests of faith and faithfulness: "real" Christians can believe such things without breaking a sweat, so what's the matter with you?

I judge it to be bad practice to require people to pretend that they have not learned the hardest lesson of all, the lesson that in many cases marks the transition from innocence to awareness, from childhood to adulthood. Death is permanent, and adult storytellers who intend to tell true stories must acknowledge this. The resurrection of Jesus is an enormous problem.

The second problem in Mark's story is unique to Mark. For all of Mark's famous roughness, for all his much-noted abruptness and choppiness, Mark still tells a whole story. Event flows to event (with some bumps and jerks along the way), and the story traces a discernible narrative arc. And then comes the problem. The story becomes tighter and more predictable as it runs, and as it nears the end everything is knit together carefully. And then everything is chopped off. Pick any metaphor you like. The end is left to ravel, the sweep of the story is slammed into a brick wall, the story that has carefully and reliably made and kept promises from the very beginning suddenly refuses to keep the most important promise of all: that the disciples and the audience would see Jesus raised from the dead. No one sees Jesus, and the women run away silent.

This is a problem.

The ending slams the story to a halt, and with enough force that serious readers of the story continue after all these centuries to ask whether this is the intended ending or an ending imposed by the loss of pages or by the exigencies of oral storytelling or by some unknown mechanism.[28] Serious readers will always argue about the wholeness of Mark's story. The issue will not be easily settled. Even those readers who see in Mark a contemporary "self-voiding fiction" will find even this as unsettling an answer as any of the other contenders.

I judge Mark's story to be whole in the form we have it. I judge it to lack nothing that was ever needed for the story to work as designed. And as a performer, I find that the end is somewhere near impossible to carry off as written.

This is a problem.

These two considerations, the resurrection to life and the dead end, hang behind every sketch made in this chapter of the arc followed by the narrative. Every attempt to make sense of the flow of the whole story will be played out in front of the sheer impossibility of resurrection and in front of the looming dead end that comes at 16:8. That does not make these sketches less useful, or less real. But it does create a discriminator that will need to be used when it is time to evaluate the effectiveness of the proposed arcs. If Mark's story is whole, then it will have to finish by hitting its target. If the end of a story is both its target and its stopping point, if the end is (as Aristotle will have it) "that after which there is nothing," then the proposed narrative arcs will need to take into account all relevant energy and find ways that this energy is exhausted in Mark's dead end.

This is no easy task.

So we have seen the two biggest problems, and have got a glimpse of the trouble they cause. The question, then, is how do you hold Mark's story together?

This is where storytellers always start. Until they find what holds a story together, all they have is a list of scenes, a bagful of random parts. And so a storyteller, like an actor, like a director, runs and runs through the text, feeling for its texture. Texture is what allows a storyteller (of any sort) to get hold of a story. Interpreters sometimes note the presence of catchwords as evidence of storytelling texture. They surely are important, and they are indeed part of what a storyteller (or an actor or a director) feels for as she runs and runs through the text. But much more important is the narrative arc, the sweeping path that a story traces as it runs from its beginning and is pulled toward its end. In a well-crafted story, every bit of texture is a clue to the narrative arc of the text. And so a storyteller starts by running and running through the text, feeling for texture, following what might turn out to be narrative arcs, always looking for what will hold the story together. I will follow a few possibilities in Mark's story.

#1: Who Is This Guy?

If you survey the ways Mark's story has been read, you will notice that one way interpreters have held the story together is by organizing it around the character and activity of Jesus, in particular his career as a worker of wonders. If you take the wonder-working scenes as keys to coherence, what kind of texture do you find?

The first thing I notice is that the first and (second to) last wonder story resemble each other in that these are the first two (of four, total) uses of the title for Jesus that I have translated as "Netzer." See page 95 for a fuller discussion of this translational choice. If this identification of Jesus offers the hint that I think it offers, that Jesus is the sprout from the stump of Jesse, it will be important that this title arrives with the first and (second to) last wonder stories. The title brackets the set of wonder stories that may hold the story together. It may also identify these particular scenes as witnesses to Jesus' identity: because he works wonders of these sorts, he is the expected king who will turn the world right side up. This would be a bit of texture to hold onto.

The next thing I notice as I run through this string of wonder stories is that the flow is punctuated by four (largely) regularly spaced exorcisms. Since I am looking for patterns that create the texture of the text, I wonder whether these scenes mark something like measures in the music of the story. These "measure markers" can be seen above the line of the chapters in Mark's story in the figure on page 59. A look at the figure also shows that the first measure set

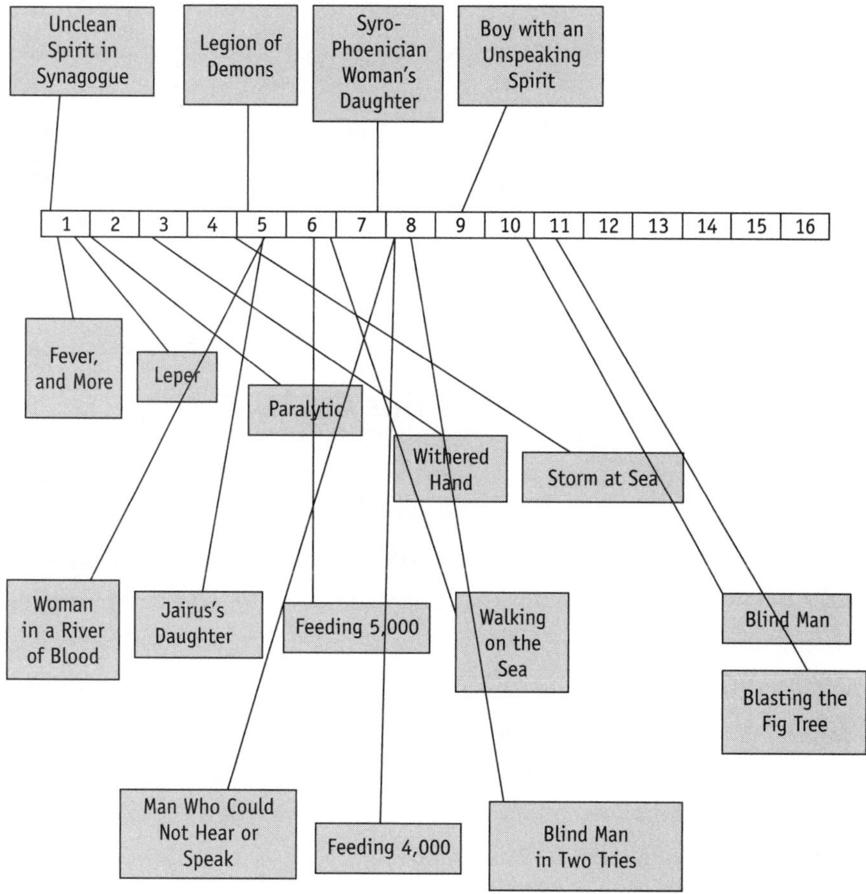

Wonder Stories

off by exorcisms contains five wonder stories, the second measure contains four, and the third measure contains three. This is also a promising bit of texture. The decreasing length of the measures suggests that the story becomes more compact as it runs along, perhaps it is speeding up, or maybe it is simply being distilled down to its powerful essence. Either option gives a storyteller something to work with.

The measures themselves show some intriguing patterns. The first wonder story in the first measure is a conglomeration of wonders, beginning with the healing of Simon's mother-in-law. This first wonder sets off a swirl of healings and exorcisms. Next Jesus cleanses a leper, raises a paralyzed man, restores a man with a withered hand to human community, and calms the sea. Thus ends the first measure. In the second measure, Jesus cleanses (accidentally) a woman with a hemorrhage, raises a little girl to life, feeds a huge crowd, and walks on the sea. This could simply be a string of random wonders, but each of these first two measures ends with a sea wonder, and each set of four wonders begins with a cleansing. This seems promising. I notice that the paralyzed man is fully as immobile as the dead little girl. I imagine that such an oddity would have been a powerful mystery in the ancient world, where such a person (assuming he was a quadriplegic, which is likely, given the description) would have been an odd hybrid of life and death: breathing and speaking and hearing, but not moving. What if both wonders constitute raising to life? I notice, further, that when the man with the withered hand was restored, he gained not only mobility in a single extremity, but (far more important) the ability to eat with others around a common table.[29] Eating, for Jewish community, is never just a matter of ingesting necessary nutrients. The table was a place to gather lost and scattered Israel. What if this wonder, then, is read as an eating wonder, along with the feeding of the huge crowd in the next measure?

This is a long string of "what ifs," but the result would be that the first and second measures share a common pattern: cleansing/raising/eating/sea. This would be good texture to hang onto as well.

The second and third measures do not share anything so regular as we have just encountered, but the presence of feeding wonders with ringing historical echoes in both measures links them tightly together. The second feeding wonder takes place in Gentile territory and likely with a Gentile populace. Mark's story brackets this second wonder with wonders involving hearing and seeing, the two senses used in chapter 4 to speak of the insight and understanding proper to the people of God. Then comes the exorcism that marks the end of the measure, and it involves speaking (also a factor in the wonder story before the last feeding wonder), and then the whole set of wonders is bracketed by a final healing of a blind man who sees very well indeed, since he is the second person to identify Jesus as the Netzer (and the first to see him as the son of David). All this makes the second feeding wonder an expansion of the work of the Netzer to include the whole creation, and the whole business is completed just in time to swirl into Jerusalem. This also is useful texture.

Then comes the final wonder story. Jesus has worked his way through the story all the way to Jerusalem. He has gone into Jerusalem and back out. The next morning, on his way back into the city, he curses a fig tree that could not possibly have had fruit, unless it were bearing out of season. When next he sees the fig tree, it is withered to its roots. How odd. The symbolic link between the fig tree and the Temple has been explored carefully. It has been noted that Jesus is asking the impossible of the tree. What may deserve consideration is whether Jesus' expectation is rooted in the kind of apocalyptic agronomy evidenced in 2 Baruch, where the grain grows so quickly that the reaper follows the sower. Is Jesus expecting the tree to be bearing the fruit of the messianic age already? Or is this a picture of a Jesus who is unreasonably demanding, condemning the tree for not doing what it could not do? Such a rootage would link this scene with the parable of the Sower, which would be interesting. Are these the roots of Jesus' unaccountable action? It is probably impossible to say, but the possibility is intriguing. That would make this a scene that culminates the explosion of Jesus' world-shattering expectations in Mark's story. Such an explosion would make the rest of Mark's story even more tense and fascinating than it already is. And that would link Jesus' teaching and wonder-working even more tightly.

But the failure of the fig tree to produce the fruit expected in the messianic age undermines the coherence of this story that bills itself as focusing on Jesus the messiah. This is a problem.

#2: Galilee and Jerusalem on Forty Dollars a Day

Interpreters have noted that Mark's Jesus is a traveler, and that his story can be charted geographically and read as a travelogue of sorts. Of course, nothing is that simple. While some interpreters notice Mark's geographical oddities (for instance, a long, looping journey that takes less than one verse to complete) and conclude that Mark did not know the land of Israel and could probably not have found Jerusalem on a map, others have pointed out that his mapping of the story shows evidence of a powerful awareness of the symbolism of place. Even his geographical oddities point to an organizational scheme that is more than geographically accurate rather than less. The locales in Mark's story are symbolically loaded, charged with power, and this affects the way things happen in the story. As interpreters have noted, the story orbits around two key locations: Galilee and Jerusalem, and moves between them in ways that make clear that Mark's story knows the symbolic value of each place over against the other. Notice, in passing, that the wonder-working stories take place in Galilee almost exclusively. Only the final wonder, the shattering blasting of the fig tree, takes place in Jerusalem.

There is more than geographical movement driving this story, even more than movement through a symbolic landscape. The story does not simply move around; it is pulled from place to place by promises. The figure on page 63 combines geography and promises to show how these factors hold the story together.

The first thing to notice in our hunt for texture is the way the Passion Predictions (in chapters 8, 9, and 10) tie the middle of the story to the end of the story. Each promise of the end throws a line into chapters 14, 15, and 16 of Mark's story and pulls them in tight to the rest of the story. These chapters are also tied to the rest of the story by promises made much earlier in the story, in chapter 3, when the death plot is first hatched and Judas is first introduced as the one who will hand Jesus over. Clearly the story is at great pains to establish supportive links that will weave the story of Jesus' death

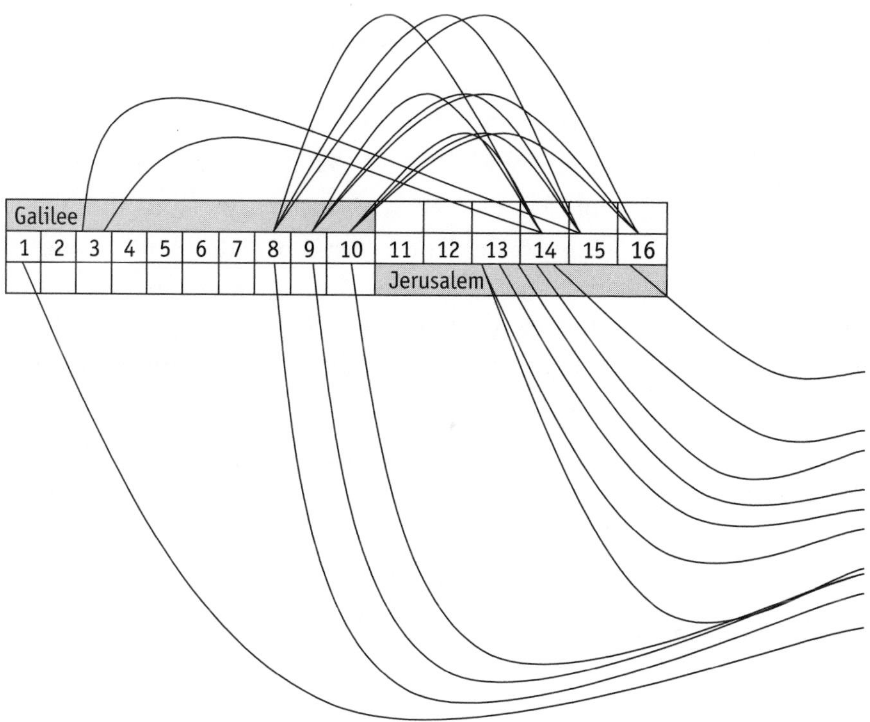

Promises Kept and Unkept

and resurrection into the narrative arc. Promises provide texture that a storyteller can hold onto.

The next thing to notice is that these promises are affected by location. Promises that are kept are made in Galilee. Promises that are not kept (at least not within the confines of the plotted narrative) are made in or near Jerusalem.[30] The bulk of these unkept promises are made in chapter 13, 14, and 16, all in Jerusalem. The unkept promise in chapter 1 is made by John the Baptist, who is near Jerusalem at the time. The apparent exceptions to this geographic rule occur in chapters 8, 9, and 10. The first two of these unkept promises involve God's coming with power; the last concerns the future of James and John promised to them after they ask for places of honor in the coming Dominion. While these three unkept promises are made in Galilee, they are made in contexts that are tightly tied to Jerusalem and the death at the end of the story. Perhaps it is not so much geography that creates promises not yet kept as it is proximity to Jesus' death?

Notice also that these promises, both kept and not kept, pull the story into its own future and beyond. This is clearly true of the promises that are kept. They create a web that suspends the whole story securely between promise and assured fulfillment. Some of the unkept promises do the same thing since they refer to events that are outside of the plotted narrative, but inside the audience's presumed experience. The Temple was indeed destroyed. There has indeed been trouble and tribulation. Thus not only the plotted narrative, but also the life of the audience itself is suspended in a web of promise. This same supportive web extends into the indefinite future, since some of the promises that are made extend beyond the boundaries of any possible world to the coming of God's final Dominion. This deep hope is also suspended in the web of promise.

The Ending and Its Completions

There is a final oddity to be accounted for in this outline. It is the most notable Markan oddity of all, the ending. If you were to suppose that the story is incomplete for whatever reason (remember the hypothetical Roman arrow?), then you need not make sense of the ending as it stands. If you suppose, however, that the gospel is complete as it stands, the oddity presented by 16:8 must affect how a storyteller charts the story. It is not enough to say, as did C. E. B. Cranfield, "Presumably Mark meant his words to be understood in a limited sense — their silence was only for a little while."[31] It is not even enough to agree with A. Stock and many others who see the ending as aimed to improve the discipleship of the reader.[32] The end is more disturbing than that, and the shock of the absent Jesus is greater. The encrustation of ancient alternative endings (Mark 16:9–20, with the various additions) is eloquent testimony to this.

What is interesting about these endings, especially the longer ending, is the way it completes the sweep of the narrative, the way it keeps the promises given in the narrative but not kept, though it does so in terms obviously borrowed from elsewhere.[33]

Promises made in the early narrative indicate that the audience should expect a rounded, concentric story. Promises are made and kept. Jesus, in particular, speaks authoritatively for the future of the narrative and of the world of the characters in the narrative. Certain expectations are raised, and rightfully. After all, Jesus is the Christ, the son of God; he is the stronger one, the one who will baptize with the Holy Spirit. He heals, he teaches with authority. He gives out the details of his own suffering and death, but he never does so without including mention of his subsequent resurrection. After his resurrection the remaining promises in the narrative will be fulfilled, and the rest of the story can come into play.

The rest of the story will involve the keeping of the pending promises. Some of these promises involve coming on the clouds with angels and power. These promises represent a promised future more secure than the troubled present (no matter what the circumstances of Mark's community). Others of the promises are normally to be fulfilled in the ordinary course of things — for instance, the destruction of the Temple.

One of the promises, that made to James and John (10:39), must be fulfilled, but can only be fulfilled if these two disciples (and by extension, the rest of the disciples) are rehabilitated. (Note that the disciples have, by their abject flight, disqualified themselves as followers of Jesus in the terms offered in 8:34–9:1.) Two more of the promises are essential for the completion of the narrative world, and for the existence of any community of Jesus' followers in any world at all. These two are the appearance of Jesus, seen by his followers just as he had promised, and the baptism with the Holy Spirit, promised by John at the beginning. When these promises are kept the story can go on.

The longer ending keeps these promises. Jesus is seen. He is seen again. He is seen yet again, and this time he scolds the hard-hearted disciples. Having settled the business of their unbelief, he sends them out, not this time for a limited journey (apparently in Galilee) as he did in chapter 6, but rather to preach the gospel to all the creation. Signs will attend their preaching. One of these signs, the speaking in new tongues, resembles the phenomenon accompanying the pouring out of the Holy Spirit as related in Acts. The narrative concludes with the audience being given a vision of Jesus seated at the right hand of God and of the faithful disciples preaching everywhere, the Lord working with them. This picture balances the identification of Jesus given in the first verse of the gospel, only now making it fully clear what it means to be the Christ, the son of God. This longer ending is not simply a fuller ending to the story; it is not simply built on the model of the other gospels in response to a gospel that neglected to include resurrection appearances. Quite the contrary, it would appear that the model for the fuller story (but not the source of the fill)[34] was the story itself—in particular, the unkept promises in the story.

These promises are kept, one by one, proceeding outward from the center of the universe of the story, from Jerusalem, specifically, from the cross. The result is the rounded, concentric narrative that has been promised.

The ending, however, is clearly secondary.[35] Mark ends at 16:8, in silence, flight, and incompletion.

The Ending and Its Incompletion

The narrative, and Jesus in particular, have orbited around its center, Jerusalem and the cross, like a comet, with each tug from Jerusalem, each approach, adding energy and speed to the story. The story comes to its close with Jesus dodging in and out of Jerusalem, like a ball in a gravity well, like a comet close to the sun. The speed increases, and the promise of a future in Galilee leads to the expectation that the final swing around the center in Jerusalem will produce the momentum needed for the jump back out to Galilee and thence to the whole creation. But this comet slams to a halt at 16:8. "They said nothing to nobody." The piled negatives make this an even stronger statement than it appears in English, where it is simply bad grammar.

The result is that the narrative, which has promised to be fully rounded, is not concentric at all, but eccentric.[36] The story crashes into a wall with Jesus raised, never to be seen, because there remains not a single human agency, not even that of the women whose ministry stretched from the beginning to the very end, available to carry on the movement promised by the narrative. As far as any human character is equipped to say, Jesus is dead, forsaken by God, and the story is at an end, a dead end.

This, of course, does not explain the telling of the story. This, of course, does not explain the audience that hears the story. This, of course, does not explain the faith, faith precisely in Jesus raised, Jesus, the king at God's right hand, that led to both the telling and the reading of the story in the first place. All of this must be explained by something else, also within the story, something else driving the story, something strong enough to account for the existence of the story and of the believing audience in the face of absolute human impossibility. But what could that be? We started with a simple question about how you hold Mark's story together, and finish with a much larger question about how we could know, tell, or hear the story in the first place. Perhaps we ought to go back and start again.

#3: So That They Not See and Not Understand

This third try at establishing a narrative arc for Mark's story returns to a consideration of the character and activity of Jesus, concentrating this time on Jesus the teacher and storyteller. This attempt has the virtue of pulling the first two attempts together, as you will see. It also has the virtue of catching the title most often given to Jesus in Mark's story: Teacher.

This attempt also poses an intriguing problem for a contemporary storyteller. If Mark's story holds together around the figure of Jesus the storyteller, a contemporary storyteller is telling the story of a storyteller, and will have to decide how to tell these embedded stories along the way. The question, of course, is how these embedded stories affect the story that carries them.

Parable as Plot Synopsis

Several recent interpreters have addressed this question. For instance, Mary Ann Tolbert and John Drury have heard the parables as offering a plot synopsis[37] or "programme notes to a drama."[38] These notions are so tightly similar to each other as to be nearly indistinguishable. Both, for instance, see the parable of the Sower as revealing "what . . . is going to happen in the story"[39] "before the actual telling of the tale begins."[40]

It is interesting here that Drury and Tolbert read the allegorical pointing of the parable somewhat differently. In Tolbert's construal, Peter and the disciples represent the rocky ground, not without cause, and not least because of the meaning of Peter's name.[41] Drury, however, sees Peter as pathlike in that his confession at 8:27 is immediately afterward plucked away when he begins to rebuke Jesus.[42] The tale has been told ahead of time, but it appears that there is still room for differences in interpretation.

More interesting, however, are the differences that emerge more clearly as the construal of the functioning of the parables continues and expands. These differences result from the differences in background that each interpreter has chosen. Because Tolbert works with models drawn from Hellenistic popular novels,[43] Mark's parables can only function as allegorical plot synopses. This is a valid role for the parables to play, but it is a small one. Just how small a role this is may be made clear by quoting one such oracle cited by Tolbert, that from Xenophon's *An Ephesian Tale*.

> Why do you want to know the cause and final outcome of the illness?
> One disease afflicts both youngsters, and one remedy will cure them both.
> Before the suffering is over, I predict terrible experiences for them.
> Pirates will pursue and chase them over the sea;
> And they will wear the chains put on them by seamen;

A grave will be a bridal chamber for both, and there will also
be a terrible fire.
Then later by the banks of the Nile you will deliver up
Rich gifts to holy Isis, the savior
After all their suffering, both will enjoy a happier fate.[44]

The difference between this flat-footed plot synopsis and the parable of the Sower ought to be immediately apparent. Though both point ahead to the coming story, there is no allegory in Xenophon's oracle, and little suggestive power. There will be a nautical chase scene, complete with chains and pirates, and, oh yes, a terrible fire. Some other things will happen as well. With the parable of the Sower in Mark's narrative, Drury and Tolbert could differ productively and interestingly in applying it to the story, but there is no room in Xenophon for such productive ambiguity. A fire is a fire. A grave is a grave. A happy ending is a happy ending. While it is clear that such bald foreshadowing is appropriate to the genre (and it is Tolbert's able discussion that makes this apparent), it is not clear that Mark's parables closely resemble this oracle, either in form or function.

Drury's construal is more promising, if only because he notes that Mark's parables are, in fact, parables, and not merely "third-degree narrative." Drury says, "From a standpoint outside the narrative, allowed by the break in narrative which is always made by a parable, it clarifies the narrative's overall thrust."[45] It is the "break in the narrative" that is crucial.

Gospel in/against Parable

I now turn to two scholars whose work is similar (though the titles of their studies would not immediately indicate that similarity): John R. Donahue and his *The Gospel in Parable*,[46] and James G. Williams and his *Gospel against Parable*.[47] Both read the parables in their narrative context, as did Tolbert and Drury. Neither develops the allegorical connection between the parables as extensively as did Tolbert and Drury. Both continue in the same stream as Drury: the parables are interpreted not only as "plot synopses" but as parables, and therefore as independent, assertive texts in their own right.

Donahue seeks "a more secure context for interpreting the parables," having noted that "the original context of the parables and sayings is no longer accessible to us."[48] He finds this "more secure context" in the individual gospels in which the parables are found. In that he will interpret the parables as parts of the narratives in which they appear, his work is similar to that of Tolbert and Drury, but his work marks a significant advance beyond theirs in at least two ways.

First of all, Donahue works with a richer sense of the connection of the parables to the narrative in which they are embedded. His sense is richer than Tolbert's in that he treats the parables not principally as "plot synopses" but as parables. His sense is richer than Drury's in that he finds the power of the parables not primarily in their connection to the history of the use of parables in Jewish Scripture, but in their function as "an entree to the theology of a given Gospel and as a reflection of its major themes."[49]

Second, Donahue brings to his study a strong awareness of the independent power of the parables to shake and disorder too-staid, too-stable worlds. Donahue seeks to preserve this power even as he works in a "more secure context." A parable, he says, must be allowed "to exercise its own power on the hearers and not be reduced to moral precepts or theological ideas."[50] He says, "The parable is a question waiting for an answer, an invitation waiting for a response."[51]

It is this perception of the power of a parable that creates the most problems, and the most interest. It is precisely this perception of polyvalence that Tolbert and Drury avoid, and thus make parables less vivid, less powerful, less intriguing than they are in themselves. Donahue's intention to treat the parables in context, while yet remembering and respecting their polyvalent force, makes his study most promising. In Donahue's understanding, "Mark not only contains the parables of Jesus; it is a 'written parable.' "[52]

Williams senses, more acutely than Donahue, the tension between the parables and their narrative context. He argues that Mark "tries at times to implode the gospel narrative into the parables as though they are microcosms of the whole."[53] At the same time, Williams notes that "given the very character of the parables, they are never completely at home in a larger narrative context."[54] The parables, thus, are both "necessary and dangerous"[55] in Mark's view. Because they are necessary, Mark presents the parables in his narrative. Because they are dangerous, only a few are presented, and these few come only in a narrative context that functions to control the parables, that acts as a "reliable guide to the parables."[56] As Williams puts it, "The written gospel is the bulwark against disbelief, anarchy and obscurity. It is a better guarantee than the apostles themselves!"[57]

At the same time, Williams understands the parables as "protection of the gospel narrative, keeping it opened up to the unstoried dimension of reality, to the beyond, to the transcendent."[58]

The parables and Mark's story need each other. Without the larger narrative, the parables threaten to shatter the world, especially in unauthorized hands. Without the parables, the larger narrative threatens to become closed and ordinary. While I do not find Mark's story to be in any danger of becoming ordinary (the problems caused by Mark's odd ending need controlling fully as much as any parable ever could), Williams has caught something important here. The parables and the story that contains them always rub and bump against each other.

Parable as Mirror, Gospel as Crystal

I turn now to a final pair of interpreters, Yvàn Almeida and Paul Ricoeur, who have presented yet another, tighter understanding of the relationship between the parables and the narrative.

Almeida, in *L'Opérativité sémantique des récits-paraboles*, presents a detailed, fully articulated study of the longer narrative parables (*récits-paraboles*: the parables of the Sower and the Vineyard) in Mark's narrative. His definition of a "narrative parable" begins at an exceedingly general level, "a narrative related by a character in another surrounding narrative."[59]

These two embedded stories, one near the beginning of Mark, one near the end, flow in opposite directions. The flow of the Sower he calls *euphorique*, that of the Vineyard, *dysphorique*.[60] (In French, a disease that is following a *parcours euphorique* is on a trajectory that will lead to a positive outcome. A *parcours dysphorique* would lead to the opposite outcome.) Almeida argues that these two narrative parables constitute together

> a semantic micro-universe that crystallizes the principal categories of the surrounding narrative. From this point of view . . . one could say that they constitute a sort of mirror, more schematic and thus more striking, of the narrative and semantic structure of the whole of Mark.[61]

Note the striking force of the metaphors Almeida has used to understand the relationship between the narrative parables and the larger narrative. The gospel crystallizes around the narrative parables. The narrative parables mirror the structure of the larger story. These metaphors promise to be productive. They clearly are richer than the notions seen in Tolbert and Drury, plot synopsis and program note. Donahue looks through the window of the parables to see the theology and themes of the gospels. Williams watches the struggle between the parables and the larger narrative, with one side pushing toward open freedom, the other toward closed control. Almeida's metaphor more adequately renders both the conflict and cooperation between the parables and the larger narrative.

Ricoeur's treatment of the narrative parables in Mark flows in very much the same channel. They even share the metaphor of the mirror. There is, however, a basic and important difference. Ricoeur carries out his study in a fashion "that yet notes the dynamism to the work in the narrative [parable], in order to understand how this dynamism is transgressed through being set [in a larger work]."[62]

Both the narrative parables and the larger story have a powerful force and flow, and it is the pattern of eddies and swirls of conflict that must be studied if you are to understand either the parable or the story. To complicate things further, these two narrative parables flow in opposite directions. These two directed flows cross each other inside Mark's story, and they clash. And then they swirl and clash with the larger story, which, Ricoeur notes, "tells the story of the one who told the parables."[63]

In his charting of the narrative arc, Ricoeur traces two inversely related processes. The first flows toward recognition of Jesus as the Christ.[64] The second flows from Jesus' early success as a wonder worker to his own death.[65] It is these processes, seen in the larger narrative and mirrored also in the narrative parables, that connect Mark's parables and Mark's narrative. As Ricoeur says:

> One sees, thus, springing up a certain parallelism between the global narrative structure of the Gospel and that of these two parables taken together. This is that parallelism instituted by the text — through the text — that gives rise to the process of mutual parabolization of the surrounding narrative and of the narratives set in it.[66]

The flow toward death and disaster (traced by both Ricoeur and Almeida) seems well-charted. It is the *parcours euphorique* that seems questionable. Both Almeida and Ricoeur see this trajectory reaching its culmination in the "confession" of the centurion at the cross.[67] While it is clearly true that what the centurion says is ironically true, and while it is possible to construe his words as being one more instance of oddly unmotivated faith in Mark's narrative,[68] there are compelling reasons to suppose, with Donald Juel, that the centurion's words are not a confession but a taunt.[69]

First of all, note that the centurion's words complete a series of three equivalent identifications of Jesus, each spoken by a determined opponent of Jesus: the High Priest, Pilate, and now the centurion.[70] Further, this scene is properly viewed in conjunction with two other scenes in Mark's narrative: Jesus' baptism and the Transfiguration. These scenes, placed at the beginning, the middle, and the end of the narrative, each present Jesus in the company of an Elijah figure: John the Baptist in the first, Elijah himself in the second, and the absence of Elijah in the last. The tone of this last scene is particularly important for the construal of this series of three connected scenes. Elijah is present only because Jesus' enemies oddly misunderstand him as crying for Elijah. Elijah is not coming, and his absence is palpable. Jesus' cry and the centurion's words complete the set of connections between these scenes. In the first two scenes, God speaks and identifies Jesus as God's Son. In the last scene, Jesus cries out, accusing God of having abandoned him. In the midst of darkness and death, God is silent. It is the centurion who speaks, and though he says what God should have said (had God spoken), his voice sounds different. He is, after all, not merely some unidentified Gentile whose insight is surprisingly unmotivated. He is the centurion in charge of the soldiers who have tortured and crucified Jesus.

The centurion's words could still be understood as a confession if they marked a channel in which the story would flow subsequently. In the estimation of Almeida and Ricoeur, they do, but this is only because each includes Mark 16:9–20 as part of Mark's narrative.[71] If the story flowed on toward the rehabilitation of the disciples, the mission of Jesus' followers, and the seating of Jesus at the right hand of God, then the centurion's words could be taken as the culmination of a *procés euphorique*. If, however, Mark's narrative ends properly at 16:8 and Almeida and Ricoeur have read the rounded, concentric narrative that was promised, they have not read the story that Mark wrote. The ending of Mark's narrative makes the completion of the promised rounded and concentric narrative impossible. At the end of Mark's story, there is silence, and this silence is no proper culmination of the progressive recognition of Jesus as the Christ.

I would even ask whether there is in the larger narrative a discernible flow toward increasing recognition of Jesus as the Christ. I might rather argue that the flow runs in the opposite direction. At the beginning of the story, Jesus' disciples are presented as insiders who are given explanations (though they show no consistent comprehension). At the end, the male disciples have all run off, and even

Jesus is outside, abandoned even by God. The flow of comprehension in Mark's story is erratic and unpredictable. If this is true, the construal of the *parcours euphorique* offered by Almeida and Ricoeur is open to serious question. Once again, the ending of Mark's story is causing trouble.

#4: If the End Is Always the Problem, Perhaps...

Always the end causes the trouble. The ancient manuscript tradition attempts to solve the problem of the end by changing the end. So do Ricoeur and Almeida. So does the bulk of the interpretive tradition.

What if the brokenness of the end is what holds Mark's story together?

What if the certainty of the impossible event is the sun at the center of the orbit of the narrative arc?

Because the event is impossible, this should lead us to expect an eccentric story. The careful promises of concentricity set up the shock of the story's eccentricity. Because of the way hope is structured in Jewish Apocalyptic texts (and faith), we should expect Mark's story to create the proper ache, to provoke the proper demand for fulfillment. The careful withholding of the central event-that-cannot-be-an-event provokes exactly this.

All this implies that a proper telling of Mark's story is careful not to deliver what is demanded.

Interpreters have heard something like this. For instance, interpreters frequently hear in the portrayal of the disciples (especially at the end of the story) a call for the audience to "out-disciple" the failed disciples. This is a useful reading of the force of the end, but it misses the careful twisting of the story.

At the end of Mark's story, Jesus is clearly raised, but nobody sees him, not even the storyteller as she runs and runs through the text hunting for texture.

This leaves the audience (and the players) in a world that is clearly changed by the resurrection of Jesus, but just as clearly unaffected by it. The end of the story leaves the audience (and the players) in the hands of the God who raises the dead to life. Remember the paralytic? Remember Jairus's daughter? Remember the boy who fell to the ground and people said: "He's dead!"? In Mark's story, God raises the dead, including Jesus, but never makes it clear *how* this raising happens.

This is the place to which Jewish faith is always driven.

Now Gentiles are initiated into this faithful waiting, into holy impatience, into the life-giving demand for life even out of death.

But this only happens if the story is broken at the end, with the brokenness serving as a witness to the event-that-cannot-be-an-event.

The coherence of the story depends on exactly the same factor as does the story's authority: this is a story that holds together when it provokes the audience to wrestle. This is a story of Israel.

And in the end, really, there's nothing much to say about a true war story, except maybe "Oh."[72]

Chapter Three

TEXTS IN THEIR CON-TEXTS

Section 1: ADVENT, CHRISTMAS, AND EPIPHANY

1. Advent 1 Mark 13:24–37

(see translation, p. 318)

Ritual Text: The Life of the Worshiping Community

The school year has begun. Thanksgiving is past. Stores have been counting the days until Christmas since Halloween at least. Sports commentators will soon be making real predictions about who will play in the Super Bowl. Sunday school children will be practicing for their Christmas programs. The calendar is filled with Christmas parties and open houses.

Each of these "end-times" comes with a set of rituals: rituals of waiting, rituals of expectation, rituals of arrival. They all follow predictable paths. That is the useful thing about rituals. They create moments of predictability in the middle of rushing chaos.

In the middle of this crush, Christians tell each other this scene from Mark's story as they prepare for the ritual celebration of Christmas. Though Mark's story has no birth scene at all, the gospel buzzes with the insistence that God make good on promises that have been made, but not sufficiently kept. Most of these promises are implicit in creation before they are explicit in Torah. Because beauty and joy and nurturing love are basic experiences of life, even in the midst of disaster, Jewish faith expects that these experiences ought not be the privilege of only a few lucky people. Deep in Jewish notions of what it means to live in a world crafted by God is the expectation that the obvious goodness of creation should be visible from every angle, from every possible perspective. That is what it means to have God be the one who says that the creation is, day by day, good and exceedingly good. God is, by definition, the One who sees all things from every possible perspective. Before God can say, "It is good," it has to be good no matter where you stand. Throughout Mark's story the characters of the story encounter limitations on the experienced goodness of creation, and expect that these limitations will be removed. "Heal my daughter," says one woman. "Rabbi, I wish to see," says a man. In the scene for this Sunday's text, all of these expectations, these demands crowd together and Jesus tells those who wait with him for God to keep the promise of creation, "Chase sleep away." No one knows when, but Jewish faith knows that, with reminders, God may be counted on to keep the old promises.

Advent is a time for Christians to practice hoping bigger hopes, to practice raising their eyes to see the parts of creation that no one (least of all, God) could look at and proclaim as good. Advent is a time for Christians, every year, to practice being part of the people of God in a damaged creation. Part of this practice includes faithful and sharp-eyed examination of the realities of life in this world. Part of this practice ought also to include meditation on the situation out of which Jesus spoke the words in this scene in Mark's story. Jesus lived late in the messy aftermath of the Maccabean rebellion, a complicated mix of victory and defeat, of freedom and bondage. Jesus lived in the shadow of the Roman Empire in a family and faith uneasy under foreign domination. Jesus embodied the tensions that lead to the first and second Jewish revolts against Rome (70 CE and 135 CE), and Mark's story achieved fixed form sometime between these two revolts. That means, at the very least, that the Jesus we encounter in this scene is shaped both by the rich, insistent hope of Jewish faith and by the wise realism of Jewish faith. The Temple, which is very much the center of Jesus' world in Mark's gospel, was a heap of rubble long before Mark's story received its final telling. Christians, as they prepare for Christmas, have a lot to learn about hopes that shatter the skies and about realism that remembers the deep pain of real loss. This small scene from Mark's story can help.

Intra-Text: The World of Mark's Story

Some of the promises that stretch beyond the boundaries of Mark's narrative world stretch beyond the boundaries of any possible world, stretch all the way to the culmination of all things. This scene from Mark 13 holds such promises. The images create a scene of decreation, with the stable markers of the heavens being moved from their places. The images promise to gather all of lost and scattered Israel. The images call for watchfulness. Because the promises extend not only beyond the borders of the story but also beyond the world as presently constituted, a storyteller must pay careful attention to how this structure holds and shapes the audience. The story is using the reliability of the rhythm of making and keeping promises to hold the audience in a web of promises that extend out beyond the disastrous aftermath of the First Jewish Revolt. Wherever Mark's story had its natural home, its shape reveals that the destruction of the Temple mattered enormously to the audience. Mark's story warns of the destruction of the Temple, and that warning was borne out in the experience of the audience. Now they wait, somewhere, shaken by the experience, expecting something more out of all the expectations stirred by the career of Jesus. In this scene, the storyteller gathers those expectations and points the audience's eyes out beyond the horizon.

Of course, Mark's story has carefully complicated the matter of keeping central promises. In telling the story of the resurrection, Mark's story promises that the disciples will see Jesus, only to carefully withhold exactly that encounter. The last link that could have passed on the promise is broken when the women are forever silent. This, of course, raises the question of how anyone knows the story to tell it at all. They said nothing. But the audience is hearing the story of how they said nothing. How can that be?

Inter-Text: The World We Think We Live In

Gathering from the four winds is no mere image. In 722 BCE, after a brutal fight, the Northern Kingdom fell to the Assyrian army and was obliterated. The army was destroyed. The cities were sacked. The people were ripped from their houses and lands and scattered into Exile. Exile, in Assyrian practice, meant that all the people would be uprooted and dispersed throughout the Empire. Exile, ideally, meant that conquered peoples would be broken into pieces, crushed together with all other conquered peoples, and separated forever from their families, their lands, and their stories. Hobbyists and crackpots will continue to hunt for the scattered remnants of the Northern Kingdom, but they are gone, vanished. Jewish faith, from ancient times forward, insists that God must regather what Assyria scattered.

Assyria, of course, was not the last scatterer. After Assyria came Babylon, which conquered the Southern Kingdom in 587 BCE. After Babylon came a long parade of overlords: Persia, the Seleucid Empire, Rome, the Turks, the Crusaders. Jews were scattered, too, simply by economic and social forces.

Provoking the Story

How do you tell this as a true story? In workshops, people often play this scene as if they were revivalist preachers. In the northern United States, people usually affect a heavy (and phony) southern drawl to do this. (I don't know what they do in the South; I've never taught this text there.)

This is revealing. Northerners who use a southern drawl indicate that they view the promises in this scene as suspect and even impossible. Perhaps ancient audiences were predisposed to agree. Perhaps Mark's story comments, with bitter irony, on the likelihood that lost and scattered Israel will ever come home. If so, a storyteller would do well to figure out how this bitter irony shapes the rest of Mark's story, and then apply these discoveries to playing this scene. Skip the phony accents.

It is also possible that this scene represents the tattered, but still living hopes of a community shocked by the failure of the First Jewish Revolt. They look to the horizon with skepticism and hope combined. Played this way, the lines about chasing sleep away imply that hope will be hard to see without intense alertness.

Or perhaps Mark's ancient audience was spared the cataclysm of the destruction of the Temple and was congratulating themselves on their good judgment and luck. As an old song says, "It's not hard to get along with someone else's trouble." If so, then this scene is inhabited by people who need to be awakened before they can be enjoined to chase sleep away.

The question, as always, is how to tell this as a true story. It is not an easy question to answer.

2. Advent 2
Mark 1:1–8

(see translation, p. 255)

Ritual Text: The Life of the Worshiping Community

This scene from Mark's story is selected because John has the power to raise eyes to larger views of God's creation. John appears and gives voice to hopes that he shared with Jews throughout his world. People went out to hear John because of the strength of their hopes.

How strong was that hope? Mark tells us that every person living in Jerusalem went out to hear John. Mark gives us no reason to be suspicious of these people. They swirl out of Jerusalem and spin around John because they have been raised to hope that God would act to heal creation, to make straight the roads that lead out of slavery into freedom and promise.

I have always wondered whether this text was chosen because of all the people who crowd in during Advent and Christmas. A friend calls them "amateur Christians." For some this will be their last practice until Easter. But my friend understands the word "amateur" carefully. They may well be out of practice, but they are in church because there is something that they love. He prepares these services carefully so that they, like the people drawn out to John at the Jordan, can raise their eyes to the needs and hopes of God's whole creation.

Intra-Text: The World of Mark's Story

This is the beginning of the good news. It is also the beginning of the making and keeping of promises. The storyteller announces the beginning of the story, but before the story can begin, Isaiah must be summoned to deliver promises. Exodus and Malachi are also drawn in, but the story calls only Isaiah's name, only the prophet from the time of the return from Exile, the return to the land to rebuild the Temple that had been destroyed. Remember that Mark's story is being told after the Second Temple had been destroyed when the Romans crushed the First Jewish Revolt. The ancient audience knew this, and it will have lent a certain poignancy to this scene.

Isaiah enters, carrying the old composite promise of someone who will prepare the people for restoration. John appears; he draws the whole region to him, and every person in Jerusalem swirls around him. The storyteller is creating a world that swirls and races in response to the promise of restoration and rest.

As soon as John begins his work, he speaks a promise. Another is coming, another stronger than John. This note means that John's career (briefly but vigorously described) is itself a promise of what is coming next. If John can make the region jump and run, what will this other do? If John appears in clothing coded for Elijah, what will this other do? If John washes people to prepare them to participate in old, old promises (long delayed and deferred), what will this other do?

Of course, in the whole story John collides with Herod (Rome's puppet), and is crushed. At the end of his last scene, his headless body is dragged out of the story. If John is killed because he is inconvenient to the Empire (and thus is marked as either a martyr or a fool or both), what will this other do? Do not assume too easily that you know the answer to this last question.

Inter-Text: The World We Think We Live In

The Exile in Babylon was the crucible in which both Jewish identity and Jewish assimilation were formed. When Cyrus the Persian issued his edict that allowed the Jewish community to return to the land, some did and some did not. Both instances are remarkable.

For the Jewish community to have remained sufficiently coherent and self-aware to be able to stand up and go home to rebuild the Temple after seventy uncertain years of Exile is an astonishing accomplishment. Read Psalm 137 for a glimpse of what the crushing weight of Exile felt like. The strategies that preserved the Jewish people shape the creation stories told in Genesis 1 and 2. Both stories show an awareness of Babylonian origin stories, chiefly the story of the violent conflict between Marduk and Tiamat. Both Genesis stories refuse the violence that creates the world out of the slaughter of a female deity. The Jewish community in Exile knows Babylonian violence up close, and they tell a story that refuses to create the world out of domestic abuse. God does not slaughter the world into being; God speaks to it as a mother speaks to her unborn child.[73] Woman and man are not victim and savage; they are together equally the image of God. Human life is not formed from clotted blood. God forms life from soil and water and breath, and the apparently androgynous mud-creature becomes a living, breathing, desiring being.

The promise sung by Isaiah was that the roads to rebuilding would be smooth and straight. They were not. Read Ezra and Nehemiah to see how crooked and complicated it all became. Paul D. Hanson sees the dawn of apocalyptic in the disappointed and blocked hopes of some members of the returning community. The promises that the storyteller calls into the story are thus tense promises, promises that remind the audience that there are promises that God has not been so good at keeping. To call such a situation to mind at the beginning of the gospel of a messiah creates a strange tension in the room. Is this going to be a story that settles old scores and finally makes good on old promises? Or is this going to be a story about how things come up just a little short yet again? Do not assume that you know the answer just because you are a Christian or because you believe that Jesus is the right answer to every question, whether in Sunday school or out.

Provoking the Story

How would the story be told if it were a story of deferred promises that will be deferred yet again? Explore this narrative arc carefully. The standard telling of this scene bubbles with joy and demand. The standard telling is worth exploring, too, but it is easy. There are more surprises in exploring the deferred promises.

3. Baptism of Our Lord
Mark 1:4–11

(see translation, p. 255)

Ritual Text: The Life of the Worshiping Community

This day catches a central oddity in the church's spiral: just three weeks ago we celebrated the birth of Jesus, just a week ago we celebrated the arrival of outsiders at his birthplace, and now this day we celebrate an event in which he is fully an adult. Time is quite compressed.

Before we race on, we ought to ask: What happened to Jesus' childhood? A decent theology of the Incarnation requires us to ask what led him from his birth to John the Baptist who called Jews to remember the hopes and disciplines that set them apart for good in the world. When Jesus looked at John, what in his upbringing prepared him to see someone like Elijah?

These are not idle questions, and they spring not simply from vague curiosity, but from a theological commitment to the human reality of Jesus' incarnate life. Mark's story helps us with them not at all. Jesus may step into churchly stories as the right answer to every question, but he steps into the beginning of Mark's story mostly as a question. Where did he come from? Why is he here? What is he up to? The teller of ritual stories must, from time to time, be not only a theologian but also a historian. The historian must examine the environment, culture, and social movements that lead up to and flow out of this scene. This examination matters for a storyteller because tone and stance and rhythm grow out of decisions the teller makes about the backstory of the characters in the story. It will not do to simply call forth the usual immutable and impassive Jesus fresh from the heavens. Such a figure fits into pagan notions of a god who is unaffected by the world, but they do not fit into either Jewish or Christian biblical stories in which God (and Jesus) have hopes and anger and sadness and compassion and a backstory. When the voice in this scene claims Jesus as offspring, the voice claims a normal human being who came from somewhere.

So where does Jesus come from in Mark's story? A storyteller who needs an answer to this question will begin to tell this scene with a sense of disorientation and active puzzlement. That's often a good place from which to begin. An alternative: a storyteller who needs an answer to this question will tell this scene many ways, will hand the audience the task of sorting out the tensions with which Mark begins his story of Jesus. That would be a good gift to any audience.

Intra-Text: The World of Mark's Story

This scene grows out of the promises with which the story begins. John appears in the story, drawn by ancient promises. Jesus comes to John, drawn by the promises John spoke when he made the world spin. And now, as Jesus is coming up out of the water, a storyteller can see links that bind this scene to the exact middle and to the very end of Mark's story.

In the middle of Mark's story a voice again comes, and the voice again identifies Jesus as "my son, the beloved." A storyteller will have to wonder why it is that the voice is given two speaking parts in the story and chooses to say the same thing both times. If this is God speaking, the repetition of the line about the beloved son indicates either that God in this narrative world has little imagination or freedom, or that the line is so important that it bears repeating. In the middle of the story, the audience hears the voice in the presence also of Moses and Elijah. While I see no evidence of Moses in chapter 1, commentators note that John wears clothing coded for Elijah. This is yet another link between the beginning and the middle of Mark's story.

The heavens are ripped. They are not "opened," as in Luke's story. They are ripped, and the violence done to the dome that separates (in Genesis 1) the "waters from the waters," or (in first-century Judaism) God's dominion from the dominion of creation[74] is figured as permanent damage that will require mending. The barrier between the inexorable and the ordinary is breached. What will this mean for the telling of the rest of the story? Good question. It will have to mean something.

Nothing rips in the middle of the story. Perhaps Moses and Elijah have access to the narrative world because the barrier between realms has been broken, but that is a guess (worth exploring) and not an assured conclusion. Nothing is ripped in the middle of the story, but something is ripped at the end. When Jesus is tortured to death, the curtain in the Temple is torn in two, and a voice speaks about a son of God. There is even a mention of Elijah. But these are strange similarities. Elijah is mentioned because he is absent. The comment about the "son of God" is a vile taunt delivered by the person in charge of the torture.[75] And the voice speaks, not out of heaven, but out of the darkness that surrounds the murder, and this voice makes it clear that it is unwise to draw Rome's attention. Rome can do whatever it wants, and in this case it wanted to make an example of a pretender and a rabble-rouser by torturing him to death publicly.

These three scenes tie Mark's story together, but this is a strange bundle when it's done. The last scene shoots tension back into the other two scenes, and compromises the sunny brightness that fills those scenes. The question for a storyteller will be how to tell this first story so that it can be tied to its mates. The torture scene at the end must cast its shadow over the earlier scenes, just as the earlier scenes must inject a certain oddity into the death scene. These tensions are crucial. Do not let your awareness of the resurrection weaken your telling of these scenes. The story as a whole will stumble if you do.

Inter-Text: The World We Think We Live In

"This is my son."

These words come from many human contexts, from graduations to morgues. The words carry power and pain in each of those multiple settings. In this scene, tied both to creation imagery and to Mark's crucifixion scene, the words name Jesus in a way that will be decisive in Mark's story. Christians are accustomed to hearing Jesus' divinity in these words. However important that theological notion might be, the words say something far more important about Jesus in Mark's story.

As Donald Juel (among others) has convincingly shown, these words identify Jesus as God's messiah.[76] There is a scriptural argument being made here, one that links together passages according to rules developed to help Jews find out how to "turn and turn" the Bible, because "everything is in it."[77] These exploratory practices give depth and dimension to what would otherwise be thin ideas. In place of isolated bits of Scripture, there emerges a richly woven tapestry in which Psalm 2 is linked to Psalm 110, and to 2 Samuel 7, and to other passages that can be brought to surround the issue being explored. Jesus is called "son." So is the king. The king is anointed. So is, if by name alone, messiah; so is a priest; so is a prophet. To call Jesus "son" is to identify him as a prophet, a priest, a king of Israel, a king of the Jews, which is what Pilate names him at his execution. All of these interwoven passages are brought to surround this scene as Jesus is coming up out of the water.

Bat qol or divine voice

> It has been taught: R. Jose says: "I was once traveling on the road and I entered into one of the ruins of Jerusalem in order to pray. Elijah of blessed memory appeared and waited for me at the entrance until I had finished my prayer. After I finished my prayer he said to me, 'My son, what sound did you hear in this ruin?' 'I heard a divine voice [*bat qol*] cooing like a dove and saying, "Woe to the children on account of whose sins I destroyed My house and burnt My Temple and exiled them among the nations of the world!" ' And he said to me: 'By your life and by your head! Not in this moment alone does it so exclaim, but thrice each day does it proclaim thus . . . ' " [B. Ber. 3b]

The "daughter of a voice," the echo by which God still speaks into a world that no longer hears God's voice, sounds in this scene from Mark 1. The image deserves careful consideration. The scene from Mark contains a voice, a pigeon (or dove, the word is the same), and an Elijah-like figure. So does the scene from the rabbis. Other *bat qol* scenes contain rushing wind (remember that wind, breath, and spirit are all translations of the same Greek and Hebrew words) and fire.[78] The scene from the rabbis takes place in the ruins of Jerusalem. It is arguable that each of the gospels, and perhaps especially Mark, takes place in those same ruins.[79] If the destruction of Jerusalem and the Temple are the depredations that give rise to the echo of a voice in Jewish life and thought from those centuries, then it will be wise to reflect on how the telling of the story of Jesus also reacts to those devastations. If the echo of God's absent voice pronounces woe to the children, why does that voice also name Jesus as son? Is this a contrasting opinion, or is there something else operating here? Christians need to practice remembering that more was expected of a messiah than was delivered during the career of Jesus.

This practice comes hard for Christians, who are accustomed to projecting Jesus' glory into the heavens and the screen of eternity. Such projecting may be necessary and appropriate, but Christians who tell this story must practice noticing that this defers the effect of God's care for creation. To name Jesus messiah (as "reinterpreted" by God) is to abandon creation in favor of re-creation. This abandonment leaves behind only an echo of God's promised redemption, and no redemption itself. If this is how one ought to view this scene with its *bat qol*, then there is a sense of loss, even of tragedy, here that must be honored if the scene is to be played truthfully.

Provoking the Story

Experiment with the voice that speaks from the heavens. The standard playing is to hear the voice as a warm baritone (so appropriate for God, don't you know?), and to make the scene into an astonishing theophany. It can indeed be played that way, and perhaps ought to be. But note that only Jesus sees the heavens being torn, and that there is no record of the crowds (presumably on hand) being affected by the *bat qol*. Is this entire event experienced only by Jesus? What does that do to the way you play the scene? If there is a crowd, do they share the view that we see later in Jesus' family, that he is out of his mind?

You might also explore what happens if the voice is too small, too feminine, too loud, too weak, too "something else" to be heard as the cinematic voice of God. What if the voice were that of a child? The scene changes with the voice, and it is time we explored what happens when God's voice is not simply an attractive masculine voice.

Alternatively, explore the possibility that God shares the sense of incompleteness that goes with Jesus' messiahship. What if God also thought there should be more substance to the one who would bear that hope-filled title? "This is my son?" asks God. "I had hoped for more." Remember that Isaiah is called (by Christians after the crucifixion) to describe Jesus as messiah and he speaks of how insubstantial and marred he looked, how unworthy of further attention

(Isaiah 52:14). Remember that Paul speaks of the crucified messiah as scandalous and moronic. One way to take this scriptural and orthodox judgment seriously is to hand it to the audience in the voice of God. Conversely, the surest way to teach people to ignore and forget Paul's words is to make God's voice in the baptism scene so reassuring that no one could ever imagine that there would be a problem with naming Jesus as messiah. Remember: this scene is tightly tied to the Transfiguration and to the crucifixion scenes. Whatever else it might be, this is therefore a scene about the crucified messiah, whom Paul calls scandalous and moronic. The wisdom of God may be wiser than what people call moronic, but this is an ironic statement whose bite must first be felt.

4. Third Sunday after the Epiphany Mark 1:14–20

(see translation, p. 256)

Ritual Text: The Life of the Worshiping Community

The net is in midair. Simon and Andrew are waiting for it to hit the water, just as it does many times, every day. They wait in the brief moment of rest within their work, that fraction of a second when people who know their trades catch the only break that is available, the break that long experience has taught them to catch. That moment allows even a casual observer to catch the difference between rookies and people who know their trade. Catch that moment in telling this story.

It is skilled human life that makes everyday life possible. Stop and watch a construction job site; stop and watch a meat cutter, or a nurse, or a physician, or a farmer, or a salesclerk, or an electrician, or a truck driver backing her rig into a space with ten inches clearance on either side. Watch any people who know their trade especially well. Life in human community requires all these people, and many more. If all of those necessary activities had to wait for "people in general" to carry them out, nothing would happen. Nothing. Nothing. Nothing.

Catch those moments in this scene and think about them in light of the Incarnation. Notice that as you watch Peter and Andrew throw their nets, as you are surprised at the offhand skill of the act and the wise conservation of energy, Jesus stands next to you as surprised as you are. When you stop by a job site and say, perhaps aloud, "I don't know how people can do that!" whether you are looking at plumbers or high-iron workers, recognize that Jesus also would stand with his mouth open as he watched. If Jesus, according to orthodox Christian faith, takes on all the limitations of bodily existence in the Incarnation, he stands there certain that he also would get too dizzy ever to walk out on a girder with the riveters. And he would be right. If the season of the Epiphany explores the surprises contained in the notion that God comes in limited human flesh, then this text provides an occasion to reflect on the notion that this epiphany is reciprocal. Stories like this one, where Jesus meets skilled tradespeople, are occasions when God learns something about the reality of differing skills, separate trades.

No Christian who understands Jesus to be God in the flesh should ever tell stories about Jesus until she notices Jesus' jaw hanging open as he stands, amazed, watching at a job site. This should be a theological requirement.

Intra-Text: The World of Mark's Story

BANG he called them.

BANG they left their net.

BANG the spirit threw him into the wilderness.

BANG he saw the heavens being torn apart.

This is a word that enters Mark's story when Jesus does, and it follows him all the way through it. Things happen quickly around Jesus.

In this scene, what happens quickly and intensely is that people abandon their families. Immediately. BANG. There is no indication of how the families react. Perhaps the larger family heard in Jesus the same thing that led Simon and Andrew, James and John to drop everything and leave. It could be that this scene should be played as a sort of "patriot-volunteering-for-service" scene. But it is also possible that the families did not see things that way at all. It is possible that the father left on the shoreline with the hired help sees only the future of his family business walking away without a thought. Remember that there was no Social Security in those days, no IRAs or pensions. Children raised to honor their fathers and mothers were the only support that aging parents had when their days became long on the land that the LORD their God gave to them.[80] Zebedee watches his sons, his future, his partners-in-training as they walk away. The storyteller does not tell us how he looked or what he said. Explore all the possibilities.

Mark's storyteller could have planted hints later in the story about how to play this scene. That is surely what Matthew's story does. In Matthew's story it is the mother of James and John who comes to Jesus and asks for positions of power and honor for her boys. Such a scene, if it were in Mark's story, would imply that the family (or at least good old mom) was a big backer of the boys' adventure. In Mark's story, however, it is James and John who ask for power and honor. Their mother does not show up. Maybe she's still on the shoreline expecting her boys to remember their duty and come back.

Are there any other hints about how families might have viewed Jesus and his project? One may come from Jesus' own family. In Mark 3 Jesus' family comes to see him. It is not a casual visit. They come because they have concluded that he has lost his mind. They come to bring him home, settle him down. His response is telling. When told that his mother was asking to see him, he asks, "Who is my mother?" Interpreters often comment that Jesus here broadens the notion of family by his answer to his own question. That is possible, but it does not adequately recognize the effect those words will have had on the woman who gave him birth. Would your mother take it that way? Mine would not. I'd rather not imagine my father's reaction, if you don't mind. This is where telling Mark's story requires a little courage and willingness to experiment. It is possible that the families of Simon and Andrew, James and John react the same way Jesus' family reacts to his career: they've lost their minds.

Mark even drops a hint of this sort in the first words of this scene. "After John was handed over," he says, and then tells this story. The audience knows what this bit of foreshadowing implies. They draw their own conclusions. A contemporary storyteller must make sure not to restrict the conclusions that the audience members, and the family, are permitted to draw in response to the sudden departure of these young men.

Inter-Text: The World We Think We Live In

According to a story told in my family, my grandmother, when she sent two of her boys off to World War II, resolved not to pray for them. This was not from a lack of love, nor was it from a disinclination to pray in the first place. My grandmother was a praying woman and firmly convinced that prayer was efficacious. That was why she refrained from praying for her boys, one flying torpedo bombers, one in the 82nd Airborne. She knew the risks of the war, the risks that every mother's children would face while they were in for the duration. She believed that her prayer could shield her sons. And since she feared that another mother might not know to pray for her own children, my grandmother chose not to pray since it could mean that another mother's boys were exposed to greater risk as a result.

I do not tell you this story for the purpose of debating theology with my long-dead grandmother. I judge that anyone who has been through the agony of sending her children off to possible death has the right to save her life and faith any way she can.

I tell you this story because I wonder whether the parents of Simon and Andrew, James and John felt the same sense of certain loss when their boys went off to follow a teacher who had been baptized into action by John the Baptist, John the beheaded. Do you suppose that their parents and grandparents prayed for them?

Provoking the Story

When you play this scene, whether you do it as a solo or as an ensemble, do not forget the family that surrounds every character in the scene (maybe even Jesus?). They will have had a reaction, and the reaction will be germane to the playing of the scene. The best way to catch the possibilities might be to have an actor playing the role of Zebedee. This player ought to explore what happens if he approves, if he disapproves, and if he is simply puzzled. These three possibilities ought to give you a start.

Imagine the scene if Zebedee objects to the sudden departure of his boys. Each of the characters will have a goal, an obstacle, a set of tactics, and an expectation in this scene. Jesus might be aiming to convince James and John to join him. Though the scene does not give him lines that spend much time convincing, you can convince without speaking. His obstacle might be Zebedee, but just as likely the obstacle is the natural tendency of responsible people to attend to duty. He has to overcome the sons' training in honoring their father. What tactics might he choose? Here is where the experimenting begins. The actor will have to try many things to see what might work. What might he expect? This is early in his career, so he may not know what to expect yet. Or, like rookies the world over, he may simply assume that everything will work out well.

How about Zebedee? His goal at the outset is simply to get the day's work done. When it becomes clear that his sons are being drawn away, one may assume that his goal is to draw them back. The obstacles in front of this goal could be many. He could have a history with the boys that gets in his way. If the boys were unhappy with their lack of responsibility, Zebedee is in trouble. If they are thoughtless airheads, he will have trouble getting their attention. And then there is the religious appeal of Jesus and his project, not to mention whatever personal appeal is part of the equation. Zebedee may well share Jesus' sense of what God ought to do in the world, but at the same time he needs his sons to carry on his business. That would mean that one obstacle could be Zebedee himself. What tactics might he adopt? He will need to catch the boys' eye somehow to give them a chance to look him in the eye and make a real choice. He might stand in front of them as they leave, or he might call after them. He might touch one of them silently on the shoulder. What does he expect? My guess is that Zebedee is a realist, and he knows the game is over.

5. Fourth Sunday after the Epiphany Mark 1:21–28

(see translation, p. 257)

Ritual Text: The Life of the Worshiping Community

The season of Epiphany offers glimpses into the structures of life. In this scene, the audience encounters a character, identified as an unclean spirit, who can see deep into Jesus' identity. He calls him "Jesus Netzer." The usual, and probably preferable, translation is "Jesus of Nazareth," which gives the first fragmentary answer to the question of where Jesus has come from. "Jesus Netzer" grows out of having noticed that the phrase in Greek does not smoothly yield "of Nazareth," and has consequently required commentators to apologize for Mark not knowing the proper way to say "from Nazareth" in Greek. It responds to the hint mixed into this name: in Hebrew, "netzer" refers to a sprout or a shoot of a plant. The experienced reader of the Bible might catch the echo. Remember the shoot "out of the stump of Jesse"? This old fragment of a line from the prophet grew into a reference to God's intention to send a ruler, a leader who would replace David's failed descendants (see 1 and 2 Kings to hear the repeated phrase "did what was evil in the sight of the LORD") with a new beginning, an anointed leader who would begin it all again as a new David. If the unclean spirit can see deep enough into Jesus and into Scripture to see Jesus as this new David, he has good eyes indeed. This is a revelation.

It is normal enough to encounter unclean spirits in stories and plays. It is normal enough for an actor or a storyteller to be required by the story to embody characters and realities that are only convincing inside the play, inside the story. But such moments require delicacy and careful thought. How will you embody this character? Customarily unclean spirits are made into raging, drooling, stereotypically evil characters. The text of the scene even helps in this direction. But I am suspicious of such portrayals, if only because they are so cartoonlike, so stereotypical, so obviously false. The actors I work with tell me that the first task when playing an unpalatable character is to find what is ordinary in that character. The second task is to find what is loveable. But this is what is hard.

So how might you play this scene with its impossible character? Perhaps you make him truly dangerous, not just stereotypically evil. Of course, true danger is just as likely to be still as it is to be riotously loud. You might want to ask someone who has been in a bar fight. I don't know many people who do such things, but I have known a few over the years. "Danger wears different faces" is what they have told me, and the worst face of all is one that doesn't care whether it lives or dies. "When you see that on the guy's face," one person told me, "you run. Fast." Or maybe the character is played the way evil is more often encountered: in the deadly dull carrying-out of orders. Watch the movies of the Nuremburg war crimes trials, and you will see mainly the faces of functionaries, bureaucrats, dull and unimaginative people who just did what was next on the list of tasks. Maybe the unclean spirit looks and sounds like that.

Whatever you decide, remember that Epiphany is the season of revelations. Remember that just because ordinary life is lived without spirits and demons, that does not mean that evil is not real. Remember that part of your responsibility is to participate in a revealing of what opposition to the goodness of creation looks like, for real.

Intra-Text: The World of Mark's Story

This scene is the first in the sweep of events leading up to the healing of the man with the withered hand (Mark 1:21–3:6). In this swirl, Jesus is repeatedly found in the synagogue, on the Sabbath. After this swirl of scenes, Jesus is only discovered in the synagogue one more time. In addition, after this swirl, there are only two more days that are identified as Sabbaths. Whatever else holds these scenes together, they are bounded by scenes that take place on the Sabbath in the synagogue. Beyond that, Jesus' activity in these passages is set to the rhythm of Sabbath and synagogue: Mark makes it clear that both Jesus and his disciples have regular practices associated with Sabbath after Sabbath. What is worth noting is that these practices include not only habitual attendance at synagogue (1:21) but also habitual violation of the Sabbath (2:23). These scenes establish a pattern of activity that is laid down under all the story that follows. Though the mix of behaviors is a bit puzzling, it is worth noting, for a storyteller, that Mark emphasizes the regularity of the activity, and that this activity is set to the rhythmic beat of the Sabbath. The way Mark tells the story, even patterns of sloppy observance of Torah are set in the rhythm within which God created the world. How odd.

Teaching in synagogues is a regular practice of Mark's Jesus, but an interpreter must note that Mark has not even hinted at this point that Jesus goes to the synagogue to dispute with the "arthritic representatives" of the "legalistic religion" conjured up in too much Christian interpretation. On the contrary, it works better in the flow of the story to suppose that Jesus is in the synagogue (this Sabbath as on all others) for the same reason he (along with people from the whole region, and the entire population of Jerusalem) went out to be baptized by John. John appears in Mark's story as a native growth, erupting out of old, reliable tradition and expectation. People (including Jesus) went out to John because their faith (and their faithfulness) led them to expect that God would work something larger and more life-giving in a world that was distorted by dangerous foreign powers and those that consort with them. In Mark's story, the most likely interpretation puts Jesus in the synagogue, teaching, because that would have been the place he would have found other people ready to hear that God's dominion was "so close." In Mark's story, the most likely interpretation expects that Jesus' teaching will grow out of the same fertile, hopeful Jewish faith as did John's teaching and arrival on the scene. There is surely conflict with Jewish characters and Jewish practices in Mark's story, but it is important not to prejudge this conflict, not to preinterpret it and thus miss the real clash of the story.

In Mark's story, at least at this early stage, the most likely interpretation has Jesus teaching people who, like him, are deeply rooted in a faith (and a faithful practice) that expects God to nurture life in the creation. Jesus goes, habitually, to synagogue, and teaches there, also habitually, because there he finds people who are hoping and waiting precisely for what God can be expected to do. These habits, protected through generations of difficulty, have created a people ready to jump up and run to John. They have created a community of faithful people who hear Jesus and hope for something big, not because he is new, but because he is rooted in something very old.

And BANG the man in the unclean spirit is in the synagogue. What an odd place for such a character. When Jesus next encounters a man overpowered by demons, he meets a Gentile living among the tombs. This is where one might expect to encounter unclean spirits. So in Israel even the unclean spirits go to shul? It could be that the spirit is an infiltrator, an enemy in disguise, but what if Mark's presentation means something else? This unclean spirit has good and accurate knowledge of Jesus and his identity. Somehow he has heard what only God, Jesus, and the audience have heard: Jesus is the Holy One of God. When a voice from the heavens identifies Jesus as the son, the beloved, we assume the speaker to have been God. When an unclean spirit calls Jesus the Holy One of God, we notice that unclean spirits agree with God. How odd.

It takes a while, but Jesus succeeds: the spirit convulses the man, cries out, and comes out of him. The other people who also (habitually) are gathered on the Sabbath in synagogue are amazed and, in the translation chosen for the NRSV, they "kept on asking one another" (συζητειν). This choice allows the reader to hear the crowd gathered in the synagogue as being favorably impressed with Jesus' first wonder, as commentators typically do. The problem comes when συζητειν is translated in its other occurrences in Mark's story.

In 9:14 and in 12:28, the NRSV translates the word as "argued" or "disputing." Both readings of the word are clearly possible, though the flavors differ sharply, especially in a culture that sees arguing as inherently negative and aggressive. What is interesting is that translators reveal by their practice that they assume that where the crowds or the disciples might question, the scribes can only argue.

There is another question here. When Jesus was trying, at the time ineffectively, to cast out the unclean spirit, Mark also presents him as trying (also ineffectively) to silence the spirit. This is the beginning of the much-studied "messianic secret," and of much consternation among students of this gospel. Was Mark covering for a nonmessianic Jesus? Was Jesus trying to avoid uncontrolled publicity? Or was he trying, indirectly, to spur the exploding publicity that (in fact) went out everywhere? In telling a story it is crucial to maintain close touch both with the overarching narrative arc and with the small details of the scene at hand. No matter what one makes of the overall purpose of Jesus' commands to silence, a storyteller will have to make sense of (and with) the bodies and voices in this scene.

How does Jesus say these words? And out of what posture and understanding? And to what end? These are crucial questions. Maybe Jesus' command to silence is motivated only by the fact that the unclean spirit is making noise and disturbing the proceedings in the synagogue. We are not told that the spirit is noisy, but stories of exorcisms in the ancient world (Jewish and otherwise) include frequent mention of loud, inhuman cries and frightening behavior.

There is another possible reading to consider. The unclean spirit, however disruptive he was, had correct information. Amid all the disturbing shrieking, he says something crucial and correct. What if the very correctness of the speech is what motivates Jesus' attempt to silence the spirit? We are not told in the baptism scene how Jesus reacts to the voice that speaks from the heavens. The usual reading of the baptism scene supposes that Jesus' reaction resembles that of the reader who knows that this is the voice of God and that the voice speaks good news.

What if Jesus did not hear the voice that way? What if Jesus reacted to the voice the way one might expect a Jewish friend to react: with shock, or even horror?

The spirit, we discover in the next scene, cast Jesus out into the wilderness. The word is the same as the word used in the exorcism scenes. Unclean spirits are cast out. The implication is that they are thrown out violently, not simply shown the door. Now Jesus is cast out. A coherent interpretation will need to create a scene that honors the surprising violence of the language. Maybe Jesus' experience of the voice foreshadows his experience of the spirit. Maybe when Jesus hears the unclean spirit speak in the synagogue, he is reminded, unpleasantly, of the voice at the river. Maybe, for all his evident commitment to the cause that brought him to John in the first place, Jesus rejects the claims being made for him, claims that are made by powerful, but untraceable, voices.

Some interpreters have followed something like this line through this scene. Such readings find support in Jesus' command to silence after Peter called him "messiah" in chapter 8. If Jesus is actively resisting the application of impossible titles to a career devoted to sanctifying The Name, then the scene in the synagogue would be a powerfully painful scene. Or, to twist things a little further, what if Jesus' discomfort is rooted in his own unwillingness to be drawn into this kind of conflict? Jesus went out to John, according to the reading we are exploring, because of a powerful devotion to Torah, and to the hopes that have given life to Jewish communities through the centuries. Jesus goes about teaching, on this reading, to carry this project forward, and that project has brought him now into the synagogue. The unclean spirit not only interrupts the synagogue service, he threatens to draw Jesus into a conflict with unclean spirits, to draw him into the practice of exorcism, which would lead to charges of involvement in magic, which, at least, would distract from the project that has led Jesus so far in the story. Such a reading raises the possibility that Jesus saw a disjunction between being a wonder-worker and being a teacher. Mark insists on calling him a teacher, and maybe Jesus insisted on the same thing.

But BANG there in the synagogue was a man in an unclean spirit. And Jesus was stuck with working an exorcism. In the synagogue. On the Sabbath, no less. So, on this reading, Jesus attempts to get the spirit out of the synagogue and out of the scene as quickly and quietly as possible so as to get back to his work of proclaiming and teaching. But the spirit resists and slows the process. And the spirit speaks, stopping the action and addressing Jesus as an old familiar friend, claiming a connection with Jesus that no other character in the scene could understand.

Inter-Text: The World We Think We Live In

In Mark's story Jesus encounters "unclean spirits" and "demons." Interpreters need to approach both terms carefully. Demons, in customary usage, are often nothing more than cartoon figures, little devils suitable to be team mascots or military insignia. They are, in customary mythology, the underlings of the devil, serving some Screwtape[81] or other in a regulated hierarchy. The first thing to notice about these notions is that they seem not to line up with available ancient ideas. Demons, it appears from Wendy Cotter's compilation of exorcism texts, were living entities that afflicted human beings, but there is no great clarity about who is in service to whom.[82] That might matter for interpretation, because importing an imagined coherent hierarchy into our reading of Mark's story could distort our view of the clash within the story.

The next thing to notice is that "unclean" is a notion difficult to translate into a culture that does not trade in transactions between clean and unclean. One of the best, and most accessible, treatments of this matter in recent studies is offered by Paula Fredriksen in *Jesus of Nazareth, King of the Jews*.[83] Fredriksen notes carefully that "unclean" does not mean "sinful." There is a kind of moral uncleanness, but most of the uses of the term refer to "ritual" uncleanness. As Fredriksen notes, given the regular state of daily affairs, most people most of the time would have been in a state of ritual impurity.[84] In this sense, "unclean" simply refers to the state of being ordinarily engaged in life, carrying out the functions that go with living: bearing children, ejaculating, menstruating, burying the dead. These activities are not sinful; they simply involve human beings in what is called "uncleanness."

This distinction is crucial. But we need to notice, with Jacob Neusner, that the matters that are marked as unclean are in many instances matters that touch on the mysterious. It is here that Neusner's work adds something crucial. He notes that faithful Jews come into contact with uncleanness in another way. If you have been to synagogue you may well have noticed that the Torah scroll is carried by people who wear gloves, or who take pains not to touch the scroll, using their prayer shawls as a buffer between hand and scroll. And when the scroll is laid open to be read, the reader will follow the words, not with a finger, but with a pointer. This all makes sense when one considers the expense and fragility of a Torah scroll, but Neusner indicates that these practices do not have their roots only in simple practicality. Observant Jews do not touch the Torah scroll, says Neusner, because the scroll "renders the hands unclean." How odd. But this is odd only if one imagines some association between uncleanness and sin. How could the Torah make one sinful?

But if one dispenses with the notion of sinfulness, and notices that uncleanness is the mark of contact with the mysteriously powerful, then it is not so very surprising that the Torah scroll would render hands unclean. There is a mystery in Torah, so powerful that the rabbis understand that even God was bound by Torah in the activity of creating the world. In some rabbinic readings, God knew how to create because God had a Torah scroll open on the desk, available for continual consultation. Torah is a powerful mystery, so powerful that it binds even God. And Torah makes the hands unclean.

So what are we to make of the unclean spirit who seizes the scene in the synagogue? First, that this character, because he is marked as unclean, is powerful and mysterious. While it is possible that Mark understands something like moral uncleanness to hang about the man in the unclean spirit (note the way Gentiles in the ancient world are spoken of as unclean because of cultural and dietary practices rejected by Jews), it is more likely that what is meant is that the spirit brought power, mystery, and the uncontrollable into the synagogue when he burst upon the scene. The unclean spirit stands apart from the human characters in the story. More precisely, he stands above them, toying with them or afflicting them as he pleases, doing what they cannot prevent, knowing what they cannot know. Thus it is that the spirit knows who Jesus is. He has access to information known only to God (the presumed speaker from the heavens), Jesus (who may or may not be glad to have heard what God said), and the story's audience. How odd.

Provoking the Story

Mark 1:21 says that Jesus teaches with authority (εξουσια) and not like the scribes. Customary interpretation makes the scribes into a detached elite, distant from real people and real life, soulless bureaucrats who trade grammatical niceties with each other while drawing fat salaries. Or, customary interpretation figures the scribes as the last, fading representatives of what nineteenth-century (mostly German) scholars called "late Judaism," as if this old and durable faith community had long since vanished, leaving only fossilized remains. In any of these cases, the comparison between Jesus and the scribes is figured as a conflict, not a contrast. As a result, Jesus can go about doing what heroes do in story after story, movie after movie. He can bring a breath of rebellious freedom. He can bring a glimpse of nonhierarchical life. He can succeed without paying any dues to any authority other than that of his own genius. In such a scheme, Jesus becomes the hero of one more B movie.

Interpreters have to wonder if this interpretive line offers enough return to be worth the investment. Interpreters have to wonder whether there might not be another, more productive reading of this comparison, one that honors the story the Mark has handed us. Consider the possibility that the comparison between Jesus and the scribes, between Jesus and tradition, is not a conflict at all. Consider whether it might not work to read Jesus as the eruption of what the scribes had long taught and described. The scribes teach and preserve and prepare; Jesus blazes, explodes, and erupts.

It is one thing to read about volcanoes. It is another to find oneself close to an eruption. Volcanologists do both, of necessity. But there is a difference. To shift the illustration, it is one thing to read the Declaration of Independence; it is another to encounter Martin Luther King Jr. But the one gives rise (and bite) to the other, as may be heard in the echoes of tradition in the speeches of Dr. King. The work of the scribes prepared people to hear John (and then Jesus), but Jesus is a real eruption of long-nurtured Jewish hope. This will stir a reaction, and will give rise to comparisons. Just so.

And so, BANG there in the synagogue is a man in an unclean spirit. The spirit speaks. The voice of the spirit creates a person over against Jesus. "What to you and to me?" he asks, cryptically. The usual translation takes this as a whining demand that Jesus stop harassing him. "What do you have to do with me?" asks the translated demon. "Why's everybody always picking on me?" he could just as well ask, echoing an old popular song from the 1950s.[85] Read this way, the demon and all the forces arrayed against humanity are bullies who are used to getting their way. Now they have met someone stronger, and they don't like it.

Or perhaps they themselves are victims of bullying, first by assorted exorcists who meddle in matters above them, and now by Jesus who disrupts the normal operating of the world by throwing his weight around, bullying demons and diseases who were only doing their jobs. Translated this way, the spirit asks a question worth asking: if the meddling starts here, what will we do when it stops? If Jesus intends to cast out every unclean spirit in Israel, and cure every leper, fine, but he does not, and his selective intervention is the kind of insult that makes theodicy necessary in the first place. Why should my sister die when yours does not? Why should old smokers attached to oxygen tanks attend my neighbor's funeral, my neighbor with lung cancer and no cigarettes? If wonders cease, why do they cease when and where they do? Good question.

There are other ways to tell the story. One of the most interesting was suggested to me by an old, badly made war movie. I don't remember the title or the actors. I do remember the setting. An English officer and a German officer, gentlemen both, found themselves trapped together in the midst of tense battle. They had each taken refuge in the same small farmhouse. Their units were scattered, maybe destroyed; the outcome of the battle was altogether uncertain. At first they tried to kill each other, but achieved only a standoff. They watched each other, stalking each other in words. And they talked. Initially this talking was part of the stalking, part of looking for an opening. Exhaustion wore them both down. Neither would relax, neither could sustain it any longer. And so their talk changes. Families emerge. And peacetime interests and concerns. And music and art and good food and fine wine.

And then the enemy officer asks the question the audience has been waiting for. The battle outside is maybe over, maybe not, and maybe has slid into the final determined and pointless brutality of private programs of revenge. The skirmish inside has made the two enemies aware of how much they have in common. And so in the midst of tension and uncertainty, the enemy officer asks his fellow gentleman, "What's all this to you and to me?" The question has a honed edge. It seeks to establish common ground raised above the common brutality of the herd of humanity carrying out the pointless slaughter outside.

"Politicians start the wars, the animals outside fight them because they'd fight and kill in any case, and this gives them a sense of being worthwhile and valuable, part of a cause," says the German officer. "But when it's over, you and I will be asked to put the world back together again. And we will do it because it's what we always do. But what's all this brutality to you and to me?"[86]

What if the demon is addressing another officer, another gentlemen, another who should be above the common brutality of humanity? Now we have real trouble. Now we have a context in which we can productively explore the wonder stories in Mark's gospel. What, indeed, is all this to you and to me?

6. Fifth Sunday after the Epiphany Mark 1:29–39

(see translation, p. 258)

Ritual Text: The Life of the Worshiping Community

The question to ask in any Epiphany text is: "What is the surprise here?" Of course, finding a surprise does not mean that you've found (or understood) the epiphany in the text. That normally takes more doing, and more waiting.

One of the best ways to listen for surprises, it seems to me, is to practice hearing the text as an ordinary story, not as a story about THE SAVIOR OF THE WORLD. As soon as you need to use ALL CAPITAL LETTERS for a character in your story, you make yourself unable to see and react to the most ordinary of situations. Think about the people who look up on the subway or in a restaurant and there is ______ (fill in the name of some overwhelming celebrity). Even time I hear such stories, I notice that people report suddenly becoming unable to carry on the simplest of conversations. They can't say hello, they can't comment on the weather or the quality of the food, or anything else. Somehow they imagine that they ought to make some memorable comment about the quality of the celebrity's last work, or deliver some penetrating insight about the inner workings of some character played by the celebrity. And they lose all of the abilities that make them delightful in any other setting.

Be careful not to let the same thing happen to you when you perform and interpret stories about Jesus. Play the scenes as they would be played if the central character were somebody named Bob. You will encounter surprises. For instance: if Simon's mother-in-law is sick enough to be in bed, why does she have to serve company as soon as she gets up? Doesn't she even get to rest? You can answer these questions many ways, but all of those ways grow out of the original surprise. Maybe she has to serve her company because the only other characters mentioned are male, and maybe none of them could cook.

Or maybe the surprise in this scene is that the word "serve" could mean something besides activities that involved cooking.

Intra-Text: The World of Mark's Story

The effect of the last scene is dramatic. BANG, his fame goes out into the whole surrounding region, it goes out (in Mark's timing of the story) even before he goes out of the synagogue. And, just as suddenly, Jesus is drawn into a sudden swirl of healing and exorcising. First, it is Simon's mother-in-law, who is lying down with a fever. When the fever departs, she rises and "deacons" to them. Elisabeth Moltmann-Wendel has noted that the translation of this word requires some rethinking.[87] When this word is used with a female subject, it is most often translated as "serving" or "waiting table." When the word acquires a male subject, however, it acquires a whole different field of operation. Then, as Moltmann-Wendel notes, it is suddenly translated as "serve as deacon in a church." Behind this disparity lies a collection of assumptions about what roles were proper to women in the ancient church. Perhaps Simon's mother-in-law did rise and feed the people in her house. She would be acting in the tradition of Sarah and Abraham, who entertained angels unaware.

But what if διακονεω is here loaded with some of the content that it carries when it has a male subject? What if Simon's mother-in-law "deaconed" to them? A deacon in the ancient church filled an important role, one of two named functions in the oldest sources available to us. The επισκοπος oversaw the preaching and teaching of the congregation. The deacon, usually considered a subordinate figure, saw to the congregation's ministry of care and concern. The deacon was in charge of connecting needs with resources. If someone needed food, the deacon was in charge of making sure that those with food to share were connected with those who needed it. If someone needed clothing, or shelter, or anything at all, the deacon was charged with connecting them with the resources of the congregation so that none would be hungry, thirsty, or naked. Set in the context of Jewish understandings of the abundance that God created when making the world, the deacon was in charge of enacting God's created intentions.

If this is what a deacon does, then the story of Simon's mother-in-law takes on considerable power. That would explain why so many people knew where to show up at sundown with all those who were sick or possessed by demons. This would mean that she motivated Jesus' development into a worker of wonders. Whether Jesus made the connection between his teaching and healing at the beginning or not, this first deacon made the connection and insisted on it. And all the city gathered to the door.

At the end of Mark's story, we suddenly see a large group of women who are watching as Jesus is tortured to death. They have followed him from the beginning, from Galilee, and they have deaconed to him. That surely means that they supported him and his project. If Moltmann-Wendel is correct, it may mean much more. It may in fact mean that they were the link who connected need after unexpected need with Jesus' ability. Some readers have even guessed that these deacons may explain why women approach Jesus in this story. A woman approaches him in a crushing crowd; a mother (a Gentile!) approaches him to ask for help for her daughter. How did they come to approach a male? Perhaps the crowd of women told them that there was some hope in making the approach. It is a guess, but if such a guess proves productive, the scene with Simon's mother-in-law marks the beginning of this larger arc in the story, an arc that extends all the way to the final scene in the story.

Inter-Text: The World We Think We Live In

The whole town gathers to the door at sundown. Why at sundown? Because that is when Sabbath ends. The town is a Jewish town, and they observe Torah. People found out about what Jesus had to offer them sometime in the afternoon, and they waited to come to see Jesus.

Christians need to practice understanding what that means. In Gentile Christian ears, it sounds like a penalty to wait until sunset. But imagine the anticipation in those houses through that day. Imagine the excitement, the sense of impending culmination. I remember the two years my fiancée (now my wife) and I lived about six hours apart. Those years were difficult, but I remember vividly how time tightened and squeezed as we got closer to seeing each other. We always knew how many weeks it was until our next time together, but time started to change when weeks changed to days, and changed even more when days changed to hours, and hours to minutes. We could feel the seconds dripping as we waited. I have never had a more intense experience of time. I am guessing that families in Capernaum also felt the seconds drip, felt time become more and more alive, felt God's promise warm as the time drew nearer. They would have notified everyone in the extended family, gathering everyone who might be even a little interested in the case, making sure that everything was ready for the miracle. It would have been more than sick people and their immediate attendants who gathered to the house that evening. It would have been quite a celebration afterward. Some things get better when you wait for them.

Provoking the Story

What does it mean that the people of the town showed more restraint than Jesus did? They waited until sundown, and he did not. They needed someone to cook as much as he and Simon did (the gathering at sundown would surely have required a hot dish), but they waited and anticipated. It was because of Torah.

Torah is a word often translated as "law." This misses almost the entire point of the word in Jewish life. The word is better translated as "teaching." This at least catches the flavor and tone of the word for Jewish life. It is not a word with penalties attached (like "law" would be). Rather, it is a word with learning and practice involved. It might even be better to translate it somehow so that the physical metaphor behind it comes through. The metaphor back behind Torah is the act of aiming a bow and arrow. This is an act that takes years of practice to do well and responsibly. If you have a friend who hunts with a bow, ask her what it takes to aim a bow. She'll tell you that it requires a careful effort to focus everything you are doing toward the end of releasing the arrow responsibly.

Torah requires the same kind of focus, the same kind of careful attention. Torah is the way that an observant Jewish community aims itself so that every act, every interaction, everything that the community says and does adds up to a witness to the stable and orderly love of God for creation. In a world tripped and tricked by too much chaos, Torah observance amounts to a public argument for the goodness and loving-kindness of God, something all of creation needs to hear, especially when it is exhausted, worn out by the grinding unpredictability of life. In the midst of such a world, as the Israeli author Achad Ha'Am said, "It is not so much that Israel has kept the Sabbath, but that Sabbath has kept Israel." So why does the community keep Sabbath more carefully than Jesus does?

7. Sixth Sunday after the Epiphany
Mark 1:40–45

(see translation, p. 259)

Ritual Text: The Life of the Worshiping Community

"Go show yourself to the priest," Jesus said, "and offer for your cleansing what Moses commanded."

Interpreters often choke on this line. Christians tend to imagine that it is superfluous to offer anything for a cleansing that has already occurred. This misses the importance of the ritual dance that is revealed in the scene.

Remember the distance between now and the first century CE. Remember that ritual tends the network that communities establish to balance the world. Such networks can indeed be oppressive, but it will not do simply to write them off. The ritual networks that communities establish make life as comprehensible as it can be in the middle of ordinary chaos. In the face of the assaults of the inexorable, these ritual dances allow human beings to maintain connectedness, orientation, and some sense of purposeful action, even when such action is finally ineffective. The priest is at the center of this dance. While the Temple still stood, the priests were responsible to tend the still point of the universe. Alan Segal notes that the Jewish symbolic world was organized in concentric circles of holiness centered on the Holy of Holies in the Temple. In a chaotic world, safety and stability (along with the terrible mystery in which they are rooted) revolve around the place where God's finger touches the world and holds it still. Around that essential place is the Temple, and around the Temple is the city of Jerusalem. Around the city of Jerusalem is the land of Israel, and around Israel is the vast and chaotic Gentile world. With each step toward the mysterious center of the world, Jews drew nearer to that which kept them safe and stable, that which allowed them to keep their balance in a world that still held the Temple.

It was the responsibility of the priests to tend the stability of the Jewish world as it moved in its ritual dance around the Temple. In this scene, Jesus sends the man to the priest. Jesus' world dances steadily around the Temple,[88] and in this scene he sends a man who had been touched by chaos, marked by the inexorable, to a priest whose task it is to tend the ritual of reincorporation, that dance of rejoining his cleansed body to the body of the people.

Intra-Text: The World of Mark's Story

The leper at the beginning of the scene cannot go into villages, and consequently lives in wilderness places. Then Jesus touches him. The man is cleansed and he is sent off to see the priest, who lives somewhere with human company. Jesus, on the other hand, can no longer go into villages and is driven out into wilderness places. He does not lack for human contact, to be sure, but as a result of touching the man with leprosy Jesus has become a functional leper.

The condition that led to the man's isolation was most likely not Hansen's disease; more likely it was one of the skin conditions that were called leprosy in the ancient world. What matters for this scene is not making the proper medical diagnosis; rather, what matters is the notion of fluidlike "uncleanness" that flows from the man to Jesus. Jacob Neusner calls "uncleanness" an "analogical fluid."[89] By the end of the scene, Jesus has absorbed this "fluid" and the man has it no more. This will not be the last scene that involves this act of metaphorical absorption. The same thing happens when the woman touches him from behind in the crowd. The same thing happens when he touches the little girl who was dead. A question to ask when considering the whole story that Mark tells: What happens to this "fluid" when it flows into Jesus over and over? Does he process it and expel it? Does it stay in him? Does he pass it along somehow? If so, how and when? (See 14:24.)

Inter-Text: The World We Think We Live In

Texts with lepers are hard to interpret. We find it easy to dismiss the whole thing as ancient overreaction to superstitious notions of contamination. We imagine that Jesus' touching the man makes him just like us: a person unaffected by superstition. This willfully ignores the ways we react to skin conditions. Psoriasis makes us uneasy. Even simple things like port-wine stains[90] on people's faces make us unlikely to talk to people who have them without uneasiness. How odd.

There is also "uncleanness" here. Things that are "unclean" are things that have been touched by the inexorable, the uncontrollable, the uncanny, and people who had been touched by these forces found themselves suddenly on the outside edge of human society.

This outside edge was a managed and regulated part of the whole community, but it was a part of the community that was managed away from the normal center, away from normal connections and supports.

Before contemporary interpreters get too happily antisuperstitious, it ought to be remembered that it is still very easy to land on the outside edge of human community. As I write this, Christopher Reeve, the actor who played Superman in the movies, has just died. Not long ago he made my point for me. "All it takes is a slip on a wet floor," he said in an interview, "and you'd be right where I am." All it takes is one catastrophic illness and all financial plans are out the window, and (with not too much bad luck) any one of us is out of our house and on the outside edge of a community that had been our home. We may (or may not) have overcome the superstitions that haunted the edges of ancient communities, but we have not overcome the tendency to push people out if they seem to have been touched by something uncanny.

Jesus' touch brings the man back inside normal boundaries. He no longer represents that which must be held at bay. The community has a regular procedure by which he may be brought back into the normal, and Jesus sends him off to attend to that procedure.

Provoking the Story

According to most translations (mine included), Jesus is "moved." This is a workable translation of the word used here, σπλαγχνιζομαι, and probably the one that ought be chosen. But the word in Greek plays on a bigger synonym field than it does in English. English has lost the sense of what was moved when Jesus was "moved." In English we think of people who are "moved to pity," or perhaps "to tears." The image is weak, and loaded with notions of pale sympathy, and seems to establish either a protective distance between the one who pities and the one who is pitied or an unwelcome and useless connection: "I don't want your pity." The Greek word is stronger than this. Behind the word σπλαγχνιζομαι in Greek is the word σπλαγχνα, which means bowels, or even guts. To catch the full vigor of this image, you ought to translate it as something like "Jesus felt his stomach turn," or even "Jesus thought he was going to throw up." This is the word used to express the powerfully physical sense of connection that surprises us, and about which we can do nothing. The word surely means that Jesus felt all of what we'd call pity, but it means that he felt it deep in the pit of his stomach. "I choose," Jesus says. And the man is cleansed.

Now comes a real problem. Translators have had fits over the next bit of this scene. Jesus has cleansed (not healed, notice) the man. And now he snorts at him indignantly and casts him out. Translators have tried hard to make sense of this by softening it. Jesus is translated as "sternly charging" the man and "sending him away." This is clearly inadequate. The words used are vigorous, even violent in their metaphorical power. We have already seen the spirit cast Jesus out into the wilderness after his baptism. While in every language words must be allowed to wiggle back and forth, to have different shades of meaning at different times, it is a risky matter to begin to translate by softening words when they touch Jesus and sharpening them when they touch demons. What if both are soft? Or, more intriguingly, what if both are sharp?

The word εμβριμησαμενος, in its metaphoric roots, refers to the snorting of a warhorse about to go into battle. As typically used, it means "snorting indignantly" or even "snorting angrily." Whatever translation is chosen, it will be important not to lose the snort, the sound, the physical reality of this word.

But how could Jesus snort at a man he had just cleansed? That question does not have an answer yet. It is a question that will have to ring over future attempts to interpret and tell Mark's story. For now, we only know that he surprised us by snorting.

8. Seventh Sunday after the Epiphany Mark 2:1–12

(see translation, p. 259)

Ritual Text: The Life of the Worshiping Community

Why does Jesus announce forgiveness of sins in this scene? Is he forgiving the man (and his friends) for digging through the roof and wrecking it? That would make sense if it were his own house that now had an unauthorized skylight installed. Is he making some link between the man's condition and his sinfulness? If so, the scribes were right to argue about whether this is a dangerous theology or not.

The issue for faithful Judaism is not whether or not human beings can offer forgiveness, but whether or not YOU can forgive someone for a wrong committed against ME. The ritual associated with Yom Kippur is significant. Faithful Jews seek to right the wrongs they have done. They ask for forgiveness in person. The person who was wronged has control of the situation. There are wrongs that can be forgiven. There are wrongs that cannot, either because the damage was too great or because the apology was too little. Faithful Jews are required to accept this reality, and to ask again later. And if forgiveness is still impossible, they are to ask yet again. If after three times reconciliation is not possible, then God may be approached for forgiveness. But not until the victim has had three occasions to consider the option and reject it.[91] Ask a victim of abuse what it feels like to be informed that the pastor has forgiven the abuser, so why can't the victim? Victims are frequently pressured to give in and forgive. The pressure is applied because of the indiscriminate practice of others. The scribes ask a good question.

Intra-Text: The World of Mark's Story

This wonder story seems different from the others in this swirl that we have examined. It does not take place in a synagogue, on a Sabbath, or involve some aspect of uncleanness, though the paralyzed man has surely been marked by the uncontrollable. But, as we will see, it fits tightly into the narrative arc that Mark is developing here. It fits, first of all, because, although Jesus has resumed teaching, he is again interrupted by people with a request for healing. Already this early in the story it is clear that teaching and wonder-working will be tangled tightly together, no matter what Jesus might have wanted. If wonder-working is an unwelcome interruption, he is again interrupted. If wonder-working is to be taken as a proper accompaniment to his teaching, then his project is developing nicely.

Once again the person needing healing erupts into the scene, this time through the roof, courtesy of friends who demonstrate a talent for breaking and entering. When Jesus sees this talent, he interprets it as πιστις, a word that Christians love to read as "faith." While that may finally be the best word to choose as a translation, it is wise to stop and remember that this is a Jewish story, with Jewish characters and Jewish vocabulary. The word "faith," through long Christian use, has picked up a set of synonyms and antonyms foreign to its origins. In Christian settings, πιστις means "faith as opposed to works," and works are specifically understood as "works of the law," and the law in question (for Christian texts) is the Torah, which is (mis)understood as a way to earn God's favorable attention. There are multiple problems with this developed reading. For one thing, it compresses centuries of interpretation into a small packet attached to a single word. Notions of faith rooted in political, religious, and even economic conditions at the time of the Reformation are made to govern words rooted in a very different world. An argument amongst Christians is remade into an argument between Christians and Jews. But the problem comes with the fact that in Jewish settings πιστις is probably best translated as "faithfulness," faithfulness to Torah, which is not a law but a way of life. In such a setting, Torah is not a demand imposed by an angry God but a gift of life from a God whose own activity is also shaped by Torah, which shapes and nurtures all of the universe.

If πιστις is translated as "faith" in this scene, it becomes a story about believing the impossible, about the inward disposition of the friends who believe that Jesus can heal the paralyzed man. This is a good story, and this reading has yielded good and fitting sermons over the centuries.

If πιστις is translated as "faithfulness" in the scene, however, the story changes. Now the focus of the story, and of the πιστις, is not Jesus but the man on the pallet. His friends act faithfully. That means that they have set aside all things (including the roof) to care for their friend, their neighbor. They have known out of their tradition that God intends for all life to flourish, and they have taken drastic steps to include their neighbor in that flourishing. Jesus is impressed. So is everyone else in the room. They have seen faithfulness to Torah acted out in an extraordinary way.

Jesus' response is rather surprising. "Child, your sins are forgiven," he says. Commentators seem surprised by this response, probably because they know (with Rudolf Bultmann) that this story is a healing story. As a result, interpreters often spend time understanding forgiveness as a kind of healing, perhaps even the "real" healing.

There has been productive work done along these lines, but I'd like to suggest another possibility, one that seems to fit better into the narrative arc. What if this scene is another scene at the crossroads, a site from which Jesus' project goes two ways? Is Jesus a healer and an exorcist like the others who ply this trade, or is he a teacher, a proclaimer, an announcer of God's dominion on the model of John the Baptist? If Jesus understands himself to be engaged in a project consonant with what John began, his response makes perfect sense. People dropped everything and swirled out to see John, to be baptized, purified from their sins.

Now that John is off the stage, Jesus proclaims God's dominion, and people drop everything to find him and follow him. On this model, the four friends have shown extraordinary faithfulness not only to their friend (and thus to Torah), but also to the hopes that have caused the central characters in the story to jump and run. They have shown faithfulness by bringing their paralyzed friend into that excited swirl around the expectation that God was preparing to keep old promises. Even a paralyzed man will be part of the movement to prepare the road of the Lord. Jesus sees this, and does what John had done for so many others: he purifies him so he too can be part of the movement that is being prepared.

Inter-Text: The World We Think We Live In

Once again, I'd like to suggest another way of seeing this scene. Christians have sometimes imagined that Jews live with what Christians call an "Old Testament God" who is figured (by Christians) as wrathful and demanding, unwilling and unable to forgive, able only to punish sin absolutely with death. This picture of God comes as quite a surprise to Jews, who know God as loving and merciful, slow to anger and abounding in love (Psalm 103:8). The notion that God has nothing to do with forgiveness can only be surprising to people who find in Yom Kippur a time for serious reflection on one's manner of life, a time to take seriously the wrongs one has done, and a time to forgive wrongs that one has suffered. Jews, now and in the ancient world, are quite clear that forgiveness of sins is both necessary and available.

But Jews will argue about the supposition that any human being has the right or responsibility to forgive someone for sins committed against another person. And so the scribes do, indeed, argue in their hearts, and they call this action blasphemy, which is a serious and well-aimed charge at this point. If God should choose to intervene and forgive without consulting the victims, that is God's business. God is God, and we are not. And so the scribes argue. Remember, arguing is also an act of faithfulness.

I can imagine them arguing also with John the Baptist. And well they should. People of faith owe each other an argument in the face of such momentous issues, all the more so since the whole region jumped and ran to John. To stifle questions at such a time is to guarantee that bad decisions will be made, and that damage will be done. So the scribes argue.

Provoking the Story

This is a scene with clash. That is the best kind, because without clash, the audience won't be able to think of a reason to keep watching. The scribes argue with Jesus. This is a gift, a sign of respect. And so Jesus responds to them. "Which is easier?" he asks. What a strange and inappropriate question. How is his question about what is easier relevant to the discussion that must go on? To take his question seriously for the moment, neither one is easier. If one supposes that words are cheap, it is much easier to announce that sins are forgiven because it is an uncheckable statement. The audience will be able to tell if the man walks, but not if his sins are forgiven. But Jewish culture has never thought that words are cheap.

Any faith that knows that God spoke the world into being will not gladly assume such a thing.[92]

But what does ease have to do with any of this? And how does Jesus' ability to restore the man to mobility offer anything useful to the argument about forgiveness? The challenge in playing this scene will be to make Jesus' response seem as odd as it is. The temptation among Christians is always to give Jesus the benefit of more doubts than anyone could possibly entertain. Jesus always gets to be right, at least in most Christian interpretation. Play this scene, if only experimentally, in ways that allow your audience to explore the possibility that Jesus' response simply does not follow properly in the argument.

9. Bonus Scene
Mark 2:13–17

(see translation, p. 261)

Ritual Text: The Life of the Worshiping Community

Torah, in its most restrictive sense, refers to the first five books of the Jewish Bible (which are also the first five books of the Christian Bible). But Torah is one of those stretchy words, one of those words so valuable that it comes to refer to a whole range of beliefs and cultural practices. Torah refers also to the entire Bible. It refers to the entire Bible and also the Talmud. It refers to everything that goes into living a Jewish life that witnesses to God's stable and orderly love for creation. And Alan Segal calls it the constitution of the Jewish faith.

This last image pulls together all the others and explains why argument about what Torah would mean is so important in Jewish life. The constitution is the root and regulator of all of a community's shared life. In the United States, arguments about civil rights and matters of equal opportunity shake the earth, and the rulings of the Supreme Court shape the course of American life. A decision about what is, or is not, constitutional will have enormous implications.

This scene from Mark's story presents an argument about the Jewish constitution. Interpreters often understand this scene to be about inclusivity versus exclusivity, and on a certain level it is. That would be a constitutional issue for Jews. But this misses the real constitutional issue. This is a scene explicitly about what it means that the Jewish homeland is occupied by a hostile foreign power that does not honor God. Levi is a tax traitor. That is the translation I have chosen of the Greek word τελωνης, usually translated "tax collector." Levi certainly collected taxes, so the customary translation is adequate in a descriptive sort of way, but the usual translation misses the constitutional impact of Levi's occupation. Levi is not just a government official to be resented (which seems to be a popular hobby of people in the United States); he is a traitor, a betrayer who violates Jewish life and faith at a most basic level. Treason, says Article Three, Section Three, of the Constitution of the United States, "shall consist only in levying War against them, or in adhering to their Enemies, giving them Aid and Comfort." Levi has surely adhered to the enemy of God's people.

Intra-Text: The World of Mark's Story

The surprises begin early. Jesus is teaching, he is beside the sea. So far nothing is new. He sees Levi. He calls him to follow. If ever a character should be paralyzed by such a call, Levi is that character. He ought, by all rights, to sit still, frozen into immobility by the social effects of his treacherous occupation as much as by the treachery itself. It is hard to imagine that the crowd following Jesus — the crowd who had jumped and run to see John, the crowd looking for purification — would allow a tax traitor to join them. He was a willing ally of Rome, a reminder of the real role played by power in the world that enveloped God's people. Even if Levi could have risen to follow Jesus, the crowd should have frozen him out.

Except that's not what happened. Levi left his booth and followed, as did many other such people. Jesus ate with them.

Jewish meals are moments for remembering the goodness of creation and the strength of the promises of God. "So now he eats with tax collectors and sinners?" ask the Pharisees and scribes. It is a fitting question. Christians who have taken the forgiveness of sinners as the center of their faith world will hear rigid legalism in the words of the Pharisees and scribes. Before drawing that conclusion, however, remember that tax collectors were traitors, collaborators with the power that destroyed the Temple.

Inter-Text: The World We Think We Live In

A colleague of mine served as a pastor in a congregation in the southern United States some years ago. He had not been at the congregation long when local neo-Nazis began agitating in the area. At a congregational meeting one of the agitators stood up to address the congregation and to invite the youth of the church to a camp where they would be taught the true Christian faith. My colleague was terrified. He did not know how the congregation, which he had barely begun to understand, would respond to such a group and such an invitation. And he did not know what he would do if they responded favorably. As he sat, wondering what he could do, what he should do, a member of his congregation rose to speak.

The man's name has gone from my memory, but I remember what my colleague called him: Bubba. He was a crude man, dressed in overalls, not always clean, and had not visited a dentist in his life. Bubba stood up. This was a frightening development, especially given my colleague's assumptions about the politics of backwoods southerners.

Bubba walked to the neo-Nazi agitator, lifted him by the front of his shirt, and carried him out of the church building. After depositing him unceremoniously on the street, he returned and said simply, "I had enough of fighting Nazis back in the war. We don't need them causing trouble here."

And that was it. My colleague learned things about his congregation, and things about people in torn overalls. And he had no more trouble with neo-Nazis.

The problem is that, for an audience first hearing Mark's story at the end of the first century, the words of the Pharisees would likely sound a lot like what Bubba said. They, too, were people with a memory. They remembered what the war against Rome had cost, and did not need to fight it again. This reading lays on the characters a later view, one familiar to Mark's first audiences if not to the Pharisees in the scene, but we must assume that Mark was aware of this when he told this story this way. There is a powerful offense here.

In this context, Jesus' response is fascinating. "Healthy people don't need a healer, but sick people do. I did not come to call righteous, but sinners," he says. Here he continues linking his healing and his proclaiming. But now he is calling tax traitors to join a project that, to this moment, seems to have attracted the faithful in Israel, people who had been waiting for God to keep promises on which they depended, people he could find in synagogue. And suddenly a great many of them are following him. This will be a problem.

Levi rises and follows Jesus, just as did Simon and Andrew, James and John. But in contrast to these followers who become central to the story, Levi vanishes as soon as he rises. We never hear of him again. In fact, we never again hear of tax collectors or sinful men in the story. Is this a failed part of the project that Jesus then abandons? Or does it become the unstated trademark of his work from this point on? Mark does not tell us. It would be worth asking, though.

Provoking the Story

Popular imagining of this scene usually includes seeing Levi as overwhelmed and repentant. He may well have been, but the scene does not mention it. Levi sits, he rises, he follows, and he is presumably among those who sit back down and eat. Meals center the Jewish world. For Pharisees, every meal should be eaten as if the family were gathered around the altar in the Temple. To include such a traitor at table, even if he were truly repentant, would be searingly difficult for any faithful Jew.

The scene does not say that these traitors were repentant. Jesus only says that they are sick, and identifies them as sinners. Again, popular interpretation leaps in here with the reminder that "we are all sinners," and "before God, one sin is just as bad as another." While this may be true, this scene can only be played honestly if you remember that no one actually believes such things, at least not when it comes to something like maintaining a directory of convicted child molesters and where they live. If all sin is equal and we are all sinners, people should be equally concerned to maintain directories of people convicted of traffic violations and of lying to Congress. Such people live their lives freely. Some even run for Congress or appear regularly on the radio.

Find a way to play this scene with tax traitors who are most definitely not repentant, just to find out what it looks like. Is Jesus a Roman collaborator? Or is he a faithful Jew who also finds contact with traitors to be painful? Experiment with the wide range of possibilities.

10. Bonus Scene
Mark 3:1–6

(see translation, p. 263)

Ritual Text: The Life of the Worshiping Community

Sabbath comes every Friday evening. The sun sets, the family gathers, the women of the family recite the blessing, "Blessed are You, Lord our G-d, King of the universe . . . ," and the candles that have been lighted are discovered. It is as if a queen has come to visit. And then the family eats. The eating is wrapped in careful rituals of delight: the wine is blessed, the bread is blessed, the children are blessed; above all, God is blessed and thanked for such a joyful day, such a joyful meal.

I live in an area with a small Jewish population. Jewish friends and colleagues tell me that it is difficult to maintain this centering meal when the surrounding culture plans its events for Friday evenings. School activities, concerts, celebrations are regularly scheduled over the top of Sabbath mealtime. My friends tell me that sometimes

Sabbath gets squeezed out. And sometimes it does not. They tell me stories of the freedom they find in having a day that is not subject to the racing pace of the rest of the week.

And all this starts with the meal.

This is crucial for interpreting the ritual elements of this scene for reasons that are obvious, and for reasons that are not so obvious. The scene takes place on the Sabbath, at one of the services that mark this holy day. The whole community is there: the Pharisees, Jesus, the disciples, everyone. All of them are gathered to remember that Sabbath comes into the world as a reminder that God promises something more than dreary workdays followed by dreary workdays followed by dreary workdays followed by exhausted death. This is an important thing to remember, especially in a land under foreign domination.

The man with the withered hand is also there. He is also a Jew, also a member of the community that remembers God's promises every Sabbath and waits for them. But this man who has only one working hand is also not quite there. Because he does not have both a public hand and a private hand he embodies the lack that Sabbath promises to fill. This lack will have been felt at the time of the Sabbath meal.

Intra-Text: The World of Mark's Story

Between this wonder story and the scenes in the previous section comes a small set of scenes that echo themes that have been developing in Mark's story. The scenes hand us occasions to wonder about Jesus' relation to tradition. After eating with tax traitors, Jesus and his disciples decline to fast. After declining to fast, Jesus' disciples choose to gather food on the Sabbath. "The son of adam is lord of the Sabbath," says Jesus, a statement so surprising that I might be glad if the old assumption that this refers to a transcendent, glorious figure proceeding from God were true. No such luck. The "son of adam" is a human being. Jesus has just asserted that human beings have a freedom over against the Sabbath that the rabbis say God does not have. "Why did God rest on the seventh day?" ask the rabbis. "Because it was Sabbath," they answer, settling things. How can a human being have control over the Sabbath when it is incumbent even on God to observe it?

Now Jesus is yet again, and for nearly the last time, in the synagogue. This time we are not told that he is teaching. Perhaps he was, perhaps he was not. What we are told is that there in the synagogue is a man with a withered hand.

They were watching him, we are told, to see if he would heal on the Sabbath. Perhaps the "they" in this case is the shadowy embodiment of opposition, familiar to those who are paranoid and to those who are persecuted alike. Perhaps it is a way of naming those who do not need to be named: the Pharisees who emerge at the end of the scene. Or perhaps it simply refers to everyone in the synagogue. We are not told, and we have no sure way of knowing. What we do know, from the last string of scenes, is that Jesus takes some watching. His practice has been a little sloppy, or a lot offensive, of late. Who could predict what he might do next?

Apparently the gathered faithful in the synagogue had a feeling about what might happen when the man with the withered hand was spotted. Even if Jesus had healed unwillingly, almost inadvertently, on the Sabbath when he was surprised by the unclean spirit, he has lately done and said things that establish a pattern of practice not like the one that led him, along with the people of that region, out to John the Baptist.

This development would not be welcome to the faithful who had waited so long, the faithful who, some years later, would recognize and welcome the rabbinic notion that if only all Israel would keep one Sabbath truly, messiah would come.

So they are watching him. Jesus gives them something to watch. He calls the man forward. He asks a pair of questions that make less sense even than the questions he asked when the paralytic came through the roof. He asks, "Is it lawful on the Sabbath to do good or to do evil? To save a life or to kill?" The people in the synagogue are silent, as well they might be. These are not the options between which Jesus must choose. They are not even options. Who is going to answer that one ought do evil rather than good, kill rather than rescue, on the Sabbath? Beyond that, it is in keeping with Torah to do good, and not to do evil, whether it is Sabbath or not. Why bring the Sabbath into the matter at all?

And beyond that, Jesus casts the issue as if it involved life and death. It does not. The man has a withered hand. If he were in danger of imminent death, Jewish practice has always been clear: saving a life takes precedence over all else. But the man is not dying.

And no one is contemplating killing him. He's just there in the synagogue with all the other faithful people. I can imagine that the man with the withered hand was as puzzled, and as silent, as the other people in the synagogue. How would one answer such questions? Argument and disputation are highly regarded in Jewish tradition, but these questions offer no way forward, no possible answers, no productive discourse. So they are all silent.

Jesus calls this silence hard-heartedness, and he becomes angry. He has been angry in the context of healing before, when he healed the leper. It makes little sense either time. He tells the man to stretch out his hand. The man does. It is restored. I can imagine that this was a surprise to the man, and not necessarily a pleasant one. Though he himself had done nothing out of keeping with the Sabbath, he became inextricably linked with Jesus' apparently heedless actions on the day of rest. Nothing would have been lost by waiting until sundown brought the end of the Sabbath. That is what the people of Capernaum did back in Mark 1. It would have demonstrated the work of God who keeps promises if Jesus had invited the man, and the whole synagogue, back to witness the power of God as the sun set. He does not do that. He picks a fight that he did not need. Probably the man with the hand did not need the fight either. We are left to imagine his reaction.

Inter-Text: The World We Think We Live In

Telling this scene requires a basic understanding of what this particular disability would have meant in a world that ate with its hands.

This is not simply a remnant of the distant past. My mother's father grew up in Sweden in a family that had no silverware to eat with. Pieces of bread worked very well. In a culture that eats with its hands, the right hand is the public, clean hand. It is used for all the shared activities of human life, from gesturing to greeting others. It is the hand with which one eats, especially if the traditional food of the community is placed in the common midst, shared by all who are welcomed to eat together. The left hand, by sharp contrast, is the hand for private functions, especially including wiping oneself after defecation. This hand is never used to gesture unless a powerful, violent insult is intended. This hand is never used to eat, it is never even placed on the table.

For the man with the withered hand it did not matter which hand was affected or how severely affected that hand was. With only one hand that worked easily, he would not be able to engage in any of the regular public, clean, shared interaction of human life. Any gesture would be an insult. Any handshake would be revolting. And eating with others would be impossible. Lacking a public hand, he would have lived in private isolation. When Jesus healed him, he restored him to communal life, which is crucial if one shares the apparent assumption of anthropological and sociological work: human life is shared life. That assumption has a corollary: life split off from community is damaged life, perhaps not even human life. Jesus makes it possible for the man to live as a relational being, which is to say as a human being. Could a man who could not eat with others live as a Jew? Good question.

Provoking the Story

This is another scene with clash. Jesus seems to pick fights that he did not need to have. How odd.

When the scene ends, the man with the hand disappears from the text. If you are working with an ensemble of players on this scene, the man with the hand will still be on stage, and you will have to figure out how he reacts to all that has happened. Is he thrilled? Puzzled? Speechless? Annoyed to have been made into an illustration of ignoring the Sabbath? You will have to experiment with what his reaction might be, because we are not given so much as a glimpse of how he reacted to all that happened.

Another reaction is narrated, instead. Mark's story has not needed ευθυς since Jesus healed the paralytic. Now he needs the word again, not for the healing of the man but for the reaction of the Pharisees, who go out BANG to the Herodians, unlikely co-conspirators if ever there were such. A death plot is hatched. This is the only reported reaction to this wonder story, which makes this one stand out from the scenes we have encountered so far. Before this scene, the wonders had caused the world around Jesus to spin in joyous anticipation. Now the reaction is different. Why? Maybe the faithful who came to John, came to Jesus, and came to the synagogue have grown nervous about the course things are starting to follow. Maybe the Pharisees act as they do not because they are implacable foes of the life-giving work of God in the world (a slanderous caricature of customary views of the Pharisees), but because they share the hope spurred by John and they fear that Jesus will divert that hope unhelpfully. The death plot is excessive, to be sure, but remember the circumstances. In such delicate times, putting a foot wrong can have dreadful consequences. Mass movements are easily diverted, turning like a flock of birds following invisible clues as they zigzag in flight. Nothing serves those in power better than an opposition that zigzags, moves aimlessly. Perhaps the Pharisees are acting, regretfully, to protect the hopes of God's people against a dangerous zigzag.

It would be easy to play this scene with the Pharisees breathing self-righteous fire and panting and growling in hypocritical rage. Centuries of sermons and a lifetime of Sunday school lessons have prepared us to play this scene that way. For the sake of historical integrity (and the liveliness of the telling of this story), resist the easy tellings of this story. What if the Pharisees were adherents to John's movement who saw Jesus as betraying the promise of that movement toward devotion to God?

11. Transfiguration Sunday
Mark 9:2–9

(see translation, p. 293)

Ritual Text: The Life of the Worshiping Community

Why is Transfiguration the pivot point before Ash Wednesday?

It is now roughly two months from Christmas (the calendar that governs these things varies from year to year). It is now something like two months until Good Friday. If your congregation uses ritual colors to adorn its worship space, you have been using white for about two months. Starting next Wednesday, Ash Wednesday, you will be using more somber colors. This day stands in the middle of the sweep of events between the two great celebrations of the church's ritual year. This day, along with Ash Wednesday, marks the pivot point in this ritual exploration of the Incarnation, the distinctive Christian doctrine that holds that in Jesus' career, God joined creation and experienced it as a creature. This paradoxical notion shapes the ritual course that the church will follow for the next two months: this scene from Mark's story takes place on a mountain; the next time Jesus is lifted above the flat land will be at his execution by torture.

Kurt Vonnegut (that great accidental theologian) considers this ritual paradox in his book *Slaughterhouse Five.* A character (an alien from Tralfamador, actually) is considering what caused Christianity to go wrong. That it has gone wrong is clear enough: any time a religion of love willingly tortures heretics, something has gone wrong. The problem, it turns out, is that Christianity has misunderstood the ritual paradox set up by the juxtaposition of the Transfiguration and Good Friday. As Christians have read things, the point of Good Friday is that Pontius Pilate tortured Jesus to death because he thought he was a nobody. Crucifixion, after all, was reserved for nobodies.[93] The point of Easter, Christians have concluded, is that Pilate was wrong. Jesus was not a nobody; he was the ultimate SOMEBODY, and thus Pilate was in real trouble. The deadly part comes, says the character, when Christians draw the conclusion that people should strive to never crucify a SOMEBODY. The corollary, however, was the problem. If you cannot crucify SOMEBODIES, you CAN crucify nobodies. You'd just better be sure that you actually have a nobody on your hands before you nail him up. Thus was laid the basis for the Crusades and the Inquisition. Vonnegut's character argues that the real point of the Christian ritual journey is that Jesus was actually a nobody. The point of Easter, then, is that God raises Jesus from the dead in order to say that in God's creation you can't crucify nobodies.

This is not a bad theological conclusion. In fact, it mirrors a conclusion made by no less a figure than Rudolf Bultmann (in another book not much like *Slaughterhouse Five*), who said that the Transfiguration was a misplaced resurrection account. Just so.

Intra-Text: The World of Mark's Story

This scene is woven into Mark's story at almost the exact middle of the story. That alone does not mean much since no one would have been timing the storyteller, then or now, if the story was being told well. What does matter is that this scene echoes the first scene in which Jesus appears. When Jesus comes from Nazareth of Galilee to the Jordan to be baptized by John, a voice speaks, a *bat qol.*[94] The voice in the first scene identifies Jesus as "my son, the beloved." In this scene there is again a voice, presumably the same voice, another *bat qol*, echoing God in a world that can hear only the echo, not the voice. The voice repeats the same identification. Also present for this scene are Moses and Elijah, which repeats another facet of the earlier scene, at least so far as Elijah is concerned. As Jesus strongly hints on the way back down the mountain (Mark 9:11–13), John the Baptist is to be mapped onto Elijah. These repetitions are important for the telling of the story. God is given two chances to speak, a great opportunity for any actor in any story, and God repeats the same line with only minor variations. This indicates either a remarkable lack of imagination, a monumental case of stage fright, or a powerful fixation on a crucial message that must be delivered. While each of these possibilities ought to be explored when developing a way to tell this story, the last seems most promising.

This scene echoes the first scene so substantially that an audience would catch the echoes and draw interpretive conclusions. This is a story that trades in divine identifications of Jesus. In each case, these divine identifications follow a significant human identification. In Mark 1, John says that "one who is stronger" is coming, and then Jesus comes into the story, is baptized, the heavens are torn, and the *bat qol* speaks of Jesus as "son," "beloved." Here in the middle of the story, Peter says that Jesus is the messiah, Jesus and a select few disciples go up a mountain, he is changed in form, Elijah and Moses appear, and the *bat qol* speaks out of the presumably still-torn heavens. Jesus is "son" and "beloved." This repetition confirms the connection between these two scenes. It also creates an audience that has been rewarded for remembering and for letting memory shape their expectations as they listen. These audience traits will matter when next this scene sounds an echo in the story, in chapter 15.

Inter-Text: The World We Think We Live In

Moses and Elijah can enter this scene because they never died. Elijah was caught up to heaven when the "sweet chariot" swung low. Moses was taken by God to see the land of promise, and was borne away by angels, his grave never found. Along with Enoch (who walked with God, according to Genesis) these characters were considered to be in a special category, different from all other human beings. Characters who had died were beyond human experience, out of reach until whatever came along in the way of a general resurrection. Enoch, Moses, and Elijah, because they were understood never to have died, were eligible to be sent back into human experience as special agents (usually of revelation and communication), sent by God to accomplish special purposes. Thus Enoch is the origin of revelatory oracles,[95] Moses is spoken of as something like an angel,[96] and because Malachi expects Elijah, Mark delivers him back into the human story.

That both Moses and Elijah appear in this scene marks the scene as one of terrific importance. Something important is being revealed in this scene.

And you might want to ask why Enoch is not in this scene. Or is Jesus Enoch?

Provoking the Story

Be careful with this scene. Moses and Elijah are real characters in it, and need to be made real even if you are telling this as a solo. But this is not a sequel to *The Night of the Living Dead.* And it is not an occasion for hokey awe and wonder.

What would Moses and Elijah look like when they show up in this scene? Maybe they glow like Jesus, but the text does not tell us that. Maybe they look just like everybody's idea of what these old religious figures ought to look like, though ancient Jewish culture avoided representational painting and sculpting, so there would not be a standard "Moses look," no visual code[97] that would immediately make Moses look just like himself. This is hard for us to imagine. I have heard students assert that while we don't know positively what Jesus looked like, it is striking that "all the artists portray him the same way, so there must be something behind this." Jesus, in the minds of many American Christians, anyhow, has to look just like himself. Maybe Moses and Elijah would look ordinary. If so, the first reaction by the disciples would be to count their own party to make sure that these two other guys are not just some of the usual bunch. The next reaction will be one of surprise to find two extraneous tourists trespassing on the most stunning event of their time with Jesus up to this point. And the next reaction will take place when they find out the names of each of the random tourists. There were other people named Moses and other Elijahs, but somewhere in the sorting out, someone will have realized that the two intruders were not just named Moses and Elijah, they were THE Moses and THE Elijah.

Explore this scene with these possibilities in mind.

Section 2:
LENT AND EASTER

12. First Sunday in Lent
Mark 1:9–15

(see translation, p. 256)

Ritual Text: The Life of the Worshiping Community

This scene is packed with ritual elements. There is a ceremonial washing in the Jordan, the river that God's people crossed to go into the land of promise. The washing is preparation for something, but the text does not tell us specifically what. The scene before this scene makes it clear that whatever it is, it grows out of promises rooted in the time of the return from Exile. Those promises were always too large to fit into the world (requiring as they did drastic changes in geography and a nearly physical presence of God, who would walk on the roads made flat and straight), but they had been preserved and conveyed both a sense of the overwhelming goodness of God's restored creation and a reminder of how little the world as currently constituted resembled the world that was promised. The promises therefore create both hope and dissatisfaction. This is an important combination.

That potent mixture, hope and dissatisfaction, feeds the work of Lent that began on Ash Wednesday. This Sunday (which is, according to traditional distinctions, a Sunday IN Lent, not a Sunday OF Lent) marks a step in the church's annual spiraling path deeper into its stories and its traditions.

After Jesus is baptized, he makes a ritual crossing over the Jordan back into the wilderness in which Israel was formed, and he is tested there forty days, tested by the *satan*, that ally of God who inspects all of creation to detect flaws that could lead to trouble. This also is part of the preparation.

Christians who observe Lent also engage in a forty-day period (the forty-six days from Ash Wednesday to Easter minus the six Sundays in Lent) of testing and strengthening.

Intra-Text: The World of Mark's Story

For a discussion of this scene, see the exploration of the Baptism of Our Lord on page 84.

If the tester is Satan, this is an attack launched in an isolated place, an ambush set up to destroy Jesus. The capital letter makes the tester into a deadly enemy, the representative of everything evil in the world. This is a possible way to translate and read both this scene and the whole of Mark's story.

But if the tester is the *satan*, the scene is different. The *satan* is an agent of God, and is given the task of testing all parts of creation to ensure that all things are as solid and sound as they appear to be. The *satan* is the building inspector charged by God with testing every structure, every person, to be sure that nothing shady slips by. Building inspectors are frequently a nuisance, and people in the building trades will tell you stories about inspectors who are petty, corrupt, rigid, or foolish. Despite even the worst stories, and despite the worst inspectors, however, building inspectors are an essential part of stable human life. Imagine living in a community where there were no effective building inspectors, a community where "imaginative" and "electrician" were not mutually exclusive words. I am VERY glad to have building inspectors around.

In this scene, the *satan* performs an essential task: he is testing Jesus to see what he is made of. If Jesus is to carry the title "messiah" through this story, he will have to be solidly made. How does the testing turn out? We are not told. Maybe the results have not come back from the lab yet. Maybe the testing continues until the middle of the story when Jesus calls Peter a *satan* when Peter urges Jesus not to waste the title "messiah" on a fool's errand against Rome. Maybe the testing continues to the end of Mark's story. If so, the audience will have to figure out how the test went. The last time Jesus appears in Mark's story he accuses God of abandoning him. This is both a cry of despair and a protest rooted in Jewish faith,[98] but the audience will have to decide whether the cry indicates that Jesus has proved himself substantial enough to carry the title "messiah" or not. The broken end of the story may indicate how hard it is to answer this question.

Inter-Text: The World We Think We Live In

Again, see the exploration of the Baptism of Our Lord for a thorough discussion of this scene.

Provoking the Story

This scene appears in the RCL two times, once during Epiphany and now again near the beginning of Lent. If you are performing this scene both times, how will it be different this time from last? Different occasions do indeed change the shape and nature of performances, even if the script is identical. For example, imagine listening to Billy Joel's song "New York State of Mind" back when it was first written, and then remember how it sounded when he performed it as part of the *Tribute to Heroes* telethon to honor the firefighters and others who were killed in the attack on the World Trade Center. The script is the same, but the occasion changes everything.

Let the difference imposed by Lent provoke your performance of this story. The forty days become more significant since Lent lasts for forty days (from Ash Wednesday to Easter, excluding Sundays), and the wilderness emerges as significant. The period of wandering in the wilderness is remembered as the time of testing and preparation (lasting forty years) before Israel's entry into the land of God's promise. The word for "wilderness" in Hebrew is *midbar*, which means something like "wordless." This could either render the silence of a true wilderness, or it could reveal that such areas are places to which God has not yet spoken a creative word to make them blossom and flourish and leap into life. This adds a different note, both to this scene from Mark's story and to the notion of what might be going on in Lent.

If this part of the baptism scene takes place in the *midbar*, what does that look like, feel like, and sound like? Is it a place of eerie silence? Or is it a place of rushing wind, hissing snakes? Remember that it was the πνευμα (spirit, breath, wind; in Hebrew, *ruach*) that blew Jesus out into the *midbar*, just as it was the *ruach* (spirit, breath, wind; in Greek, πνευμα) that blew over the waters before God spoke to the chaos and made a beautifully ordered cosmos. Do you hear this rushing, this hissing, when Jesus is in the water earlier in the scene? If you do, what does this chaos/creation imagery do to the figure of John the Baptist who lives in the *midbar* and washes people in the water? Chase the implications of these images as far as you can.

13. Second Sunday in Lent
Mark 8:31–38

(see translation, p. 291)

Ritual Text: The Life of the Worshiping Community

This scene echoes the wilderness testing scene from the First Sunday in Lent. That link is obscured when this scene is played as if Peter is somehow being cast as satanic, devilish, demonic. The scene plays better, and the ritual echoes are stronger and more productive, if Jesus refers to Peter as a *satan*, rather than as Satan, with all the mythological baggage that goes with that in Christian imagination.

Such a reference is not without its problems, however. It fits nicely into the testing and strengthening that are ritually appropriate to Lent for Christians. But it will require careful exploration to decide what, exactly, is the nature of this particular instance of testing. Here is where having an ensemble of players becomes especially helpful. Play the scene (with the scene immediately preceding this one) to see what the dramatic possibilities are. Does the testing begin (as is customarily supposed) with Peter's scolding of Jesus? Then the transformation that takes place in this scene involves Peter moving from approval to disapproval between his identification of Jesus as Messiah and his scolding of Jesus. You will also have to figure out exactly why Peter is scolding Jesus. Is he seeking to protect him from rejection and death (saying, in effect, "The messiah must never die")? Or is he scolding Jesus for his casual courting of death in the hands of the Romans (saying, in this case, "Do NOT waste the hopes of the people by making cheap jokes about crucifixion")? The two scenes are quite different from one another.

Of course, you might also explore the possibility that the testing began with Peter's identification of Jesus as Messiah in the previous scene. Maybe that is the test, and Jesus plays with it throughout the beginning of the scene for this Sunday. His immediate response, "Tell no one!" is described as scolding. This works best if the testing begins with the overzealous identification of Jesus as Messiah. Perhaps Jesus is mulling this identification, playing with the possibilities, even as he sketches the historical probabilities that will attend anyone on the course that he is on. When Peter scolds him, perhaps this is the trigger that sets off the remark about the *satan*. The question that is not answered, no matter which way you play the scene, is whether Jesus tests out solid or not, and whether he claims the identification as Messiah or not.

It will be hard for Christians to leave these possibilities open, maybe especially during Lent, which moves steadily toward Good Friday and Easter. But a proper Lenten discipline of testing, examining, and strengthening may require precisely this exercise in reexamining basic notions of what Jesus' career meant and means for those who find their life in his story. What if Jesus is significant, precisely for Christians (we are messianists, after all), because he would choose to resist the messianic notions that have grown up around him in the church?

Intra-Text: The World of Mark's Story

Here, near the exact middle of the story, Jesus promises what will happen at the end. As soon as Jesus finishes with this scene of promising, the story moves him up a mountain and into a scene that recalls the scene of his baptism. From that elevation, Jesus and the audience can see all the way to the end of the story, and all the way back to the beginning.

This short scene, however, lacks the breathtaking view of the mountaintop scene that follows it and the piercing, hopeful insight of the scene immediately preceding this one. This scene is full of hard details — suffering, rejection, killing — all in some detail. There is also a too-brief mention of rising, which passes almost without notice through the thicket of painful details. What if Peter is rejecting not the death, but the resurrection of Jesus? Martyrs are frequently more useful and trustworthy than living, fallible human beings. John F. Kennedy, safely martyred, is a symbol of a lost idealism. JFK, alive through his whole presidency, would likely have taken the United States into Vietnam.

Inter-Text: The World We Think We Live In

When reading these words about following, it is wise to consider who could follow someone who is carrying a cross. You could follow such a person as a torturer who was moving from the first part of the ritual of illustrative death to the last. The parade through the midst of the conquered people was essential to the ritual because it emphasized that you and the force behind you (Rome) were dominant. Brutality teaches a lesson that conquered people are taught by their oppressors over and over.

Another option open to you would be that of being a member of the crowd along the way. This crowd would be a mixed lot, because the parade to death was designed to cut through the heart of everyday life and make it clear that Rome had the power to cut through the entire world if it so chose. Some of the people in the crowd who followed this parade would be people who could not avoid doing so because their everyday business forced them to follow the same route. Jews in Jerusalem who hated Rome and its brutal political lessons still had to go about their work. Others would perhaps be people who could not deny their connection to the ones being crucified, but also could do nothing to help them. Family, associates, comrades: for all of them it would be dangerous to follow the parade of death, but impossible not to. Rome also calculated the effect of such enforced feebleness. It taught a lesson: no one can stand against Rome.

And there would have been people who followed who were part of the brutal, inhuman segment of every population in every culture, people who save their own lives by cheering as others lose theirs. The ugliness of such behavior does not make it less common. Some of them will have followed Jesus to his execution as well.

The only other followers would have been those who were likewise crucified. This was not a heroic lot, neither were they martyrs. They were people who had been caught and could not struggle free. Maybe they were notorious criminals or brutal bandits. Maybe they were simply slaves who were being executed because it was possible to dispose of property in any way that seemed fit. In any case, all that remained of their lives was a public exhibition in which they were made unable to cover or defend themselves until they finally died. Even if these victims were somehow resisters to Rome's domination, none of that mattered any longer. If they struggled, it was the way a fly struggles on flypaper. When they died, their death had no more meaning than did the death of the baby water buffalo described by Tim O'Brien in *The Things They Carried.* It could not defend itself. It could not move. It could not even die. It could only endure the brutality pointlessly until it finally ended.[99]

Against this background, hear Jesus' words about how losing your life makes it pointless to gain the whole world. There is a painful logic to what he says. Far less clear is how his words about saving your life make any sense at all. Do not jump too soon to a customary and comfortable metaphorical reading of this matter. Hear Mark's story carefully and slowly before you pull its punch.

Provoking the Story

Hunt carefully for the voice and body out of which Jesus speaks in this scene. The language is offensive: in the first century CE the word "cross" was a vile obscenity, and here Jesus is using the word freely. When people use vile obscenities, how and why do they do it? Children who are pretending to be adults often make their language as coarse as their experience will allow. They use vile words while affecting a casual attitude that aims to say to anyone who cares that they talk this way all the time. They look like children who pretend to have been smoking cigarettes for years, only to nearly set their noses on fire trying to light up.

When else do people use vile and violent language? Sometimes people use it in response to pain or fear, but in my experience they use it in such settings when the provocation is frustration or embarrassment. Real pain calls forth deeper, quieter responses.

People also use language that shocks others when the language describes their everyday reality. Everyone should have the experience of eating lunch with nurses. These professionals who bring health and nurturance to a part of life that involves vomit and blood and deep uncertainty will often speak casually about things that drive other people screaming from the room. I remember how the head nurse at the nursing home where I worked mentioned autopsies while we were eating liver for lunch. Apparently the organ is sliced in similar ways for analysis and for sautéing with onions. I found that fascinating. Others did not. Perhaps the language in this scene is professional language: shocking but necessary, given the realities.

Tim O'Brien says that war makes people use vile language. Read *The Things They Carried*. Perhaps this scene is part of a war story.

14. Liturgy of the Palms
Mark 11:1–11

(see translation, p. 306)

Ritual Text: The Life of the Worshiping Community

In my experience, Palm Sunday has always been uncomfortable. Even as a child the day seemed awkward. Always they gave us palm fronds. Always the fronds went home with us and were tucked behind a picture in our living room until next Ash Wednesday. These parts of the ritual made some sort of sense.

The part that didn't make ritual sense was everything between those two moments. Sometimes they expected the whole congregation to march around the church building. Sometimes they just made the kids from Sunday school, along with their teachers and a few uncomfortable adults, walk up the aisle carrying the palm fronds. Always they insisted that we should shout "Hosanna."

That was where the real problem started for me. The forced shouting seemed useless. Usually it was only a few people who said anything at all, and usually they were people who made me uncomfortable. They tended to be those people who wore their faith the way poorly trained clowns wear squirting flowers. You can see the fake flower, you know that if you express any interest at all in seeing a clown up close they will take aim at you and hose you. And then everyone will laugh, though they won't be too sure if they are laughing because the tired old trick was funny or because it was you instead of them that got hosed.

I felt like that especially when our pastors made us traipse around outside the church, sometimes all the way around the block. The clowns among us hollered "Hosanna!" at any poor soul unfortunate enough to be caught out in the open. I was always glad when they were gracious about having been singled out to be hosanna-ed.

Maybe it's only me. But if your experience is anything like mine, read the scene from Mark again. There does not appear to be anybody compelling the general hosanna-ing that is going on. The commandeering of the colt may have served as a trigger for the ritual welcome, but if so it triggered a reaction that had real integrity. This scene does not work if there is compulsion anywhere in it. This scene only works if there is some sort of internal impulsion that breaks out in cries of "LORD save us." What is this impulsion?

For a hint of an answer, you might read Paula Fredriksen's *Jesus of Nazareth, King of the Jews*. The first piece to read closely is her "Prelude 2: The Temple."[100] This bit of historical imagining catches what it might have been like for a Jewish boy from Nazareth to approach Jerusalem in the first century CE. She catches the excitement, the boiling expectation that go with approaching Jerusalem and the Temple during Passover. Such a crowd of pilgrims might well cry out.

The next piece to read closely is her exploration of the possibility that Jesus was delivered to the Romans because of the out-of-control agitation of a crowd overheated by Passover hopes.[101] In Fredriksen's thought experiment, Jesus is a teacher who has lost control of his audience.[102] The hopes of the crowd of pilgrims, particularly the Judeans, sweep Jesus into Jerusalem and into Pilate's court.

This imaginative reconstruction is persuasive. The cries of "LORD save us!" erupt out of the fissure that breaks open when Roman power, Jerusalem's mythic meaning, and Jesus' teaching about the nearness of God's dominion grind against each other and shift. Playing this scene truthfully will require discovering what hopes burn beneath the surface in a contemporary audience. This is a risky scene. Remember, if Fredriksen is correct, Jesus lost control of his audience at precisely this point.

Intra-Text: The World of Mark's Story

With this scene Mark's story moves into Jerusalem. It has been circling around Jerusalem from the beginning of the story, which is not surprising since Jerusalem is the center of the world. The tug of the Holy City can be felt throughout the story. Scribes arrive from Jerusalem to question Jesus. Jesus travels toward Jerusalem. Now he enters the city for the first time.

This entry is tense, especially if you read Jerusalem the way many interpreters do, as the origin of all opposition. While Jerusalem is the place where Jesus meets his death, it is also the place where Jesus meets enthusiastic support. The city is mixed in its reaction to Jesus. In Mark 1, every person living in Jerusalem spins out of the city to hear John. In Mark 3, the great crowd that follows Jesus comes from Jerusalem, among other places. And now an enthusiastic crowd greets Jesus as he enters. In this scene you can feel the tensions of the story coming together. You can feel the tensions that go with approaching the center of Jewish hope and history as Passover approaches. Throughout Mark's story there have been enthusiastic crowds. These crowds have followed, they have crushed together, they have raced to meet Jesus. Now they crystallize around Jesus at the edge of Jerusalem and call for God to save them (Hosanna).

It is tempting to read the word οχλος (crowd) as a signal word in Mark's story, as a word that carries special freight for the story. Because up to this point the crowd has responded positively to Jesus and individuals have responded negatively, perhaps οχλος is a flag that marks a supportive group of people. That interpretive line runs into trouble in the coming chapters because at the end of the story suddenly it is a crowd that comes with swords and clubs. This crowd is stirred up against Jesus. This crowd calls for Jesus to die.

Perhaps οχλος could still be a signal word, but not a signal simply of support. Perhaps the word is one of the places where the two trajectories that Paul Ricoeur sketches meet and cross. The *parcours euphorique* and the *parcours dysphorique* (the flow toward a good outcome and the contrary flow) meet and clash throughout the story. Perhaps they meet and clash in the word οχλος as well. This possibility creates extra tension. Responsible playing will call for finding a way to represent the dual nature of the crowd so that this dual nature can also be seen when you play the end of the story.

There is another word that needs special attention in this scene. Jesus tells his disciples who are sent to untie a colt to explain their action by saying, "The LORD has need of it." Leaving to the side the question of whether this act of untying reveals an underlying group of conspirators who had planned this entry out of the view of the story's audience or whether Jesus is just authorizing his disciples to "borrow" someone else's animal, we ought to notice the use of the word "LORD." This word translates a common Greek word, κυριος.

There are scenes in Mark's story that definitely call for κυριος to be translated as LORD. Jesus quotes the Shema in Mark 12; he tells the cured demoniac to tell people what the LORD has done for him in Mark 5. And in the scene at hand, the crowd calls "hosanna" to the one who is coming "in the Name of the Lord." These seem clear enough. But what about the business of "the κυριος has need of it"? Is this a reference to the Divine Name or to Jesus? This is complicated for contemporary Christians who customarily refer to Jesus as Lord. It is not so complicated for Mark's story, since no one in that story follows this practice. If Jesus is using κυριος as a way of referring to himself here, he is creating an innovation that the story has not prepared the audience to catch. Contemporary Christians catch it (whether it's there or not), but that's because they are Trinitarians. Jesus is, these days, the second member of the Godhead.

But is he also that exalted character in Mark's story? Good question.

Inter-Text: The World We Think We Live In

At the beginning of this scene Jesus approaches Jerusalem and enters it. At the end of the scene he will approach the Temple and enter it as well. In the next scene, Jesus will again enter Jerusalem, again approach the Temple, and again enter it. The swirl around the Temple becomes more intense.[103] Alan Segal has provided a helpful understanding of what this swirl means for the Jewish world of the first century CE.[104] That world, says Segal, was organized in concentric circles of holiness. At the center of all of these circles was the Temple. Because "holiness" is a complex construct, not a simple idea, these concentric circles map themselves onto other related constructs as well. The circles could be circles of purity (a word that differs in implication from "holiness"), and this would indicate that the approach to the Temple would require progressive acts of preparation. Such was indeed the case. The circles could be circles of Jewishness, and this would indicate that the world becomes more Jewish as you approach the Temple. This was also true. Galilee was called "Galilee of the Gentiles," and not for nothing. After the crushing of the Jewish Revolt, Jerusalem was reconstituted as a pagan city, and not by accident. But if the circles can be read as circles of Jewishness, then they can also be read as circles of Torah observance, and if they are circles of Torah observance, then they are concentric circles of safety and stability. Torah observance is the practice of living life so that every act, every word, every structure of life witnesses to the stable and orderly love of God. The world outside Israel, on this model, is chaotic and dangerous. Inside Israel, things are somewhat safer. Inside Jerusalem, things are safer still. Inside the Temple, safer still. At the center of the whole structure is the Holy of Holies, where God touches the world to hold the center still. The world spins and swirls around this single still point. That means that Mark's story in this scene is orbiting around the center of the Jewish universe, the place where God holds the world still despite all the chaos.

Of course, by the time Mark's story was told in the form we have, the Temple was a smoking ruin, destroyed by the Romans at the conclusion of the First Jewish Revolt against Rome in 70 CE. Even safety is not simple in the world of Mark's story.

Provoking the Story

So, is Jesus a lord in this scene, or is he the LORD, or is he a faithful Jew who carefully refers to the Divine Name by not saying it? Of course, the answer is yes, which doesn't help very much. Of course, I suggest playing it each of these ways, but even that doesn't help all that much since it is not altogether clear what it would mean for a human being to refer to himself as God.

At least it is not clear what it would mean for a sane human being to do such a thing.

Perhaps this is a scene in which Jesus reveals a sort of lurking insanity, a disturbing tendency to entertain delusional ideas. This way of playing, disturbing as it will be, actually will pay off in the next scene in Mark's story, in which Jesus curses a fig tree for having no fruit when it would be impossible for it to have fruit.

Or perhaps this is a scene in which Jesus does something ordinary, and is surprised when the crowd blows up his action into something that exalts him to divine status. This way of playing replicates (in some measure) traditional readings of Mark's story that have argued that Mark presents the "most human" Jesus among the canonical gospels, the Jesus least likely to be promoted to an office in the Trinity.

Or perhaps this is a scene in which Jesus and the crowd discover God working in ordinary events. Jesus plays on old code when entering Jerusalem, the crowd reads the code, and the result is that everyone sees God working in creation to keep old promises of safety and deliverance. Such a discovery requires all parties to hold onto their old hopes with a fiery intensity. Such a process of revelation will be a surprise to all involved. Jesus, on this model, triggers the whole business by his mode of entry, but the reaction goes beyond anything he has allowed up to this point.

Or perhaps Jesus always wanted to ride a donkey into Jerusalem, maybe even because he knew the old texts that had been linked with the coming of God's deliverance. And maybe the crowd's reaction is not to be played as believing but as derisive. In any case, the crowd disappears immediately upon Jesus' entry into the city. If they honestly saw him as the representative of David's return to dominion, wouldn't they follow him throughout the rest of the story? What if their acclamation of Jesus as the "one who is coming" is a joke told at his expense, told because they recognized the code that Jesus was using, told because they looked at this bumpkin from the north and laughed at his naïveté? That would explain their disappearance: having had their fun at the expense of the tourist, they went on with their lives. That would also mean that this scene foreshadows the taunting references to Jesus as king and messiah that haunt the death scene.

This last (and rather disturbing) way of playing the scene, by the way, sounds notes that may be heard in Albert Schweitzer's reading of Jesus' intentions in going up to Jerusalem. In Schweitzer's understanding, Jesus went up in order to turn the wheel of history, to provoke God's intervention against Rome by sacrificing himself. Schweitzer's Jesus discovers the futility of his fool's errand when the wheel of history crushes him and he hangs bleeding and hopeless on the cross.

Explore this scene carefully. There is more here than normally shows up in Palm Sunday parades around the neighborhood.

15. Bonus Scene
Mark 11:13–24

(see translation, p. 307)

Ritual Text: The Life of the Worshiping Community

This scene is not part of the Revised Common Lectionary. One can understand why. This scene would be played, if the story were handled consecutively, sometime between Palm Sunday and Good Friday. The tirade in the Temple could be managed in the midst of such a ritual flow. Christians would gladly imagine Jesus attacking (or, in common parlance, cleansing) the Temple as his last official act before being caught in the whirlpool that draws him to crucifixion. Such a reading even provides a sort of dramatic motivation for the attack on Jesus: it is payback.

The problem would come with the fig tree. Mark has carefully laid out the scene so that Jesus' actions are unjustified. It is not the season for figs. He has no reason (unless he feigns ignorance of the growing season) for his destruction of the tree. Because he is disappointed in his unreasonable demand for fruit out of season, no one else will ever eat from the tree again. If the tree is private property, Jesus has just committed a trespass. If the tree is public property, Jesus has just taken food out of the mouths of homeless people with no other source of food. Neither option will be palatable in the flow from Palm Sunday, the entry of the Messiah into the city of the great king, to Good Friday, when the sinless Lamb is sacrificed.

What puzzles me, on a purely ritual level, is how carefully Mark lays out the scene with the fig tree. It would appear that he does not intend to play along with the customary Christian ritual flow. In such surprises lies dramatic potential.

Intra-Text: The World of Mark's Story

This is the last of the wonder stories in Mark's story. What a strange way to finish off his career as a worker of wonders. The other wonders are customarily (and properly) read as acts that benefit the creation. Jesus heals people, he raises a little girl from death, he walks on water to come to the aid of his disciples in distress. And now he blasts a simple fig tree, and Mark makes it clear that this attack is unjustified: it was not the season for figs.

It is this careful withholding of justification that must draw our attention. Even those readers who are inclined to maintain, blandly, that this is simply a bit of historical fact (it was just not fig season, that's all) must still figure out why Mark takes pains to mention this particular detail. Storytelling demands a severe economy of its practitioners. You simply cannot mention every detail that might be historically grounded, or your audience will wander off in boredom. Mark makes certain that even audiences that know nothing about figs know how to react to Jesus' actions here. It is not the season for figs. Apparently it IS the season for unreasonable actions by Jesus.

Of course this is not the first time that a wonder story involves surprising violence. When Jesus exorcised the legion of demons, he killed a herd of two thousand pigs in the process (Mark 5). Interpreters sometimes note that this would not be a problem for a Jewish audience since pigs were not kept by Jewish farmers (for obvious reasons). This is true enough, and may reveal no more than that Mark's story does not think beyond its own cultural borders. But the story does demonstrate awareness of the effect of this destruction on the Gentile population: they ask Jesus to leave their territory. And then there is the case of Jesus' words to the mother who asked Jesus to cast the demon out of her daughter (Mark 7). She was a Gentile and Jesus calls her a dog. Even if he were to call her a puppy, that would not make this less insulting.[105] At the end of the scene, her daughter is found thrown on the bed, the demon gone. And Jesus heals a leper, only to turn on him and snort indignantly and cast him out (Mark 1).

The blasting of the fig tree points out a stream of violence in Jesus' acts that ought to be considered when interpreting this scene. Such behavior is puzzling. Of course there are other instances in which Jesus behaves in puzzling ways. He weakens Sabbath observance; he refuses to acknowledge his own mother. This pattern of unaccountable action ties this very odd scene to themes that Mark has developed from the beginning of the story. What is going on here?

Inter-Text: The World We Think We Live In

The following is a quickly gathered collection of readings of the cursing of the fig tree that were available on the World Wide Web. Note the flavor of these readings and their implications for playing this scene. The dangers of anti-Semitic readings have not diminished.

The following were all accessed on November 27, 2004. All relevant access, copyright, and update information is included, when it was available. No spelling or formatting has been corrected or altered. The quotations appear here just as they did on the Web on the day of access.

> Jesus was not out to condemn a non-bearing tree; he was pronouncing judgment against the religious barrenness of the nation. The tree is not in trouble, the nation is. The tree has not rejected its Messiah, the nation has. The tree is being used as a symbol, not the object itself, of the judgment. If it had been the season for figs, then the tree would have itself borne certain responsibility, and its judgment would have applied as much to itself as to the nation, watering down the force of the symbolism. But Jesus is not interested in judging fig trees. The focus is, rather, on the nation, the temple, the Jewish leadership.
>
> —*www.wcg.org/lit/bible/gospels/figtree.htm*
> Copyright © 2000 *Worldwide Church of God*

> The fig tree is Israel which will be judged for a lack of repentance. They have the pretension of life, but not the substance of life.
>
> —*www.bible.org/page.asp?page_id=2245*
> Copyright © 2004, Bible.org—All rights reserved

And that's a perfect symbol of the nation of Israel at the time Jesus was born into the world. They had a form of godliness, with the religion of the Pharisees, Sadducees and scribes being openly practiced in the temple at Jerusalem. But where was the reality, the fruit of godliness? Their religion allowed rejection of their Messiah....

Or in the case of the fig tree, He cursed it and caused it to wither away. Which is exactly what happened to the nation of Israel, which ceased to exist from A.D. 70, when the Romans destroyed it, until this very generation today, which has seen the nation reborn.

—*http://johnmyers.com/bible14.html*
www.johnmyers.com © 2001, John W. Myers

Jerusalem had its time. Now it is our own time of decision and continuous fruit-bearing. What will our future be?

—*www.heartlight.org/wjd/mark/0812–wjd.html*
Copyright © 1996–2004

The religion of Judiasm [*sic*], based at Jerusalem would not bear fruit for God any longer. Like a fig tree without fruit, so too would this fig tree wither.

—*www.bibletime.com/bt/theory/time/*

Such a fruitless tree, was useless, similarly, the Jewish Nation rendered to be unfruitful spiritually, because of legalism, man-made tradition and the hunger for power by those in charge.

A fruitless tree, a fruitless people. The nation was spiritually barren. The fruitless tree had failed in its purpose and Jesus rightfully expressed anger. In Israel Jesus had only found religious legalism without any holiness.

—*www.tne.net.au/ abdaacts/cft.html, Last updated May 2003*

The curse of the fig tree is not about trees and fruit. It is about faith and fakery. When Jesus cursed the fig tree, he was acting out a spiritual lesson. He was on His way to a Temple and to a religious system that had all of the leaves of piety, but which was dead and fruitless on the inside.

—*www.angelfire.com/nt/theology/mk11–20.html*

> The Fig Tree incident is used to frame and explain what is going on in the temple, the heart of Israel's religion. Just as the fig tree is cursed for it's [*sic*] lack of fruit so the temple, the Jewish religion, stands cursed by Jesus for it's [sic] lack of fruit.
>
> —*www.thebluefish.org.uk/articles/mark11.htm*

As you can see from these quotations, it comes clear that it is wise to exercise care in playing a scene like this one. Even gentle and good people can be coaxed into anti-Semitic rants if performers are not wise and careful. Recognize the problems. Play wisely.

Provoking the Story

Be sure, whatever else you do, to play the justified reaction of the disciples to the dead fig tree. This is not just an astonishment reaction to a wonder worker. It must also be, if this is to be a true story, a reaction to the excessive anger, the excessive violence, the taking of revenge on the tree for not yielding what it could not be expected to yield. Remember that the physics of the world must be respected. In any real world, such violence will at least yield cringing, maybe even an intervention because he is out of his mind. This would not be the first such intervention attempted in Mark's story. Remember the attempt made by Jesus' family earlier in the story. Perhaps they might try again in this scene. Remember that, though the script does not give them lines, the action of the scene would provoke a response that would happen between the lines. Such inventions are not impositions on the script. Quite to the contrary, they are evidence that the script is being respected above all.

In order to catch the enormity of what Jesus has done, it might be necessary to play the scene several ways. Some of the ways will give Jesus the usual free pass to do and say whatever he wishes. Others, however, must honor the range of real human reactions to such behavior. Something needs to give voice to the physical reaction that would be embodied in the scene, something to help the audience catch what the problem might be. It is not just that Jesus blasts an innocent tree. He attacks an image of the Temple and Israel. The audience needs to be let in on this larger attack.

16. Liturgy of the Passion Mark 14:1–15:47

(see translation, p. 320)

Ritual Text: The Life of the Worshiping Community

I find myself in an odd position with regard to the Liturgy of the Passion. On the one hand, I have a strong ritual preference for allowing single days to be single days. This Sunday is the day to explore the ritual entry of Jesus into Jerusalem, and there is plenty of exploring to be had in that scene in Mark's story without having to add also the Passion into the day. On the other hand, the Revised Common Lectionary chooses John's story of the death of Jesus as the scene to be read on Good Friday. John's story is good and worthy, and (as Paula Fredriksen points out) it aligns rather well with the outline of Mark's story.[106] But Mark's story of the death of Jesus has a peculiar power and integrity that I am reluctant to lose as part of the ritual exploration of his death.

So what does one do? Of course it is always an option to displace John's story on Good Friday and work with Mark. That is, in my estimation, a good choice, though John also deserves careful attention. In any case, it is worth examining the ritual structure that Mark's story brings to this central week in the church's year.

What must be seen above all else is that Mark's death scene establishes a link back to the beginning of Lent, and from there to the celebration of the Transfiguration, and from there to the celebration of The Baptism of Our Lord, which closely follows Epiphany. This binding is rooted in the structure of Mark's whole story (and thus will be examined in the exploration of the Intra-Text), but it creates a ritual linking that is fascinating in itself. The Baptism and the Transfiguration involve Elijah (or John who looks like Elijah) and a voice, best figured as a *bat qol*. These elements make the scenes powerful.

Centuries are spanned and the "daughter of a voice" echoes into human history with an identification of Jesus that raises all manner of questions. The death scene involves a taunting reference to Elijah and a voice that is no echo. The question for a storyteller is how to play the voice. It speaks the same words, but the tone and force of the scene are utterly at odds with what has gone before. Surely one might choose to play this as a moment of ironic triumph, as is customary. But the ritual of the event is more interesting if it is played as the antithesis of the earlier moments of revelation. This is a moment of concealment and death, a moment that refuses the tearing of the heavens and drowns out the *bat qol.* Rome controls this scene according to its own well-practiced rituals of domination and oppression. Where the Baptism and the Transfiguration prompt hope that there is a power beyond the dome of the sky that may break in to straighten the world and smooth it, the death scene makes it clear that such hopes die painful deaths in a world ruled by power. When the curtain in the Temple is torn, storytellers will do well to remember that the tearing of a garment is a Jewish gesture of mourning, and that mourning is the ritual activity human beings engage in when they are reminded that their hopes and their love cannot turn back death. Perhaps the tearing of the curtain is best played as God's ritual of mourning. If so, it is wise to remember that other garments are torn in mourning in this larger scene. The ritual players in this larger scene may be different than you had guessed.

Intra-Text: The World of Mark's Story

When Jesus hands the cup to his disciples in the scene of the last Passover meal, they all drink the wine right away. This is not so very surprising. Wine makes the heart glad, so says the Bible, and this is especially true during Passover, when Jews remember God's acts of deliverance and remember also the crying need for such acts in a world that is dangerous and chaotic.

The disciples all drink because the chaos that Passover recognizes has entered even into the room where they are eating. First Jesus tells them that one of them will hand him over. The audience knows this, of course, but the disciples do not. Be careful in interpreting this moment. The easiest playing of the scene will treat the audience's knowledge as determinative. The disciples will be portrayed as dolts who have not been paying attention, and they will simply go through their routine of saying, "Surely you don't mean me!" to no good purpose and for no good reason. Even if the interpreter makes a theological/sermonic point that allows as how "everyone betrays Jesus," the scene will still be flat and dead. Embodied interpretation requires honoring the laws of physics: every event must have an adequate cause. Honor the viewpoint of the disciples. How would Jesus' words sound to them, especially in the midst of the Passover meal, that refuge from the angry swirl of heedless history? Jesus' words about being handed over intrude roughly on a moment that the disciples, observant Jews all, would have waited for every year of their lives. And then he says, "That man would be better off if he had never been born." The violence and anger of these words needs to be heard and felt. We do not often wish other people out of existence, but Jesus does it here. Perhaps some around the table remember what happened when Jesus wished the fig tree out of existence. Perhaps everyone remembered what happened when Jesus attacked the proper operation of sacrifice in the Temple. There was not evidence of shady practice that led to the overturning of tables and benches. There was just Jesus acting out a program that is hard to follow or justify. And now he issues a death sentence against an unnamed opponent. Jesus' words would have sounded jarring and out of place. For the sake of the integrity of the text, play them that way.

No sooner have the disciples got Jesus calmed down and back on the traditional track of the Seder meal[107] than he goes off again. He has blessed the bread. He has handed it to them. It is not clear what part of the service they are observing, if only because we do not know with certainty what Passover practice was in first-century Judaism. It does not matter. The bread is there, the tradition is there. He hands them the bread, and he tells them the bread that they will eat is his body. Christians immediately hear the Eucharist at this point. We eat Jesus' body every time we share that meal. This seems normal to us. But the disciples have never been to the Eucharist. They have never even been to Christian catechism class. They are Jews who are just trying to celebrate Passover, and now Jesus has introduced cannibalism into the ancient traditions of the Jewish faith. Another unwelcome intrusion. Another violent and jarring act. It will not do to save Jesus by saying that he is "reinterpreting" Passover. Imagine the reaction of a Christian congregation if the pastor "reinterpreted" the Eucharist by handing out raw meat instead of bread. (She could have taken the reinterpretation all the way and handed out bits of human flesh.) This scene cannot be played as if everyone onstage has already finished their catechism training, at least not without undermining the story that Mark is telling.

And then Jesus hands them the cup of wine. At least now the meal gets back on track and their hearts can be made glad again and they can remember the Passovers of their childhood and their hopes for the future. The wine will help. They all drink some. The wine will surely help.

"This is my blood," says Jesus.

Now he has gone beyond cannibalism. An injunction to practice cannibalism would be a relief next to this statement. "Anyone who eats blood will be cut off from the people." So says Torah. "Do not drink blood." "In the blood is the life." So says Torah over and over. The practices of kashrut include careful procedures to be followed in butchering animals so that blood will not be part of the meat that is eaten. This understanding will have been a central part of every Jew's daily practice since earliest childhood's first awareness. And now Jesus tells them that the wine in their mouths is blood. Research indicates that people will taste what they are told they should taste. Subjects who are eating (in fact) a piece of potato will taste an apple if their noses are plugged and they are told that it is an apple. Imagine the faces of the disciples when they taste blood in their mouths. Imagine their faces when they taste expulsion from the people of Israel.

This is a very odd scene.

Inter-Text: The World We Think We Live In

Why would a community of faith focus its central attention on the torture death of a single man? Storytellers, however, have to wonder. Storytellers always have to wonder. There are many ways to tell the story of a death by torture. Such stories are told to stir feelings of patriotism. I remember learning to regret having only one life to give for my country. I remember seeing posters in the American Legion post (where my Boy Scout troop met), posters that held up tortured American prisoners of war as heroes. I remember the stories and the movies out of World War II about battlefield deaths, prison-camp deaths, civilian deaths during the London blitz. All of these stories were told to shape me, to shape us all, as loyal citizens who had something to stand and fight for.

Stories of death can also be told to blow on the embers of smoking resentment. I remember reading Tertullian's statement: "the blood of the martyrs is the seed of the church." I remember being frightened by the tone and flavor, even as my colleagues and professors seemed thrilled. Any plant that grows out of such a seed will grow bloody and dangerous.

Listen to a prayer that grows out of the twelfth century CE, out of the attacks on Jewish communities by Christian Crusaders. This prayer asks God's mercies on all those killed because they honored God's Name. As part of Christian reflection on the death of Jesus, Christians ought to pause and remember the Jewish martyrs killed by Christians in the name of Jesus.

AV HARACHAMIM
(FATHER OF MERCY)

The Father of mercy who dwells on high
in His great mercy
will remember with compassion
the pious, upright and blameless
the holy communities, who laid down their lives
for the sanctification of His name.

They were loved and pleasant in their lives
and in death they were not parted.
They were swifter than eagles and stronger than lions
to carry out the will of their Maker,
and the desire of their steadfast God.
May our Lord remember them for good
together with the other righteous of the world
and may He redress the spilled blood of His servants
as it is written in the Torah of Moses the man of God:
"O nations, make His people rejoice
for He will redress the blood of His servants
He will retaliate against His enemies
and appease His land and His people."
And through Your servants, the prophets it is written:
"Though I forgive, their bloodshed I shall not forgive
When God dwells in Zion."
And in the Holy Writings it says:
"Why should the nations say, 'Where is their God?' "
Let it be known among the nations in our sight
that You avenge the spilled blood of Your servants.
And it says: "For He who exacts retribution for spilled blood
remembers them
He does not forget the cry of the humble."
And it says:
"He will execute judgment among the corpse-filled nations
crushing the rulers of the mighty land;
from the brook by the wayside he will drink,
then he will hold his head high."

Provoking the Story

How do you tell the story of Jesus' death? Some of the ways that the story is told frighten me. For instance, some of the ways Christians tell the story imply that Jesus' sufferings are greater than any other human suffering has ever been. That is not true, or helpful. Jesus' death is one of thousands of deaths by crucifixion under the

Roman Empire. Jesus' death is one among too many millions of Jewish deaths, from the Crusades to the Holocaust and beyond. When Christians tell the story of Jesus' death, they must remember that Christian preachers have used Holy Week texts as an occasion to call for Christians to kill Jews. When Christians reflect on the nailing of Jesus to the cross, they must remember that medieval art sometimes painted the picture of Jesus being nailed down with Jews holding the hammers. This is false to history, but that is the least of its problems. This lie has moved vicious people, some of them Christians, to kill Jews.

Perhaps we ought to tell the story of Jesus' death so that our eyes are lifted to see the faces of other victims of Empire. Perhaps we ought to tell the story of Jesus' cry on the cross so that we hear the death song of the millions of Native Americans who were slaughtered. Perhaps when we tell the story of the death of the one Pilate taunted as "king of the Jews," we ought to hear also the echoes of the deaths of Jews in the battles of the First and Second Jewish Revolts against Rome.[108]

17. Easter Sunday
Mark 16:1–8

(see translation, p. 332)

Ritual Text: The Life of the Worshiping Community

Easter is the heart of the Christian faith, the spring that drives every theological movement. It is the event that completes both the gospels and the tensions of the faith. It is the release that makes the agony of Good Friday into something other than masochistic wallowing in blood and pain. As such, it is the relief that the faith has been waiting for since Ash Wednesday, the hope that has allowed Christians in desperate times to dare to defy death.

And Mark's telling of the Easter story is puzzling in the extreme. Ask any Christian to tell you the Easter story, and my money says that she doesn't tell you the story out of Mark. So why does Mark tell an Easter story that is all question and no answer?

In ritual terms, most congregations (in my experience) replicate what was done as soon as Mark's story was reduced to written form. Mark's Easter story is padded and completed, and the church's Easter faith is protected from the resurrection story with a Jesus that no one sees. Often congregations read John's story instead of Mark's. Often preachers tell the story so that the incompleteness of Mark's story does not matter. Always the hymns smooth over any problem that sneaks through the pastor's defenses. Everything celebrates the joyful completeness of an Easter-based faith. And all this falsification of Mark's story is justified in the name of Easter.

The question a storyteller must ask in preparing to embody this scene is simple: what if Mark's ritualizing of the incompleteness is wiser than the church's institutionalizing of smoothness? The task on Easter (which is every Sunday for an Easter-based faith) is to tell stories about resurrection in a world where everyone dies. Any ritual enactment that implies a false easiness in this task will fail the test of truth that will be applied by the people who have found good reasons to avoid worship since last Easter. Any ritual enactment that does not treat resurrection as a problem will offend everyone who has learned that death is an inexorable reality.

The ritual for this Sunday emerges out of the tension between Mark's story and the too-stable ideology of the church.

Intra-Text: The World of Mark's Story

Without an Easter story, Mark's narrative arc cracks and breaks off just when it MUST be complete. Without a complete appearance of Jesus to someone, even if it is just the reader, the story makes a central promise that it cannot keep. Other promises might have been dispensable. Not this one. For the story to sit level and deliver what was promised from the very first words onward, there must be a resolution of the tension that has been created by the shocking death scene.

There is none.

This is no minor omission. Interpreters of all kinds have heard this all the way back to the earliest years of Mark's story. There are five different possible endings supplied for Mark's story, four of which patch the ending and complete the narrative arc. Most scholars agree that the shortest, most abrupt, most offensive is the oldest and most original. I think Mark's story was shaped to end in precisely this offense, exactly this provocation.

That means, on the one hand, that the broken end is not so broken after all. The story is whole as it sits when it reaches its stopping point at 16:8. That means that the audience could be expected to relax at the end and experience the incompleteness, to "be the brokenness," to echo a particularly unsatisfactory modern easiness with jagged narratives and broken promises. The end is not so broken as it might first appear, but the painful provocation of the broken end must still be felt if the story is to be truly experienced.

Mark's story aims from the first to create this moment of vertigo with which the story ends. Promises are made and kept carefully so that this last most important promise could be made and frustrated. The insufficiency of Jesus' career as messiah is emphasized so that the audience will need a resurrection to sense that there is yet an adequate payoff for waiting the story out until its end. The collapse that Jesus suffers at his death cries for resolution, and the only resolution that will serve will raise Jesus from his disastrous death. And that is precisely the vision that Mark withholds from us.

Inter-Text: The World We Think We Live In

There are stories in popular culture that end without ending. Movies do it all the time, especially when the studio hopes to make a sequel. The ends of such movies carefully leave something yet to be resolved, or introduce something new to be solved in an effort to create an audience for the next money-making installment of *Return of the Living Dead XXXVI*, or *Batman Forever and Ever*, or *The Matrix, Part 25*. The usual rule is that sequels are terrible.

Interpreters sometimes read Mark's ending as a plea for a sequel. Perhaps the audience is supposed to "out-disciple" the disciples, and thus provide the sequel. Perhaps the audience is supposed to "out-tell" the storyteller, and thus finish the story. Or perhaps the storyteller is supposed to improvise a conclusion so that the whole thing has no need of a sequel.

I find such proposals unpersuasive. The best of them recognize the problems created by the end of the story. The worst of them refuse to notice anything at all. All of them, to my eye, neglect the way tense incompleteness touches every part of Mark's story. When Paul Ricoeur pointed out the two *parcours* in the story, the two trajectories, he found evidence of both flows in all of the gospel. Even Ricoeur finally releases this tension by choosing to read the "internal sequel" (16:9–20) as part of the story, but this choice itself points out the way the story is whole and broken at the same time. As I note in my discussion of the parables of the Sower and Vineyard, the Sower (early in the story) provides a paradigm that expects wholeness and completion. The Vineyard (late in the story) expects brokenness and destruction. The form of the story that we have was inscribed in the tense period between the two Jewish Revolts, and in that period both trajectories proved true. Jesus was raised and the world was destroyed.

Does Mark's story promise a sequel? Since Jesus is named messiah, but does not accomplish what one ought to expect of a messiah, perhaps the unfinished business (the promises not yet kept) is actually the trailer for the sequel. Such a solution at least recognizes that the usual Christian interpretation, that Jesus "redefined" messiahship, has little to commend it. That would be like "redefining" the title "shortstop" so that I could play for the Yankees (despite my impressive lack of skill as a baseball player, noted already in my youth: I was precociously bad at the game).

Such a solution, further, misunderstands the function of God's promises in Jewish faith from beginning to end. Look at the promises given to Sarah and Abraham. When Sarah hears them, she laughs, and her laughter is justified. Old women know that they should not be bearing children, and that it is laughable to tell them that they will be the mother of a great nation. Was Sarah right to laugh? She died having borne one child, one child whom she did not see after her husband tried to kill him on God's orders (Genesis 22). Sarah was buried, not in the land of God's promise, but in a tomb purchased from someone who was not wandering toward a promise he would never see.

Look at the promises given to the people returning from Exile in Babylon. Mountains would be lowered, valleys would be raised, the desert would bloom. The actual road home was rugged and hostile. Once again the promises did not fit into the world as it actually exists.

You can see the same structure in the book of Job. Any suggestion that the end of the story balances the pain of the beginning is a provocation to argument. It seems to me that Jewish faith makes its way in the world by creating people who expect more from God, each other, and themselves, than they are likely ever to get. As a result, Jewish faith trains people to demand justice, even when corruption is the norm. Jewish faith trains people to demand that creation nurture all people, even when greed is the norm. Jewish faith trains people to expect God to be involved in every aspect of the world, even when Jesus' cry on the cross (taken from Psalms, that most Jewish book of prayers) has been the experience of Jewish sufferers through the millennia.

Mark tells a story that trains its audience to demand more than it will ever get. This marks it as a Jewish story, a story suited for the training of wrestlers.

Provoking the Story

How do you take a bow after performing Mark's story? A more immediate problem: how do you get the young man off the stage? It is simple to get the women off the stage. They just run. But they can never come back. And if you bring Jesus on for a bow, you defeat the entire show. And if you don't, you puzzle your audience.

The difficulty of the end of Mark's story emerges clearer than ever when you try to perform it. Anything you do to finish off the action implies too much finality, too neat a packaging job. You can't even really turn the lights out. Perhaps you should play Mark's story with people out of the audience. Maybe they are planted actors, but maybe they are people who don't even know their lines, just regular patrons of the performance. Perhaps John the Baptist is the only one who knows what is going on, and then he is killed. That leaves the recruited characters without a director and without a sense of the arc and resolution of the story. That means that as the story runs, the ad hoc improvisations accumulate and the characters (especially Jesus) lurch from side to side. Maybe that explains the jerks and tugs that move the character Jesus back and forth and all around. Jesus withholds service (even attention) from his mother, but also condemns the Pharisees for doing the same. Perhaps this is because the Jesus from the audience won't play some scenes the way they are written. Perhaps this Jesus refuses the scenes in which the character is nonobservant, or refuses them when he catches on early enough, and thus plays (even inserts) the other scenes of strict observance. This could be used as an explanatory note for the frequent references early in the story to Jesus' regular attendance at Sabbath services. Or perhaps the opposite is true: the script aims to make Jesus observant, and the actor from the audience wants something more rebellious or simply can't manage to keep kosher.

This strange way of playing the story would leave the young man onstage alone at the end with no clear notion of what to do next, so perhaps he finally goes back to his seat in the audience, picks up his program and coat, and goes home.

However you play it, the end of Mark's story must solve problems and puzzle the audience, it must complete the story and leave it hanging. Mark's story is completely incomplete, and the ending is the place to embody this.

Section 3: SUNDAYS AFTER PENTECOST

18. Bonus Scene Mark 2:23–28

(see translation, p. 263)

Ritual Text: The Life of the Worshiping Community

This scene is not part of the Revised Common Lectionary and thus has no natural home in the church's annual ritual spiral. It is a scene, however, of such importance, precisely in ritual terms, that it must be considered here.

The first ritual encountered involves eating. Many rituals do, both inside and outside Judaism. Since rituals dance in a ring around crucial human actions and decisive human pleasures, it is no great surprise that matters related to food would be drawn into the ritual dance. Food rituals (formal or informal) set patterns of eating that shape the rhythm of the what, where, and when of eating. Thus it is that more turkeys are consumed on Thanksgiving in the United States than on any other Thursday in the entire year. Thus it is that lutefisk is eaten at all, say my friends who can't stand the stuff.

It is worth noting that there is no ritual problem in this scene with the what or the where of the act of eating, and that the problem of the when is not rooted in the food but in its preparation. One may certainly eat on Sabbath; indeed, the celebration is welcomed into the house as a queen.[109] The problem is that the disciples are harvesting and threshing the grain on Sabbath.

This is where the problem arises, actually more for contemporary Gentile readers of the scene than for the characters in the scene. The dispute in the scene is normal enough for the characters. Because Sabbath observance is central for Jews, and because there always have been and always will be disagreements about what is *halakah* for the day, it would have surprised no one that the disciples did what they did or that they were challenged for doing it. When the rabbis argue that messiah would come if only all Israel would keep a single Sabbath perfectly, they reveal the impossibility of agreement on what constitutes a full and complete observance. "Sooner would messiah come than would we agree," say the wrestlers of Israel. All over Galilee, Judea, and the whole Jewish world on the day the scene took place, Jews were asking Jews to consider whether their own practice was appropriate.

The problem comes for contemporary Gentile Christian readers. Most of us know little about Sabbath observance, and few of us could manage it. We have not been trained to the dance. Further, and this may be true particularly for the United States, Gentile Christians have come almost to take pride in their NON-observance of Sabbath. Businesses stay open, lawns are mowed, shopping gets done. Individualistic commercial culture asserts that it is resting "in its own way." Add to that the Protestant tendency to treat ritual with disdain, and you have a recipe for certain misunderstanding of the scene.

Intra-Text: The World of Mark's Story

Mark tells his story carefully. Jesus heals on the Sabbath, does it in the synagogue. He again heals on the Sabbath, only this time in private, and possibly so that the healed woman could cook (on the Sabbath) for him. He steps into the place of God and forgives sins that were not committed against him. He eats with tax traitors, perhaps because they also had not offended against him, at least not personally. On the next Sabbath in the story he and his disciples are walking through a planted field, and his disciples are picking heads of grain. There is no record of the reaction of the landowner to this trampling of his grain field. The farmers I know would not be much amused. The reaction comes from Pharisees who continue the reaction that began in the scene with the paralyzed man. These reactions have been measured and appropriate. Jesus' observance of Torah is open to question, so he is questioned. In the next scene his questioners have had all they can take.

It is the easiest thing in the world to simply go along with Christian ideology and approve of his behavior while condemning his questioners. It is clear from the flow of Mark's story, however, that Jesus engages in a string of relatively pointless offenses. He could have waited until Sabbath was past before he performed his healings; the other people in town certainly did. He could have avoided arrogating himself to a place reserved for God, but he did not. And now he defends his disciples for what appears to be heedless behavior on at least two counts: they are making a road through the field, and they are threshing on the Sabbath. And Jesus does not just defend his (sometimes witless) disciples; he compares their activity to that of David, of all people. He did not need to make such a leap. Why does he go out of his way to pick these fights?

Inter-Text: The World We Think We Live In

"Why does it matter whether a Jew eats pepperoni pizza or not?" This was the question asked of a Jewish friend of mine by his twelve-year-old daughter. "It tastes good," she said (she had tried it while at a friend's house as part of her exploration of the world). "Besides, God made all animals, including pigs, and the food doesn't affect your heart, just your stomach," she said, sounding uncomfortably like another Jew who lived roughly two thousand years ago. My friend believes that children should discover and choose their own patterns of observance, so he asked her to find an answer to her own question.

It took a long while.

Finally his daughter came to him one day and said, "It's not that pork is bad. It's that self-control is good."

This is a very good answer.

It is not just Torah observance that takes this as a leading principle. I had a roommate during my years of undergraduate work who was studying the martial arts, although not very successfully. Colleagues who teach the martial arts tell me that the main value of the training is that they teach students to control themselves so that they would not need to fight. With that in mind you can understand their dismay when I told them that my roommate, in order to demonstrate his mastery of the martial arts, put his fist through the door of our dorm room. "He sounds dangerous," one said, speaking seriously. "He should not have been allowed to study."

I have wondered whether that might not have been the reaction of the people who question Jesus in Mark's story.

Provoking the Story

Be sure in playing this scene not to give the Pharisees evil scowls and grating voices. Everyone already knows how to play the scene that way. If you are working with an ensemble, the actors playing the Pharisees have the task of finding the solid and sympathetic reason that they do what they do. Take this task seriously. When anyone who asks Jesus a question is immediately turned into a villain, the consequences are quite serious. Audiences who are subjected to such storytelling strategies are taught that they must never make mistakes, must never ask questions, must never have doubts or disturbing ideas. The outcome of such training is either the creation of dangerously compliant Christians or (more likely) the creation of intentional unbelievers.

19. Bonus Scene
Mark 3:20–35

(see translation, p. 265)

Ritual Text: The Life of the Worshiping Community

The logic of Jesus' argument is sound. If the world is a battleground, Jesus is fighting on the side of God against the forces arrayed against creation. This is an important argument in the developing wrangle with members of his own community who question him and his activities. Such arguments are to be expected, and they are precisely how a community works through questions of what constitutes a wise course of action in a complicated world.

The issue is how best to steer a Torah-observant course through the world, and Jesus is arguing that his frontal assault on oppressive forces justifies itself. His response calls to mind a similar (but less abstract) argument that erupted during the Maccabean Revolt. There, too, the issue was observance of Sabbath. There, too, a sharp division occurred between members of the community. But in the case of the Maccabees, the Hasidim who practiced rigorous observance of the Sabbath refused to defend themselves on Sabbath and were massacred. Jesus' argument is that it is better to take the fight to the enemy, an argument that makes sense to most people, I expect.

So far, so ordinary.

Interpreters must not forget, however, that this sound argument is wedged into a scene that has powerful ritual significance for Jews. Jesus' family has come to gather him in because they fear that he has lost his mind. They apparently have looked at the same evidence as Mark has shown the audience and have seen a pattern that indicates he has lost the sense that orients a sane and faithful person, and they come to do for him what a family does at such a time. This is a ritual act in any culture and in any century, but it is particularly powerful in a Jewish context since the family is the locus for all significant Jewish observance.[110] Honoring family is the first commandment in the second table of the Commandments, and it is the commandment that sets the context for all other faithful observance. When Jesus' mother arrives, he ritually disowns her.

This is a scene to explore with a storytelling ensemble. If Jesus' words are delivered by a solo performer, the ritual impact of his dismissal of the woman who gave him birth can be lost. But if his mother's face must remain visible as he turns away from her, the impact of his words becomes clearer. In ritual and family terms, it does not matter whether Jesus meant to raise the status of his followers to something like fictive family status. Even if such an action were altogether good, he still leaves his mother alone as she watches him turn away from her. The offense of this action is essential to the development of Mark's story.

Intra-Text: The World of Mark's Story

In most of Mark's story, Jesus steps through a world filled with families, but does so with no noticeable family of his own. When he goes to Simon's house after Sabbath services, he encounters Simon's mother-in-law, which implies also a wife. No one else has a mother-in-law, no one else has a wife. Other characters have fathers or daughters or sons. The whole world is knit together by relationships, and Jesus seems to have none. This is rather surprising, perhaps, given the importance of family in Jewish faith. Sabbath is observed in the context of a family meal. Passover has its real home in the family.[111] He may, of course, have had all of these relationships and more, but Mark does not open that to the audience.

Except in this scene.

Here Jesus suddenly has a mother, and brothers, and sisters, and they want to see him. More than that, they want to take him home before he hurts himself. The story says that they were concerned that he was out of his mind.

Such scenes are hard for Christians to play. Ever since we were in Sunday school we have been taught that Jesus is the right answer to every question. Jesus has become an icon, not a character, not a person, not a son or a brother. So when Christians read this scene and see that Jesus' family thinks he might be out of his mind, we know immediately that they are wrong. At least that's what we think.

What if his family is right? One of the things impetuous young people learn as they become adults is that their parents get smarter and smarter. If you take the doctrine of the Incarnation seriously and hold that Jesus is fully and completely human, then you ought to expect that his mother knows more than he thinks she does.

So, what if she is correct in being concerned that he might be a danger to himself or others? Why might she conclude such a thing? Perhaps because he seems to have lost his sense of the proper balance and rhythm of life. Though he will have been brought up to observe Torah, he seems to go out of his way to compromise the integrity of Sabbath in the scenes leading up to this one. Remember, this does not simply mean (as it might for an American Christian) that he is a little less faithful in attendance at worship or that he takes a job that has him working on some Sundays. It means that he seems to have forgotten that Sabbath gives the world a weekly reminder of the goodness of creation, and that it was calm attention to Sabbath rhythm that kept God's people safe under persecution. Perhaps his mother is concerned because of the disruption her son caused to other families — Zebedee's, for instance. If the main result of his independent activity was to fracture the basic locus for faithful and productive life, then his mother might well be concerned and find it to be her responsibility to tend to her child. Parents often find themselves in such painful situations, and deal with it as well as they are able. Jesus' mother comes with her children to gather her son home. My grandmother used to say, "Raising children is not for the faint of heart." She was correct.

Inter-Text: The World We Think We Live In

Of course, the other side of the argument needs consideration as well. Mark's story does indeed present Jesus as engaged in fighting the forces arrayed against humanity. The repeated violation of Sabbath is not incidental, but neither is the outcome. Jewish history has not been sure how to evaluate those Hasidim who were slaughtered because they refused to fight on Sabbath. Observance of Sabbath is central, but so is attention to first priorities. If Mark tells a story of a Jesus who figures his project as the equivalent of the fight against Antiochus IV, as a fight against oppression and for the safety of Israel, then his behavior must be evaluated in those terms as well. Of course, just because Jesus views his project that way does not mean that his family does, or even should. Remember, the Incarnation requires Christians to entertain the possibility that Jesus had something to learn from his parents, and not just when he was little.

In this scene, Jesus attacks the logic of those who question his behavior. How can he be a servant of chaos, he asks, when he attacks the forces of chaos? To understand this scene, you must grant the cogency of both sides of this wrangle. His actions do result in the freeing of people attacked by the forces arrayed against humanity. But his actions also result in the weakening of the fundamental practices that protect people from the forces arrayed against humanity. Who is right? Yes.

Two issues seem central here. First, Jesus' argument that this is a battle (perhaps equivalent to the fight against Antiochus IV) relies on agreement that he is engaged in pitched battle, not simple elective forays that could be carried out at any time. If the enemy is present, sword in hand, it is not clear that Jewish readings of history finally will side with the Hasidim and allow themselves to be slaughtered. This is especially true since the Holocaust. But where is the sword in the scene of the man with the withered hand, or the harvesting of grain on the Sabbath? This is a problem for Jesus' argument.

Second, those who question Jesus understand Sabbath as (to borrow a thoroughly Christian phrase) a "foretaste of the feast to come." Sabbath is a bit of the messianic age dropped into regular history.[112] In the messianic age, all the forces arrayed against humanity will have been defeated, and everyone will have cause and opportunity to rejoice in the overwhelming goodness of creation. No one will be shut out from the community feast because of a withered hand, and no demons of any sort will harass the people. Because this is the case, they object to Jesus' actions on Sabbath not because they don't want people to be healed, but because they don't want to weaken the foretaste of the healing of the whole creation for the sake of a few random skirmishes with the enemy. If all of creation were healed, then they would have no objection to Jesus' actions. But if creation will simply go on largely unchanged, then Sabbath is too important a sign of God's promise of ultimate healing to be tampered with casually. So the question is: do Jesus' actions eliminate all withered hands, all demonic harassment, all assaults against people, or do those assaults continue? It will be important that Christians answer these questions honestly and that we not spiritualize the whole matter to save face for Jesus.

Provoking the Story

The integrity and truth of this scene depend on giving Jesus' family the benefit of the doubt. If they think Jesus may have lost his mind, truthful tellings of the story will contain evidence that could be read that way.

This will be hard. Christians have a long tradition of imagining Jesus with a beatific smile on his face, a rich and warm baritone voice, and a helping hand ready for any stranger in need. This is a good and helpful picture to have of the savior of the world. If we are honest with ourselves, however, we will have to notice that this Jesus looks a little like the late Fred Rogers who created *Mister Rogers' Neighborhood*. My guess is that Fred Rogers's mother (who knitted his cardigans) never worried that her son had lost his mind. If the scene is to be played truthfully, Jesus' mother must have cause to worry.

What might this cause look like? Perhaps Jesus' words about dominions divided against themselves need to be played as a rant. They work when played that way, if only because his examples go on and on long after the basic point has been made. Redaction critics can explain this perseveration as the result of the collecting of similar traditions from several sources. Storytellers have to come up with a way to make the scene play truthfully. It works as a rant.

Or maybe the cause is seen when Jesus refuses to acknowledge his mother. This is a painful scene, and needs to be explored. It is a powerful offense (in Jewish culture and in any culture) to turn your back on the woman who gave you birth. My Little League baseball coach would not allow us to call our mothers "mom." When we did, he stopped practice and told the whole team that, in his presence, we were not to call the woman who gave us birth anything other than "Mother." "I want to hear the capital letter," he said. I remember thinking he was a little crazy, but I also remember the look on my mother's face when I went home from baseball and thanked her for being my mother. Maybe the coach wasn't entirely crazy after all, I thought.

20. Bonus Scene
Mark 4:1–34

(see translation, p. 267)

Ritual Text: The Life of the Worshiping Community

Out of this nest of parables, one in particular has ritual significance: the parable of the Mustard Seed.

This parable has been variously referred to as a parable of growth or as a parable of contrast. These descriptions make good sense, especially given the stated terms of the parable. That which is exceedingly small becomes exceedingly large, and grows at a rate that is astonishing, if not simply impossible. The parable has also been read as a story of negative contrast, since it obviously echoes texts from Jewish Scripture that refer to a tree that provides shelter for the birds of the air. In those texts, the tree is Israel, and it is a mighty cedar. In this parable, as Bernard Brandon Scott notes, all we have is a mustard plant.[113]

It must be further noted that the mustard plant is not a neutral image. It is not simply a plant that grows large or quickly, and it is not merely smaller than the scriptural foreshadowing would expect. The mustard plant, as Scott notes, is a ritual weed, a plant that would not be sown by an observant Jew. As any farmer can tell you, it is impossible to have a little mustard in your field. Mustard is uncontrollable and disorderly, and as such it embodies an offense against Torah observance in a chaotic world. In a world of clashing chaos, Torah observance allows a Jewish community to present a witness to the stable and orderly love of God. It allows the community to act out the possibility that life does not simply come down to a clash of power. The aim is to present a sign of real hope for the sake of exhausted Gentiles who might blunder out of the chaos and see a safe and stable community, evidence of the love of the God who is God, and who is One.

Why then would Jesus say that the dominion of God is a symbol of corruption and disorder? How can the culmination of all creation's hopes be figured as a ritual weed, a symbol of chaos that undermines Torah observance? These are not casual questions.

Intra-Text: The World of Mark's Story

Mark tells a story that winds itself in frustration and impossibility. When that happens (again and again) the parable of the Sower provides one possible set of expectations that might help an audience know what to hope for. The seed falls into unproductive soil more often than into productive soil; at least that is the pattern of the parable. In real life, no field is one-quarter path, or rock, or thorns. But the rhythms of the parable suggest that even if there were a field so constituted, still the field would explode in productivity. The harvest is quite impossible. Ancient wheat yielded something like twelve to sixteen grains in a head, with perhaps three stalks tillered out of one seed planted, which yields a maximum yield of no more than forty-eightfold for the best of the best. Jesus' parable expects thirty-, sixty-, and one hundredfold yields. Such yields would be exceptional indeed. They are not, to be sure, the sort of yield one should expect in the messianic age, at least if the witness of 2 Baruch (written at roughly the same time as Mark's story) is to be believed. Then each vine will produce a thousand branches, each branch a thousand clusters, each cluster a thousand grapes, and each grape a cor of wine (2 Baruch 29:5–6). The yield in the parable of the Sower is not so stupendous as that, but it was still impossible in the ancient world. There may be miracles expected this side of the messianic age, it would appear.

Inter-Text: The World We Think We Live In

Understanding this set of parables requires a two-step process. First, you must come to terms with the ordinary miracles of life and growth. Martin Luther wrote, "If you truly understood a single grain of wheat, you would die of wonder."[114] This parable only works for those who take time to be overwhelmed by the sheer fact of growth. Small seeds grow into large plants, even huge trees. Harvests are received from fields that look exceedingly unpromising.

Second, you must notice that this parable stretches beyond what is possible. This does not negate the goodness of ordinary growth, but it makes the parable a picture of how to read the face of the impossible.

Provoking the Story

The task of playing a mass of parables is difficult, more difficult than it might appear. The stories erupt one after another, the images shift and change, and the explanation of this parable is jammed into the middle of something else. Remember to bring your audience along when you perform this scene. Groups that I have worked with have done well with parable complexes by playing them as riotously as they possibly can. If the images riot with each other on the page, the players riot with each other onstage as well. Parable interrupts parable, explanations are inserted as soon as the interrupter stops to take a breath. Try this as one possible strategy.

21. Proper 7 (12) / Second Sunday after Pentecost Mark 4:35–41

(see translation, p. 271)

Ritual Text: The Life of the Worshiping Community

There has been a long intermission since the last wonder story. In the gap, Jesus has gone away from the crowds, away from his mass of followers. He has selected from among the larger group of people called "disciples" a group of twelve whom he will send out to proclaim, to carry on the project inherited from John. Mark tells us who they are, and tells us (twice) that Jesus "made" them twelve, an odd way to put it.

And now Jesus has finished a day filled with parables, some apparently easy and open, others obviously closed at best, maybe even excluding and forbidding. He is already in the boat, on the sea, floating on chaos, which matches the implications of some of his teaching. There is a certain chaos, or at least unmanageability, implied by the parable of the Sower if soil type absolutely predetermines one's response to "the word." There is a definite kind of chaos to be expected if the "dominion of God" is somehow properly like a mustard seed, a weed which is never sown in a Jewish garden (at least in the ancient world) because of the way it grows: rampant, wild, and out of all manageable boundaries.

He is floating on chaos, and it is appropriate. Since he is already in the boat, they take him across to the other side, just as he asks, just as he is. Other boats are there, too.

Intra-Text: The World of Mark's Story

How do you not have faith? This is a question that Mark's story hands its audience. The question is a problem. It is a problem, first of all, because it is not entirely clear what he means. In most contexts in Mark's story, it seems best to translate the word used, πιστις, as a Jewish word (faithfulness) and not a Christian word (faith), though the words and notions surely overlap. In this scene it is more difficult to say how the word ought to be translated.[115]

The question is a problem, further, because no matter how we translate the word, Jesus' words imply an unreasonable demand. Whatever πιστις might be, it will be demonstrated by remaining unafraid in a storm, in the midst of deadly chaos. This is an impossibility, and never should be anything else. It is the mark of an experienced sailor to know when it is time to be afraid, just as it is the mark of an adult to know what is impossible. It was time to be afraid; it would have been impossible not to be afraid.

Beyond that, one could argue that the disciples in the boat do, in fact, show πιστις (whether faith or faithfulness) when they awaken Jesus. They, like crowd after crowd in the story, look at Jesus and expect great things. They expect not only that Jesus ought to be awake, carrying out his responsibilities, but that if he were, they would not be dying. In Mark's story, this is a reasonable expectation. And Jesus calls this expectation a lack of πιστις. How odd.

Perhaps the problem is not that the disciples were afraid, but that they were so afraid that they asked Jesus to perform yet another wonder. They, like the crowds, force Jesus into actions that potentially distract from what he saw as his central mission: proclaiming the dominion of God.

But if that's the case, look at the wonder Jesus performs. He carries out an act that begs for comparison with God's act of creation. Floating on wild chaos, he brings order to the wind and the sea. If the scribes were right to ask who could forgive sins besides God, another such question would be in order at this point in the story. The problem is that God created the world, say the rabbis, according to Torah. Serious voices in Mark's story, including those of his closest family, have asked forceful questions about Jesus' practice, especially around matters of Torah.

But how do you tell this story? Is Jesus the everlasting strong friend who swats the storm away as if it were a wintertime housefly, slow and drunk and scarcely a challenge? Is Jesus a cocky young rookie, as full of himself as he is full of power? Ideology provides an easy answer to this question, but telling Mark's story with integrity requires that the teller be actively open to the possibility that the story holds together better with an atypical rendering of even the central character, Jesus.

So, which of the many options is it to be? The answer can only come from careful exploratory telling of the story. What is clear is that this central character has enormous power in the world of this story. He does what only God can do.

Inter-Text: The World We Think We Live In

They begin the crossing in the half-light, half-dark of dusk, the time of day when sharp edges begin to blur, when clear distinctions are more difficult to make. It is a time of day when the light and the darkness are not clearly separated, a time, therefore, most like the time of chaos before God began to create. A wind begins to blow across the water, a great windstorm, not the gentle breath of God's brooding spirit. The waves beat into the boat; the boat is being swamped. Jesus is asleep.

It is odd that he should be asleep (though the mudman, Adam, also sleeps in the Genesis story). Jesus is asleep. A member of my parish when I was a working pastor had been a Great Lakes boat captain, sailing big ore boats up and down the chain of lakes. I count him as one of my most important teachers. He taught me about opera, a particular love of his, but not of mine at the time. He taught me about gardening, a love we shared. He taught me most of what I know about preaching. And he taught me everything I know about storms and big water. I asked him if he had ever been in a really big storm. I saw in his eyes a distance, a look I did not exactly understand. I asked him if he had ever been afraid. The look changed. I saw how little I knew, how little I would ever understand. And I saw his eyes change one more time as he decided to give me an answer for free, an answer to which I had no right. "Always remember," he said, "that no matter how big you are, the lake is bigger. And the lake doesn't care."

Another friend, another sailor, though in small sail-powered craft, told me that the mark of an experienced sailor is knowing when to be afraid. "An experienced sailor," he said, "is someone who tried something they shouldn't have tried. An experienced sailor is someone who will never try that again."

And so they set off from shore. Nothing is said about a storm developing. Perhaps it was sudden. Or perhaps they tried something they should not have tried, though that seems unlikely, given that several of Jesus' followers worked on the water, they were experienced. Perhaps they knew what they saw when they looked at the sky, but also knew what they saw when they looked at Jesus. Peter will not call him "messiah" for another few chapters, but they have seen plenty up to this point. Maybe they expected that Jesus would, indeed, keep them safe. Or perhaps Jesus forced them, or at least pushed them until they made a choice they otherwise would not have made.

They set off from shore. And as the day slipped into mixed half-light, half-dark, the storm blasted the lake. We do not have a distant description of the storm. We do not see the wind piling up waves far across the lake, shooting the tops off whitecaps. We do not even see the other boats any longer, the boats we were told were with them. We see only the single boat and the waves that beat into it. Storms are like that. They focus your attention. Chaos has that effect. Vast systems of intricate organization fade into irrelevance when the world skids into chaos, when the reliability necessary for life is revealed to have been no more than a shallow assumption born of a sheltered life. Notions of power, projects, and accomplishments seem laughable when the boat is filling with water, and you realize that the lake doesn't care.

Jesus is asleep. Who sleeps through a storm? Not an experienced sailor in an open boat about to sink. Not a landlubber who doesn't know how bad it is, but can see that the sailors are afraid. Who sleeps? My teacher, the boat captain, said he had always wondered about this story. "Forgive my bluntness," he said, "but it's only an idiot or an infant who could sleep at a time like that. I never could. I had responsibilities. In a storm you just need everybody to do their job."

The disciples ask, "Don't you care that we are dying?" The question is desperate. It is a rude question, but experienced sailors who know that they are dying are granted the right to be a little rude. And they are, after all, only asking him to do his job, which is all you need at a time like that. Jesus wakes up. He silences the wind and the water. And then he asks how they were afraid. He asks how they lack faith.

Provoking the Story

Play this scene so that the disciples are honored for knowing that a storm can kill you. Honor them for knowing what danger on the water would look like. The disciples who have a trade (at least the only ones who are mentioned) make their living on the water. I judge it to be good policy to always listen to the person who knows her trade. So trust the disciples when they say that they are dying. They are likely to be correct.

But this will require you to experiment with how the disciples might wake Jesus and ask if he cares whether they live or die. They might be calm and submissive, though I cannot exactly imagine how that would work. They might be terrified and incoherent. This is certainly a possibility, though it will require you to imagine that the disciples have never been in danger before. Be careful not to play such scenes to emphasize divine all-sufficiency at the expense of human strength and competence. God surely is all-competent, but human life is lived best by people who have learned to cope with any circumstances, whether God appears on time or not. Besides, it is an insult to creation to imply that God created human beings incapable of doing the tasks set before us by the trades we follow. Several disciples were fisherfolk. They know how to handle themselves on the water. Do not make them into invalids.

This scene might best be played with the disciples showing that mix of restraint and suppressed anger that you see when professionals encounter a rookie who hasn't learned how to do her part yet. When they ask, "Don't you care that we are dying?" the line works well if they are really asking Jesus to get busy and act as if he were a part of the crew. Honor this truth when you play the scene.

The tension in this scene is between people who know danger when they see it and Jesus who is asleep. The tension at the end of the scene is between Jesus who asks how they manage not to have faith and the disciples who know that the wind and the sea never ask "pretty please" before they blow up into a storm. It will not do to simply make fun of the disciples. No one can stop a storm, no matter what religious hucksters pretend.

22. Bonus Scene
Mark 5:1–20

(see translation, p. 272)

Ritual Text: The Life of the Worshiping Community

Jesus and the disciples step out of the boat, the boat that floated on the lake, the water, the sea, the embodiment of chaos, danger, and uncreated disorder. BANG, a man met them out of the tombs. In ritual terms, this encounter is the same as the encounter with the storm. In each case the confrontation is between Jesus and the inexorable, the uncontrollable, the wild. The difference between the previous scene in the storm and this one is the presence of the tombs. The man with the host of demons lives with corpses as his companions. He breathes air that smells of death. In stable human society, breathing is an act that replicates the original breathing of God that made the mudman into a living being: the air you breathe in is life shared with you by your sisters and brothers, mud creatures all. The air you breathe out shares life again with a living, breathing world. Not so for the man living among the corpses. His comrades do not share life with him, nor he with them. Death is all there is, death and uncleanness, none of it controllable.

Intra-Text: The World of Mark's Story

It is interesting that at the end of the scene the people of the region ask Jesus to leave. That could be because they do not trust the intrusion of uncanny power into their ordinary lives. It is just as likely to be the result of his having destroyed the pigs that represented their community's livelihood. This will be a Gentile community since it possesses two thousand pigs, and while it might not matter to Jesus to be party to the destruction of so many unclean animals, it did matter to them. It is odd that so many of Jesus' accomplishments come at a high price for people involved. Healings violate Sabbath and, depending on how one translates διακονεω in Mark 1, may have been conducted for the purpose of making Simon's mother-in-law able to work on the Sabbath to feed Jesus. A paralytic is healed but a roof is damaged, as is the principle that only the person wronged can forgive an offense. And in the next scene in Mark 5, Jesus stops long enough in the crowd for the little girl to whom he had been hurrying to die. Imagine the reaction of the woman who had had the hemorrhage when she heard that Jesus' delay over her healing had led to the girl's death.

And now when the man who had had the legion of demons asks to stay with him, Jesus refuses. Interpreters read this as motivated by Jesus' desire to have him spread the word among the Gentile population. This would be odd enough. Jesus generally commands silence when he heals someone. This time, when he is in Gentile territory, he commands the man to speak. But there is another oddity here. Jesus sends the man back to his family, and charges him to tell them what the LORD has done for him. We most probably ought to assume that the man was from the immediate area. That means that Jesus sends him back to the community that just lost its entire herd of swine. The man is charged to remind his family that he was the cause of their catastrophic loss, and to cement the association of this loss with the God of Abraham, Isaac, and Jacob. Why? How would this help? Is this some sort of divine cleansing action, a surgical strike aimed at unclean animals? Mark's storyteller tells us that the man, instead, told people what Jesus had done for him, either because he had made an association between Jesus' success with the legion and God's power, or because he decided not to lead people to associate their loss with God and chose to let Jesus take the blame.

Inter-Text: The World We Think We Live In

Jesus defeats demons. This is not new in the story. It is significant in this scene that the battle is not with a single demon, a scout or a skirmishing party, as it were, but with an entire legion. This is a major engagement, and the choice of words adds power to this scene since it is part of a story that achieved this form after the Roman legions crushed the First Jewish Revolt against Rome. In that revolt, Jewish forces had initial success and succeeded in destroying the twelfth legion in battle.[116] But the ultimate battle went to the Romans and the fifth, tenth, and fifteenth legions. Each legion had over five thousand soldiers in it, and was a highly effective force. If the demons facing Jesus in this story are to be understood on this model (more than simply metaphorically), then they were formidable opponents.

Because the audience for Mark's story may be expected to know both of the early success of Jewish forces against Roman legions and of the final defeat, the use of this title for the force of demons is a poignant and powerful image. If the echo of the First Jewish Revolt is assumed to shape this scene, it may shape the audience to expect victory over this legion, or defeat. It may even shape the audience to expect that this scene marks a temporary advance against forces that will finally be victorious. This last possibility is most interesting, given that in the end it is a single centurion that stands guard over Jesus. Jesus vanquishes a legion and falls to a far smaller force. How odd.

Provoking the Story

How will you embody the legion of demons? There are cartoon figures available for demons, to be sure, but the scene will be more interesting if you can avoid stereotypes. And the demon you are embodying is actually a full legion of demons. Years ago my storytellers were putting this scene together, and they hit on representing the legion by a babble of voices. Their first attempt was to get several voices (five, if I recall) to speak in unison. This never seemed to work. It always sounded like poorly done choral reading. Then they settled on having all the voices do the lines simultaneously without any attempt at coordination. Out of this wonderfully wild sound they built a sound that was wilder still. When finally they performed the piece, they had a single narrator telling the story in a flat, emotionless voice. Beneath her voice was a babble of hissing and chattering voices who repeated fragments of the lines spoken by the narrator, echoing them, fracturing them, chanting them, over and over and over, and moving along in the story only when the narrator moved on. The carefully constructed cacophony built to two climaxes, one crescendo led to the speaking of the demon's name, the other to the death of the pigs. In each case the sound built louder and louder, and suddenly cut to nothing, leaving only the voice of the narrator to speak the demon's name and to report the death of the pigs. It was fascinating to listen to.

There are many, many ways to play the demons in this scene.

23. Proper 8 (13) / Third Sunday after Pentecost
Mark 5:21–43

(see translation, p. 274)

Ritual Text: The Life of the Worshiping Community

This scene, like so many others in Mark's story, wrestles with life and death, the heart of ritual practice. The scene begins with Jairus's daughter at the point of death, at the point of becoming a corpse, at the point of becoming the physical embodiment of the inexorable, the mysterious, the unclean. Near the end of the scene she is a corpse, which introduces a complication into the scene beyond that merely of her death. She has died because Jesus has delayed too long in the crowd, but that is not the only problem here. She now embodies all that ritual exists to manage and hold back. When Jesus grasps her hand, he absorbs uncleanness normally shared only by family members at the time of a death. This sharing of the mystery of death marks him, though it is unclear what happens to that mark when the little girl rises and walks around. If the border between the realms of life and death is the place where ritual dances to regulate and protect, what exactly has happened here? The retrieval of a little girl from beyond the border will disturb things all along this fortified line. What ritual accomplishes this?

And before Jesus arrives at the border between life and death, between breath and stillness, a woman touches him in a crowd. This touch, like the one that follows it in the house of Jairus, is loaded with ritual power. The touch is from behind and can only be read as one touch among hundreds: the disciples note that the crowd is crushing Jesus. The touch is from a woman who is bleeding, perhaps it is menstrual bleeding, perhaps it is not. Nothing in the text helps us decide this matter definitively. Whatever sort of blood is involved, the scene is ritually the same. Blood is the mysterious stuff of life, the place that God's first breath is understood to inhabit in a human being, the place also from which we give life back. That it is a powerful mystery comes clear when Jesus, crushed by the crowd, suddenly stops and asks who touched him. In this story world, the rituals that dance around the mystery of life are so powerful that they do not require a person to consciously participate in them. Jesus' back is turned, and still he feels the ritual power go out of him.

This draining of power has two sides. The standard reading hears in this the flow of healing energy from Jesus to the woman in need. This is a good way to hear the story, but there is something else that must be heard here, another ritual dimension to consider when playing and interpreting this scene. The word for the power that drains from Jesus is δυναμις. This is the ordinary word for power, but because power is also potency, in the ancient world when potency drains away, males become impotent. This is worth waiting on and reflecting. If the woman is understood to be menstruating for twelve years, this loss of male potency was one of the ritual effects that was to be expected in any man in contact with her.[117] This complicates things considerably.

Is this a scene in which healing flows? Indeed it is. Is this a scene in which potency is drained from Jesus? It is more than possible. What is clear is that contact with the mystery of blood will have caused the metaphorical fluid of uncleanness to flow into Jesus and be absorbed. Anyone interpreting or playing this scene will want to explore the consequences of all of these possibilities.

Intra-Text: The World of Mark's Story

This set of scenes nests tightly together. Both scenes involve women, women whose lives overlap by twelve years. The first woman, a girl just on the edge of marriageability at twelve years of age, is at the edge of death. The second woman, twelve years in a river of blood,[118] is at the edge of community. We are not told what sort of "flow of blood" she has experienced for so many years, but because blood is a holy mystery, she will have had to deal daily with the mystery of life. This blood may be menstrual blood, and interpreters must deal with this possibility, but, as Amy-Jill Levine has pointed out, there is no reason to conclude that this can only be menstrual blood or that her culture would discriminate against her if it were.[119] There is, however, a certain power to the scene if the woman is held for twelve years in the midst of a woman's contact with the mystery of blood and life while the little girl is just on the edge of entering that mystery. These conjoined scenes may play best if the contact with blood is not just any old blood. In any case, these two scenes are tightly tied, one to the other. The story of the approach of the woman with the hemorrhage interrupts the progress of the story leading to Jairus's daughter and creates suspense. The gap holds the audience and increases their anticipation. It also tightens the interweaving of the scenes. Remember what Tim O'Brien said about magic and storytelling.[120]

Inter-Text: The World We Think We Live In

Read the poem "Down There" by Sandra Cisneros. It is from her collection *Loose Women* (New York: Knopf, 1994). The poem deals with the realities of menstrual blood and the ways they affect the border between the sexes. If the blood in this scene is, indeed, menstrual blood, weaving this poem into the text will give a sense of the physical impact of this scene that abstract interpretation will never touch.

Provoking the Story

Two moments in this scene are riveting. The first comes when the woman who has come up behind Jesus in the crowd and touched him now falls down before him and they meet face-to-face. This confrontation is easy enough to play, and is easy to imagine as a warm, joyful encounter. The woman is afraid and trembling, we are informed, and she falls down. Jesus addresses her directly and commends her faithfulness. If you are exploring this scene with an ensemble of actors, play this scene several ways, because there are several moments at which the woman could look at Jesus, and several ways they could meet face-to-face. The woman is afraid at the beginning of the scene and she could be afraid at the end. Or she could be relieved of her fear. Or her fear could mutate into an entirely different form of being overwhelmed. There are more possibilities. Play as many as you can find, and do it before you move on to the next verses in the scene.

The reason for playing many possibilities is that this encounter is the first beat in a pattern of transformation that is crucial for playing this scene. Jesus and the woman meet face-to-face: first beat. They speak to each other: second beat. While Jesus is yet speaking, the word arrives that the little girl has died: third beat. This third beat is the key to this whole scene, and to the larger development of the character of Jesus in this story. It is easy to miss this beat if you are performing the story as a solo. Then the story goes from successful healing to challenge to successful raising from death. But if Jesus has a face and the woman has a face, both faces must react to the news that the girl has died, and both faces react while still looking at each other.

What happens to Jesus' face when he hears the news? What happens to the woman's face when she realizes that Jesus' choice to delay and dither in the crowd has led to a girl's death? All she intended was to touch Jesus surreptitiously from behind while he hurried past. She had no awareness of the errand to save the little girl. She did not imagine that Jesus would notice or care about the touch, and surely did not imagine that he would turn and turn around in the crowd to find her. What happens to her face as all this sinks in? And what happens to Jesus' face when he sees the woman's developing reaction? This complex interaction gets missed when there is only one storyteller. Work with an ensemble to explore it, even if you will be telling the story as a solo.

The next moment that needs careful treatment is the moment of the bitter laugh. This is difficult for Christians to catch, I think, because we know the story thoroughly well and know ahead of time that Jesus will heal the girl and everything will be fine, so it sounds like a promise from God when Jesus says that the girl is only sleeping. As Lamar Williamson writes, "The text intends to affirm that in the presence of Jesus and under his authority death itself, real death, is but a sleep."[121] This is a powerful and elegant statement of Christian hope that springs from knowing how this all turns out, but the scene only works if you play it with integrity. The mourners are correct in their reaction. They know death when they see it, and Jesus' statement is an occasion for bitter laughter. How dare he say such a thing in the house of the parents who have just lost their little girl? In order for this scene to be played truthfully, the audience will have to be allowed to know that the mourners are right when they are disgusted with what Jesus says.

There are several ways to do this. Try all that you can think of. One that you might not think of (but should) is the possibility that Jesus is still smarting from the look on the face of the woman in the crowd when she realized that Jesus had delayed needlessly over her instead of hurrying on his way to help the girl. Perhaps Jesus is embarrassed, or perhaps he is aware that he should not have delayed. Each of these possibilities is a real human reaction to such a situation. If Christians actually are committed to the doctrine of the Incarnation, we should explore all the real human possibilities for such a scene. Perhaps the woman has followed him from her healing to the house of mourning. If she has, would she join in the bitter laugh? Explore what happens if she does.

24. Proper 9 (14) / Fourth Sunday after Pentecost Mark 6:1–13

(see translation, p. 276)

Ritual Text: The Life of the Worshiping Community

Another Sabbath, another synagogue. This time there is no ritual offense. Jesus is teaching, a good activity for the Sabbath, and the congregants are arguing about the impact and import of his teaching, which is exactly the sort of faithful response one should expect in a faith that is named "Israel," which means "he wrestles with God." To refuse to engage the ideas, to refuse to argue, would be a sign of serious disrespect, a failure of faithfulness. The congregants honor Jesus with an argument. Jesus calls himself a prophet and calls them unfaithful. Up to this point the Sabbath has been spent exactly as it ought to be spent. Why does it end so badly?

Intra-Text: The World of Mark's Story

Jesus has been regularly in synagogue up to this point. This is the end of that. With this scene Jesus' pattern of activity changes, and the tone of the story with it. He is never again reported to be in the synagogue, but his disciples and his questioners are reported to gather together to him (the verb in Greek for "gather together," συναγω, is the root of the word "synagogue," συναγωγη). It is never again reported that it is Sabbath, at least not until the very end of the story when the women who remain faithful to him observe Sabbath before risking their lives to come and anoint his corpse and complete his burial.

At the end of this passage Jesus sends his disciples out two by two, with authority and little else. When they are sent out, they do what Jesus has been reported to be doing: announcing that people should repent and healing people. There is a new note here, and perhaps it echoes that unsettled finish in Jesus' hometown. If they are not received, they are to leave, shaking the dust off their sandals. From this scene onward, Jesus also moves in wider circles than he has to this point.

Inter-Text: The World We Think We Live In

What is to be made of Jewish wandering disciples? Some have seen in them some sort of cross-cultural echo of wandering Cynic philosophers. Others have postulated a link to the Essenes as described by Josephus. Both groups were characterized by rootless wandering, and Jesus' paradoxical teaching is seen by some as akin to that of the Cynics. What these linkages miss is the urgency of this sending out. This is no rootless wandering. This looks far more like purposeful canvassing of Galilean villages in service of some mission of preparation.[122] Even without considering the utter lack of cultural fit between Cynic philosophy and the deeply Jewish career Jesus follows, the disciples do not look like itinerant teachers. They are sent out to attack demons and heal. They are sent out to call for change, just as Jesus did at the beginning of Mark's story. Their mission is continuous with what he has been doing up to this point.

As Richard Horsley points out, Jesus and his followers show every sign of being a movement of resistance to Roman pagan domination. Their sharpest conflicts are with those organs of Jewish society that were chosen by the Romans as organs of liaison: the Temple and the priesthood. While I think Horsley under-reads the impact of some of Jesus' actions on Jewish life and faith (his actions go beyond what ought to be part of a reform movement), still neither Jesus nor his disciples can be convincingly played as anything other than faithful Jews carrying out a deeply Jewish program.

Thus it is that the militant sound of John the Baptist's words at the Jordan at the beginning of the story rings through the whole story. Thus it is that Herod Antipas, Roman stooge that he was, added the execution of John to his sins. Thus it will be that Jesus will be killed by Rome at the end of the story. And thus it is that the disciples are sent out, in this scene, on a foray to skirmish with the forces arrayed against humanity. They are not given a political mission, unless one realizes that Mark's story sees demons as allies of Rome, and diseases as foes that weaken the body of Israel. In this light it is interesting to consider Warren Carter's suggestion in his *Matthew and the Margins* that Jesus' healing of the man who could not speak in the gospel of Matthew also has political overtones. Muteness, he notes, is counted among the maladies caused by subjugation to empire.[123] Perhaps Mark is working a similar angle here.

The bit about shaking dust off the feet in the face of rejection needs to be heard against the powerful symbolism associated with feet even in the contemporary Near East. Remember the pictures of Middle Eastern men taking off their shoes to pound them against fallen statues of former rulers. This is a powerful insult rooted in body metaphor. Jesus is directing his delegates to insult those who do not receive them and their mission. This is the way one rouses a rabble.

Provoking the Story

This text is a patchwork of small scenes, each with its own integrity. Scenes with integrity are easy to play. Patchworks are not. One problem you have to solve, whether working solo or in an ensemble, is how to create a flow throughout this text that makes sense of the movement from scene to scene. Another problem relates to finding the neuralgic moment in each of the smaller scenes and playing it truthfully.

In the first small scene in this pastiche, Jesus amazes and then offends the people from his village. This is difficult to play (at least for Americans) because we have a cultural expectation that involves leaving home and becoming misunderstood. My friends who are Lakota have told me that a major problem that Lakota young people have in American undergraduate institutions is that the coming-of-age story they have grown up with is different from the myth that organizes the undergraduate coming-of-age quest. European Americans expect that one comes of age by leaving home and journeying off to adventure, hence the drive to "go away" to college. For Lakota young people, they come of age by growing up among their family, their parents and grandparents, to be sure, but even more so their aunties and other relatives who have known them long enough not to be fooled by anything. In the scene in Jesus' hometown, European Americans hear Jesus pushing against exactly the force they themselves had to fight in order to become a person of integrity, an adult. Native Americans hear something else. They hear Jesus resisting those people who have the right and the responsibility to remind him that they know his brothers and sisters, and that they knew his parents when they were his age as well. This string of small scenes in Mark's story plays better, and more truthfully, if the hometown people are played the way Lakota culture would understand them.

The second small scene in this string has Jesus resuming his canvassing spiral through the region, and initiating his twelve closest followers into the task as well. They are sent out in pairs, which supposes either danger or a kind of mutual apprenticeship is required for them. In this scene these followers are given immense power, authority over unclean spirits, and otherwise no resources at all. This may function to put them at the mercy of the people they are canvassing, or it may emphasize the speed with which they are to work: no time to waste preparing, no time to dally on the road.

25. Proper 10 (15) / Fifth Sunday after Pentecost Mark 6:14–29

(see translation, p. 278)

Ritual Text: The Life of the Worshiping Community

This scene spirals from Herod's puzzled reaction to the disruptions caused by Jesus back into a telling of the execution of John the Baptist. The spiral spins the audience from an external world inhabited by men to a private inner confrontation between Herod and a daughter, a girl at the brink of marriageability. The girl dances, the male crowd is pleased. There is no necessary implication that the dance is lascivious, but that is a possibility. It is also just as possible that the little girl is simply delightful and that the crowd of banqueters is charmed by her innocence. I think the scene may play better if the dance is a little girl's happy dance because that sets up the disastrous surprise that happens in the next three beats of the scene. First Herod swears an oath anchored by the presence of distinguished guests. Then the little girl speaks to her mother. Then the little girl speaks to Herod. This final beat in this pattern changes the entire dance of the scene. Up to that moment it was possible to read the scene as a contest between Herodias and Herod, a contest that was conducted on the unwitting body of a little girl. She is sent in to dance, she is sent back to Herod, and John is executed. But the little girl adds something to the ritual dance. She asks not only for the head, she asks for it to be delivered on a plate.

Why the innovation on her part? There are at least two very different possibilities. First, she may be suddenly enjoying the whole brutal clash and may be adding humiliating details to the ritual of execution. John's head is brought out as if it were the next course in the banquet. If this is the implication, then she has just rung all the rituals that go with ceremonial cannibalism. John, the enemy, is to be treated as food. One might want, at this point, to pause and reflect on Jesus' ritual words at the Last Supper, repeated in rituals of Christian Communion: This is my body, This is my blood.

It is also possible, of course, that the little girl is up to nothing so powerful. Perhaps she simply wishes to avoid the mess that would be made if a bleeding severed head were to be brought into the room. A plate would contain the gore, she might hope in her innocence. Which is the correct way to play this scene? Yes.

Intra-Text: The World of Mark's Story

When John's name is first mentioned in this scene, he is brought in as someone who has already been executed. That means that, in order to pull him back into the story at this point, the storyteller will have to raise him from narratological death. This also helps to mark out the orbit of the whole story. John is dead, but he is brought back for a flashback appearance in Herod's prison in Galilee. And then, at the end of the scene, he is killed and buried again.

John and Jesus have been tightly linked ever since John pulled Jesus into the story with his promise that one stronger than he was coming. Now John is pulled back into the story by the report of Jesus' fame. Herod is the one who pulls John back in, because he is analyzing what he has heard and he does not believe that one of the prophets of old has reappeared, and he will not believe that anyone in his own generation could have such a great impact as John had. It has to be John, there couldn't be a second troublemaker.

But, of course, there could. So Jesus is pulled back into the story as well. As John is toyed with and then killed, the audience sees the end of the story in the distance. It is odd that Jesus' fame pulls John back in, and John's death pulls Jesus in. It is possible that the audience sees the two as a contrast: John ends up a headless corpse, Jesus rises from the dead. But if Mark's story is a story told and retold, then the audience knows that the end of the story (and of Jesus) is unsettling and unsatisfactory. That raises the question of what effect it has to drag Jesus' death and unseen resurrection back into the early middle of the story. John's death is surely a death at the hands of a hated Empire. As such it offers both a rallying cry and a moment of somber reflection on the ineffectiveness of even John's fight against Empire. Is that, perhaps, the tone of the story of Jesus' death and resurrection? He clearly is raised, but where is the victory that should bring?

Inter-Text: The World We Think We Live In

I find myself reflecting on the deaths of John and Jesus, and I hear in them something I hear also in songs of rebellion from other times and places. Most such songs are deeply disturbing. Take, for instance, the nineteenth-century Irish song "Boulavogue," which remembers the rebellion against King George a century earlier.

> At Boulavogue, as the sun was setting
> O'er the bright May meadows of Shelmalier,
> Arebel hand set the heather blazing
> And brought the neighbours from far and near.
> Then Father Murphy, from old Kilcormack,
> Spurred up the rocks with a warning cry;
> "Arm! Arm!" he cried, "for I've come to lead you,
> For Ireland's freedom we fight or die."
>
> He led us on 'gainst the coming soldiers,
> And the cowardly Yeomen we put to flight;
> 'Twas at the Harrow the boys of Wexford
> Showed Bookey's Regiment how men could fight.
> Look out for hirelings, King George of England,
> Search ev'ry kingdom where breathes a slave,
> For Father Murphy of the County Wexford
> Sweeps o'er the land like a mighty wave.

We took Camolin and Enniscorthy,
And Wexford storming drove out our foes;
'Twas at Sliabh Coillte our pikes were reeking
With the crimson stream of the beaten Yeos.
At Tubberneering and Ballyellis
Full many a Hessian lay in his gore;
Ah, Father Murphy, had aid come over
The green flag floated from shore to shore!

At Vinegar Hill, o'er the pleasant Slaney,
Our heroes vainly stood back to back,
And the Yeos at Tullow took Father Murphy
And burned his body upon the rack.
God grant you glory, brave Father Murphy
And open heaven to all your men;
The cause that called you may call tomorrow
In another fight for the Green again.

I first heard this song when a student mentioned it in a class. We were discussing old songs that were tied to ethnic and religious identity, and she told the story of this song to the class. Her family comes from County Wexford, and she learned the song from hearing her father and his father sing it. She learned to play it on the piano as a little girl. I understand how such a song stirs heroic memories. But such songs also give me chills, especially when I imagine a little girl being cheered for learning a song with reeking pikes and burned bodies on the rack, this though my student is a good and gentle person not apparently much given to dreams of revenge. And so I wonder if the stories of John and Jesus function like this song and stir pride and anger together. This scene is not a simple one.

Because the scene involves a beheading, contemporary audiences will experience this scene in terms of the inter-text provided by the beheading practiced by terrorists at the beginning of the twenty-first century. This inter-text complicates the playing of this scene. Anger and dreams of revenge will rise whether they are summoned or not.

Some of the depths of the scene will be revealed as a consequence. One of the most painful moments in the story comes when the little girl asks for John's head and adds the detail of placing it on a platter. As I noted, this could mean many things, but if it means that she is gleefully improvising on a theme of brutality, the scene becomes intensely painful. How could a child take delight in such barbarity? The inter-text that comes to mind, for me and most of my contemporaries, will be the scene of little children (seen on the news) hoping someday to become martyrs by carrying out a suicide bombing. The scene from Mark's story stirs deep and searing reflections about the separation between enemies, the gulf that encourages even children to dream of blood and death and revenge. This scene must be played wisely.

Provoking the Story

How do you play a scene like this wisely? That is easier to ask than to answer. To play the scene wisely, you must be aware as you (and your ensemble, if you work with one) explore the text that there are frightening revelations down at the bottom of this mine. If you have an actor playing the little girl or her mother, that actor will need to find a place in herself to ask for the severed head of a human being. Current situations will have made that as hard as it ought to be, but that can be disturbing. To play this scene wisely you need to remember the game of "Six Degrees of Separation." If you play the story for an audience of any size, the chances are disturbingly good that someone in the audience will be connected to someone closely involved in the recent beheadings. And in any case, if you play the scene in the United States, there will be many people in the audience who have friends, coworkers, children, or students in the U.S. military who have a personal reaction to anything that stirs memories of wartime violence. None of this means that you ought not play the scene, with all its pain. But you must play the scene aware of what intense pain might be involved, and you must play the scene knowing that your audience will be watching for any sign of irresponsibility in your treatment. Any story that is real and true will touch matters of life and death. Do not play with such issues heedlessly. Touch them reverently and wisely.

26. Proper 11 (16) / Sixth Sunday after Pentecost Mark 6:30–34, 53–56

(see translation, p. 280)

Ritual Text: The Life of the Worshiping Community

The text as assigned by the Revised Common Lectionary is a simple and direct scene: Jesus retreats and the world swirls to him. As many as spin close enough to touch him are rescued from whatever held them captive. This way of cutting the scene creates a smooth and followable flow.

The RCL has left out the middle of this interwoven scene, and it is the middle that is most interesting from a ritual point of view. In the omitted scene Jesus hosts a banquet for five thousand men (plus women and children), Jews most likely, given their place of residence. In the scene immediately prior to this one, Herod gave his banquet. It was a smaller group that attended, and most likely all male except for unseen servants and the suddenly visible Herodias and her daughter. The outcome of the banquet was the beheading of John. The banquet that Jesus hosts, by contrast, does not end in death. People are satisfied, the disciples depart, and Jesus once again shows his mastery of chaos and the sea by walking to them on the water in the midst of a storm. The contrast is telling.

Intra-Text: The World of Mark's Story

In the longer scene the disciples have calloused hearts. They have already seen Jesus control the wind and sea, and still they are afraid and amazed. They have just seen Jesus feed more than five thousand people on little food, and still their hearts are calloused. The scene as cut pays attention to the powerful swirl around Jesus. He tries to retreat from the crowds and they follow him. He tries to cross over the lake, and they recognize him. He walks, people touch him and are healed. There is no escape. And still the disciples' hearts are calloused. The scene as cut continues the theme that Mark has played from the beginning of the story: the world swirls to Jesus, even more than it did to John the Baptist. Jesus is instantly recognized, and the benefits he offers are instantly perceived. But those people who follow Jesus most closely are given scene after scene in which they act out incomprehension.

What is going on here? It may be that Mark uses the disciples to explore incomprehension because such tensions require characters that the audience knows better, characters with a little more depth. Perhaps incomprehension is harder to portray clearly, so Mark needs the core of his cast to do it adequately. Or it may be that incomprehension is such an important theme that Mark needs continuing characters to develop it thoroughly. If it were played only by hit-and-run outsiders, it would not have the same impact as it does when played again and again by insiders. Or it may be that making it a major theme and portraying it only with outsiders would defeat the whole notion that the world swirls to Jesus. Insiders could easily play comprehension, but if it became a repeated motif that outsiders do not get it, a major drive of the story would be lost.

Or it may be that there is something about being an insider that is very like being an outsider. There may be something about this movement that follows a crucified messiah that puzzles insiders more than outsiders. To commit to a faith that has its roots in the renewal of creation in the midst of a world that is insistently not renewed, insistently resistant to themes of new life and freedom may require the telling of stories about insider incomprehension. Outsiders and immature insiders may believe that Christian faith immediately smoothes all roads and raises all deeply shadowed valleys. Insiders who have seen a little more know that this is not true. It may be that the theme of insider incomprehension is a storytelling strategy through which Mark's story works out what it means to tell stories about resurrection in a world where everyone dies. And that may go a long way toward explaining the odd way that Mark tells the story of Jesus' resurrection.

Inter-Text: The World We Think We Live In

A long time ago my sister died. She was young, only twenty-five years old, and she had been married for less than a year. She was healthy and had just taken a job that held real promise. She and her husband had started to talk about having children.

And then one day she collapsed at work. A blood vessel had burst at the base of her brain. She didn't die on the spot, and didn't die in the next twenty-four hours. She didn't even die during surgery to repair the vessel that broke, though the surgeon warned us that 60 percent of people with her condition die on the table during the operation. And then, after two weeks of holding her own, one day she died. It was an outcome we knew was possible, but that's not the same thing as being ready for it. Death is always an insult, even when it is anticipated. And so we held her funeral and buried her ashes and went back to the church for lunch and stories about my sister who had spun so many stories in her short life. And then we went home. The food tasted like Styrofoam, we couldn't sleep well, and we got back to what would pass for normal.

And then came the telephone call. It was Christians. They called to comfort us and tell us the good news of the gospel.

"We're so sorry to hear about your daughter," they said to my mother.

"Thank you," said my mother, who knew that these words were the best that anyone could do at such a dreadful time.

"We're so sorry," they said, repeating the way people do when they get stuck and can't offer what they'd love to offer.

"I know," said my mother, who does indeed know.

"We're so sorry, we wish you had called us so we could have prayed for her," they said.

"Thanks for your concern," said my kind and exasperated mother.

"We would have prayed and our prayer warriors have had good success healing people in her situation," they said. "If you had called us, she would still be alive. We feel so bad."

Christians who have grown gentle and wise through long and difficult experience would never have said such a thing. Old Christians, gentle and wise, have learned long ago that there is at the heart of the faith a tense standoff between enormous hopes and powerful realism. Outsiders and people too young or immature to know might not see this tension, but old insiders know that durable faith is born in the questions that must be asked of a faith that would tell stories of resurrection in a world where everyone dies.

The Christians on the telephone had not a clue. They imagined that the world swirled around Jesus simply and easily and that disasters were the result of failure to pray or of secret sinfulness and depravity. How else could you explain and illustrate the undeniable goodness of God?

Provoking the Story

The joyful swirl around Jesus is the heart of this scene. However you end up playing this scene, the spin of the crowd as it is drawn to Jesus is crucial to the physics and rhetoric of this passage. Experiment with ways of incorporating this movement into your telling of the story. Perhaps the lines could be divided up among players placed around the performance space. Perhaps the players could themselves spiral around the space as they speak. Perhaps a solo performer could follow the swirl with her eyes as she stands still in the eye of the storm.

I think that the scene is stronger, and the swirl more truthful, when the cautionary notes out of the omitted scenes are included. If there is a way to include the disciples' honest reactions that are attributed to their calloused hearts, this will allow the joyful swirl to have an anchorage in the real world. This anchorage is essential.

27. Proper 17 (22) / Twelfth Sunday after Pentecost Mark 7:1–8, 14–15, 21–23

(see translation, p. 283)

Ritual Text: The Life of the Worshiping Community

The way this scene is cut by the Revised Common Lectionary, it is a scene that sets ethics in opposition to ritual. That surely is part of the larger scene, prior to the radical surgery that is performed. The theme is surely part of Jewish faith. The prophets give voice to the heart of ethical monotheism: the God who is God, given the choice between mercy and sacrifice, will always choose mercy. Sacrifice, for the prophets as for the entire Jewish faith prior to the destruction of the Temple, is the dance that tends the relationship between God and creation, but the heart of that relationship is the ethical and just interaction of all parts of the creation. The ritual dance of sacrifice exists to allow the creation to be brought back into balance when ethics fail, which will always happen.

The pieces amputated from this scene are essential to any larger understanding of Mark's story about Jesus, particularly in ritual terms. Torah observance is the way Jews shape the dance of everyday life so that everything adds up to a witness to the stable and orderly love of God. In this dance, as Jesus makes clear in verses 10–13, the family is the center. If one does not dance Torah with one's family, it does not matter what other rituals one performs. So far, so simply Jewish. But an attentive interpreter must ask how this clear and piercing insight squares with Jesus' own treatment of his mother and family earlier in the story. If Jesus will not give his mother the time of day (the very least he owes the woman who gave him birth), one ought ask, purely in terms of the ritual dance of Torah observance, how this differs from "saying to his father or mother Korban" (see Mark 7:11). It is not clear that there is a difference, at least not one his mother would recognize.

Intra-Text: The World of Mark's Story

All foods are clean.

Even dog?

Even cat?

Even cockroaches?

Apparently not all foods are as clean as we had imagined. American Christians who believe all foods are clean are, of course, referring to bacon and pepperoni pizza, which they eat, and every time they do it makes them glad that they are Gentile Christians. Isn't it a great thing that Jesus came to set BLTs free?

Or not.

This scene is hard for Gentile Christians to make sense of. The details of dietary practice are foreign to Gentile Christians, and can be played for comic effect. The bit about washing with a fist is odd in Greek and even odder in English, and since we don't know what in the world it refers to, we can make it into anything we choose. Resist with all your might the temptation to play this for laughs. Out of such playings comes unconscious anti-Semitism, and out of unconscious anti-Semitism comes truly dangerous theology and practice.

Before you can play this scene, you must find a way to respect the practices described. While it was surely possible for "Pharisees and all the Jews" to find ways to observe dietary practices that were legalistic and foolish, this was not the main mode of practice, nor was it the purpose of the practice in the first place. Torah observance has never been understood to earn Jews favor with God. Torah observance instead offers a witness to an exhausted world that there is a God who is stable and orderly and loving.

The oddity in this scene comes from the sections that have been excised. As the passage is cut, observance of dietary laws sounds arcane and excessive, and it is easy to wish for a world in which all foods have been declared clean. The material cut out deals with family relations and the saying of "Korban." The oddity shows up in Jesus' own practice toward his own mother. To play this scene wisely, a storyteller will have to explore along the border between the scene in which Jesus looks his mother in the eye and asks: "Who is my mother?" and this scene in which Jesus ridicules a supposed practice of voiding duties owed to parents because "it is given" to

God. What exactly is the difference between saying Korban and saying, as commentators often do, that Jesus "enlarges his notion of family out of a sense of his more urgent mission"? The longer I listen, the less I hear a difference of any sort, except that it is commentators saying Korban for Jesus.

Be careful in interpreting this text that you don't falsify it by giving Jesus an automatic free pass that allows him to say anything he wants while doing the opposite. Be careful in interpreting this text, and Mark's story as a whole, not to falsify the whole enterprise by refusing to entertain the possibility that Mark is telling a story of Jesus that requires you to argue with Jesus. Remember, the tellers of the gospel knew the stories out of Jewish Scripture, and knew that those stories require the audience to argue with Abraham, with Sarah, and even with God.

Inter-Text: The World We Think We Live In

This story comes out of the legends from the period of oppression under Antiochus IV. These stories are hard to assess for absolute historical validity. I would suggest two resources to help with your assessment: *Rebecca's Children* by Alan Segal and *From the Maccabees to the Mishnah* by Shaye Cohen.

The story comes out of 4 Maccabees.

An old man, Eleazar, old and faithful, has been imprisoned by Antiochus for refusing to acknowledge Antiochus as a god. It would have been easier to make a sham acknowledgment, bow before the tyrant and be done, but Eleazar is a faithful Jew and will not compromise the sanctification of the Name of God for a tyrant.

"Shema Yisroel, Adonai Elohenu, Adonai Echad."

God is One. Eleazar affirms the basic Jewish confession: God is God, and Antiochus is not.

In his torture Eleazar is commanded to break dietary laws. "Eat the pork," he is commanded, "and the torture will stop."

"All my life I have lived for the Sanctification of the Name, and I will not now abandon it."

The torture increases, and still Eleazar refuses.

The man applying the torture is torn by the experience. Eleazar reminds him of his own grandfather, and the torturer offers a lesser demand.

"Simply put the pork in your mouth," he says, "and the torture will end."

"All my life I have lived for the Sanctification of the Name, and I will not now abandon it."

The torture again increases, and still Eleazar holds firm.

The torturer makes the demand simpler.

"Don't even put the pork in your mouth," he says. "Simply say that you ate it and I will confirm it, and the torture will stop."

"All my life I have lived for the Sanctification of the Name, and now I should become a liar?"

And finally Eleazar is tortured to death, but only after witnessing to the honor of serving the God who is God by observing dietary laws even at the cost of his own death.

Such scenes make little sense to comfortable people living in comfortable times. Eleazar will sound fanatical and excessively obsessed with following a set of practices that comfortable Gentiles do not understand in the first place. But the issue is not whether a human being can eat pork, but whether a tyrant has the right and power to tell a Jew who he is. This is a much larger issue. Dietary observance and all of Torah observance is part of Jewish practice that maintains freedom in the face of oppression.

Several years ago a friend of mine was raped. I tell this story with her permission. During the assault the attacker looked straight into her face and said, "You are nothing. I can do anything I want to you. You are nothing."

This was the hardest thing to recover from, she said. There were many hard parts, many parts that were impossibly painful. But the truly devastating part was finding a way to stare back at her memory of his face and refuse his definition of her as "nothing."

"What I have learned," she told me, "is that if you let an attacker tell you who you are, you lose the ability to tell yourself who you are."

Now Eleazar makes sense to me. This makes sense of all of the characters in the era of the Maccabees. This makes sense of why it is no solution for Jews to "be less Jewish" in order to escape the notice of oppressors.

Against this background Jesus' words about the unimportance of dietary laws sound hollow and unwise. The stories of the Maccabean period would be lively and vivid for Jews in Jesus' lifetime. Even granting the distance and difference between Galilee and Judea, still the matter of maintaining identity in the face of oppression would still be a part of lived experience.

Provoking the Story

Playing this scene wisely requires establishing a larger sense of the point and practice of dietary laws. Gentile Christians will typically have no real sense of this. It will be a useful exercise to explore a resource such as *Every Person's Guide to Judaism* by Stephen Einstein and Lydia Kukoff. Excerpts from such a resource could be woven into a performance of this scene. You might also weave in Eleazar's death scene.

There surely is no argument that "what comes out of a person" is of more importance than "what goes in." This is basic Jewish practical theology. But in the absence of an awareness of the importance of dietary practices, Gentile Christians will simply misunderstand this scene from beginning to end.

28. Proper 18 (23) / Thirteenth Sunday after Pentecost Mark 7:24–37

(see translation, p. 286)

Ritual Text: The Life of the Worshiping Community

The scene begins across a border and inside a house.[124] The ritual dimensions of this shaped space are crucial to the scene. Jesus is outside of Jewish territory, and "outside" is always a significant place in ritual terms. Jesus is inside Gentile territory, and not just any Gentile territory, but inside the territory of the descendants of the Seleucids, of Antiochus IV, the classic oppressor from the time of the Maccabees. He is inside a house, perhaps because he is inside Gentile territory. As the scene develops, it seems increasingly likely that he is inside a Jewish house, a Jewish refuge floating in a chaotic Gentile sea. When Jesus was in an actual boat on the actual sea he fell asleep. There is no hint that he is so casual this time.

Into his space of ritual safety comes a woman. This encounter is twisted tight with ritual tension. A woman faces a man, and this implies a dance that will regulate and lead their interaction. The woman is a Gentile, the man is a Jew, and this means that they will not know the same ritual dance and will thus not be sure how to approach each other.

And just in case the ritual space was not tense enough already, the woman represents the power and wealth of the Gentiles of the area while the man is out of place and relatively powerless, at least along this one dimension.[125] Perhaps it is the complexity of the ritual situation that contributes to the deep oddity of this scene.

Intra-Text: The World of Mark's Story

In this scene, perhaps only for the second time, he speaks with a Gentile. This is only his second recorded conversation with a woman.

This scene, this conversation, is strange for all sorts of reasons. On the one hand, this is an ordinary exorcism scene that ends with a daughter freed from a demon. Jesus does such acts throughout his career. But this exorcism is accomplished at a distance, instead of up close as the others were. Why? There is, of course, no real answer to this question, but one might ask whether it had something to do with the woman being a Gentile. Perhaps Jesus IS in a Jewish home and would choose not to enter a Gentile's home. Healing at a distance saves him the trouble. Or perhaps it is because the person making the request is a woman. When Jairus tells Jesus about his daughter, Jesus follows him to his house. Perhaps there is revealed here a scruple about propriety and practice. Or perhaps it is something else.

There is more strangeness still. Throughout Mark's story, Jesus has been asked to heal or free or cleanse people. In this scene, for the first (and only) time he says no. This is a surprise all by itself, but even more surprising is the way he refuses. He insults the woman, calls her a dog. The force of this insult must be carefully felt. A dog is a metaphor for a scoundrel in rabbinic sayings. A dog eats flesh torn by wild beasts. The rabbis take this as evidence that God cares for the whole of creation, but that does not flatter the dog much. The rabbis say that a person who eats in the marketplace is like a dog, and is unfit to give testimony. R. Papa said: No one is poorer than a dog or richer than a pig.[126] None of these references becomes any easier to bear if a storyteller highlights the diminutive form of the word "dog" used in the passage. Jesus has used a powerfully offensive word, and he has used it face-to-face with a woman who had only asked him to help her daughter. The woman's response is reported only in part. An actor knows that there is more to this scene than snappy repartee. The woman in the scene absorbs the insult, waits for the bitterness to subside, and then presses her claim on Jesus' attention. "Even the dogs . . . ," she says. "Even the dogs." What does it cost her to say such a thing? Her daughter is worth more.

Jesus replies, more or less. His words are terse, chopped. "Because of this word, go," he says. "The demon has left your daughter." And with those words, Jesus changes his mind. This is a moment to notice. Vestiges of docetism[127] that always hang around the edges of popular Christian piety shatter under these words. Jesus changes, and from the tense sound of the words, he does it none too willingly. How can Mark dare to tell such a story?

One can see how the lectionary dares to include such a story. You can see it from the way the text is cut to form the pericope. The scene does not end with the girl thrown on the bed (a violent image to end a strangely violent scene). The lectionary series extends the text to verse 37, which allows the last words to be "He has done all things beautifully." This saves Jesus' character, and most congregations will choose to meditate on how beautifully Jesus has done things rather than on how cruelly he has insulted the mother in the first part of the text. But a storyteller is stuck with both. Of course, you could just ignore the tension and hope that no one in the audience catches it. That tends to be a terrible choice. You could play the scene as Rawlinson suggested years ago, with Jesus smiling wistfully as he speaks to the woman, but in my experience with the scene, that makes the insult more painful, no matter what Rawlinson thought.[128]

Inter-Text: The World We Think We Live In

Tyre and Sidon, Phoenician cities a few miles from each other, were places of wealth and power. They are also places with a long history of interaction with the Jewish people. Ahab, king of Israel (the Northern Kingdom after the split from Judah), married Jezebel, the daughter of the king of Sidon. Now the scene changes. The woman, who is in fact only a mother, only a human being who needed help for her daughter, is associated by her place of origin with Ahab and the corruption of the Jewish people. She becomes Jezebel, a name that has come into contemporary use to designate an evil woman. The history of this treatment of Jezebel is complicated and deserves careful attention. Jezebel is remembered as the one who brought foreign idols into Israel. There is surely some justification for this, but remember that Jezebel's story is being told by a storyteller in the Southern Kingdom who works out of an identifiable ideology. Remember that the practice of identifying a woman as the source of corruption is a practice with a long and dangerous history. This is not a neutral historical report. This is an ideologically charged slander directed at a character who will most likely have brought her own culture with her when she entered the court of Ahab.

Go carefully here. There is ideology and slander and violence on all sides of this matter. Jezebel brought her culture with her. This is no surprise. She also brought the power of the monarchy to bear on her opponents. This also is no surprise, but it is to be remembered that her violence was as real as is the violence of the attack on her in memory. Read the story of the contest between Elijah and the prophets of Baal on Mount Carmel to get a sense of the war that is being waged in the time of Jezebel.[129]

Ahab is overthrown, killed in battle. Jezebel is thrown from an upper-story window. She also is killed. What matters for the scene at hand is the question of how the historical memory of the daughter of the king of Sidon might shape the character of the Syro-Phoenician mother in this scene. Does Jesus look at her and think of Jezebel? If so, does it matter that Jehu (the leader of the rebellion against Ahab and Jezebel) had eunuchs throw Jezebel from the window? The implication of the scene is that any male with available testosterone would be overwhelmed by desire in the presence of Jezebel, so is Jesus afraid of being overwhelmed by desire in this scene? What does he project on the mother who dares ask for help? Does it matter in this scene that Jezebel is thrown from the window and the daughter is thrown on the bed?

And, most painfully of all, does it matter that after Jezebel is thrown from the window and trampled by horses, dogs lick up her blood and consume her corpse? Again with the dogs! This is a painful story.

Provoking the Story

So how do you play this scene? The scene is freighted with memory and offense. Jesus and the woman face each other. He is a Jew, and she is a Syro-Phoenician. He remembers the Jewish revolt against Antiochus IV at the time of the Maccabees, and she remembers that Sidon remained loyal to Antiochus during that revolt. If both of them somehow represent the socioeconomic average of their communities of origin, he is relatively poor and powerless, while she is relatively rich and powerful. At the same time he is a man and she is a woman, and they each live in a patriarchal culture. He is a healer and an exorcist, and she is a mother with a daughter who needs help. He is male, and she is female. Each represents the exotic other, the strangely fascinating, and they are inside a house, perhaps alone. The scene is tense and strained from so many conflicting angles that it frustrates easy analysis. That is a gift for anyone who will perform this scene. Finally the tension will defeat any attempt to make this into a simple melodrama, no matter who is figured as the hero or villain. Emanuel Levinas understood ethics to be born in the tense encounter between face and face. This scene, on that model, is an incubator for ethics. The crisscrossing tensions will provide the complications that ethics needs if it is to grow strong and healthy. Make sure that you explore all the ways that Jesus and this woman might look each other in the eye.

There is one last oddity to consider. This one is speculative. How did the woman know to approach Jesus? How did she dare to? You need not suppose any sort of oddly affected (and unhistorical) separation between the genders[130] in order to see the problem with this scene. Some interpreters have suggested that this unheralded approach by a woman might be rooted in the agency of the large group of women who are following Jesus throughout his career. This large group is invisible throughout the story. They only appear on the hillside watching at the end of the story when Jesus dies. Only then does the storyteller show them to the audience, and suddenly they are revealed always to have been there, deaconing to Jesus. Perhaps they only cooked for him and funded his work. This would be a huge contribution. But if the word διακονεω is to be read vigorously (as Elisabeth Moltmann-Wendel reads it[131]), then these women did the work of deacons for Jesus. That would mean that they were charged with connecting need with resource. They would have been the ones who found people who needed healing and brought them to Jesus, the healer. Perhaps the mother in this scene knew to approach because the women around him encouraged her to do so. Perhaps she stayed even after having been so cruelly insulted because the women urged her on. Or perhaps she was simply a person made of stern stuff who refused to abandon her daughter. Of course, the scene does not mention these women. No scene does, not until the end when Mark's storyteller tells us that they had always been there, had always been deaconing. We just couldn't see them was all. If anyone has eyes to see...

29. Bonus Scene
Mark 8:22–26

(see translation, p. 290)

Ritual Text: The Life of the Worshiping Community

In this scene we see Jesus acting out a ritual of healing. Many of his wonders in Mark's story are accomplished with a word and sometimes at a distance. This time he spits and he touches and then he touches again. The next time he heals a man who is blind, he does not touch him. This would seem to indicate that Jesus was variable in his observance of ritual.

The powerful physicality of the ritual of healing in this scene must be explored, including the offense contained in the act of spitting. Any storyteller who wishes to truly explore this scene must explore the physical flow that is charted through the healing. I do not suppose that the teller ought to spit at anyone, but at the least she needs to explore why it is that she would not spit. Remember, touch anchors this scene.

Intra-Text: The World of Mark's Story

Trees that are walking. This is another scene that asks careful attention of a storyteller. It takes Jesus two tries to get it right. This is the only time in Mark's story that such a thing happens. How can it happen here? Certainly it is significant, as interpreters have noticed, that this scene precedes Peter's confession about Jesus' identity, which also requires a couple of tries to get it right, but the healing scene remains strange and surprising even after it is set in a context that could embrace it. How could Jesus need two tries to get it right?

There is one more healing of a man who is blind in Mark's story, in chapter 11. That occasion lies on the other side of the three predictions of the death of Jesus, and on the other side of the disciples' repeated demonstration of their incomprehension of their responsibilities in Jesus' project. Do the two people who are blind comment on the shortsighted blundering of the disciples? This seems very likely. But go carefully when caricaturing the disciples in Mark's story. It has become traditional to notice how dull they are and how slow to understand and accept the terms under which Jesus will prove to be messiah. This has been a useful perception. But it must be noted that some of what gets called blindness is the clear-sighted opposite. When Peter refuses the self-destructive program that Jesus sketches for himself in chapter 8, he could be acting out of a sort of blind naïveté that imagines that opposing Empire will be simpler and safer than it actually will be. But it is just as likely that Peter opposes what sounds like a foolish forcing of God's hand. God has promised to turn the world right-side-up and will deliver when it is time. Forcing God's hand is not a good idea.[132] Perhaps Peter sees Jesus' sketches of the future as a fool's errand that will add one more corpse, one more demand for revenge, and nothing more. Perhaps Peter sees even more than this. Perhaps he sees that Jesus has made himself into the issue when the point of resisting Rome was, from the start, to maintain a solid and clear Jewish identity and witness in the world.

Inter-Text: The World We Think We Live In

In a rabbinic saying from the fourth century CE, R. Zera says, "We are not required to give heed to the traditions of R. Sheshet since he is blind." The editor of this volume of sayings explains: "Since R. Sheshet was unable to look at the man who conveyed a particular tradition to him and observe his face, eyes, etc., he was not altogether reliable." This is a fascinating conclusion. For one thing, it echoes the understanding of Emmanuel Levinas, who argued that encountering the face of the other gives birth to ethics. For another, it implies that the man who was partially healed (on the first try) would only become a reliable witness after Jesus finished the job.

Provoking the Story

Imagine the reactions of the people watching the healing when it goes wrong the first time. If the people in the crowd could be assumed to have heard of Jesus' performance in the past, then they will have expected something more successful from him this time, too. And then they get trees walking. Even if they have heard little or nothing about Jesus' past healings, still it is hard to watch someone struggle with their trade. If Jesus is properly a healer in Mark's story (and this is indeed part of his work from the beginning, figured as part of his teaching), then this scene looks strange indeed. The crowd will provide for your audience a picture of what this strangeness might look like. Don't avoid letting the audience see this uncomfortable picture of Jesus just because it doesn't fit into your conventional image of who Jesus must be.

What if the implication of the scene is that Jesus is blind to the danger that Peter sees, the foolishness that any clear-eyed person would see? As an exploration of the scene, play it with two blind men. One of them is the man who must be touched twice in order to see. The other is Jesus. No, the scene does not say that Jesus is blind (and it won't satisfy to note that neither does the text say that Jesus is NOT blind). But, as an experiment, use the scene as an interpretive tool to explore the possibility that the blindness noted by interpreters is not blindness of the disciples, but blindness that affects Jesus. This will sharply change the scene and may yield nothing that you will ever show anyone in the world, but, at the least, you will get a glimpse of what it would mean for Jesus to join humanity as a person who was blind. I think you might find more than that.

30. Proper 19 (24) / Fourteenth Sunday after Pentecost Mark 8:27–38

(see translation, p. 291)

Ritual Text: The Life of the Worshiping Community

"Lift high the cross, the old rugged cross, towering o'er the wrecks of time." I could go on. Much longer I could go on. Christian hymns are filled with crosses. Christian churches are filled with crosses. Even the jewelry boxes of Christians are filled with crosses. There is even a day in the church's spiraling cycle devoted to the Holy Cross.

And Christians who sing these songs, see these crosses, or wear them, or even belong (as my family and I do) to congregations with names like "Holy Cross Lutheran Church," tend on average to understand such obsession with crucifixion as an act of devotion. Perhaps it is a good thing that we do. But it ought to be kept clear when performing a scene like this one that the cross in this scene is not nicely housebroken like those in our church buildings and jewelry boxes; neither is it tightly wedged into a sadistic theological scheme like the cross is in Mel Gibson's movie *The Passion of the Christ.* The cross in this scene from Mark is simply an obscenity, an absurdity, an instrument of torture that Rome used to remind its subject people of the cost involved in resisting the Empire.

That means that the act of picking up the cross, enjoined by Jesus in this scene, is not a ritual act of devotion or honorable self-sacrifice or solidarity with the oppressed. It is an absurdity. It is an act against nature and all goodness. When you perform this scene, remember to embody the painful irony.

Intra-Text: The World of Mark's Story

"Who do you say that I am?" It is a large question. The answers that are given are large in response. John the Baptist: this is a significant guess since the story has made it clear that John is dead. Herod made this guess because John's force was so powerful that it made sense that death could not hold him. Elijah: this is a bigger guess than even John. Elijah was understood to be eligible to reenter Israel's history because he (like Moses and Enoch) were never seen dead and buried.[133] That left them alike able to serve as messengers between God and creation. Elijah was expected (at least since the prophet Malachi) to precede God's reordering of creation. To guess that Jesus might be Elijah is to see in him a sign that the disordered world in which Roman power holds brutal sway will be turned right-side-up. Both of these guesses have revolutionary impact. One of the prophets: this is a different kind of guess. It resembles the first two in that the prophets were similarly figures of power and authority, especially as they aged in memory. But the prophets are different figures from John and Elijah. Whereas John and Elijah promise to change Israel's position over against its enemies, the prophets of old challenged Israel's character in the face of her enemies. Both portend change, but the prophets change the people, not the world. This could mean that people who look at Jesus see different needs and different edges to his career.

Peter's answer could split the difference between these choices. Messiah, as sketched in texts outside the Bible, can be expected to lead Israel in battle and rule forever in the peaceful aftermath. Alternatively, messiah could be expected to teach Torah to Israel and to the entire creation. What did Peter mean when he called Jesus messiah? It is hard to tell. It is clear, however, that he takes his hopes seriously because he scolds Jesus for courting death. Messiahship is too important a contribution to the life of creation to waste it on a failed career. This scene may, in fact, provide a hint about Peter's views. Jesus' words about death in Jerusalem and his following words about carrying a cross make it clear enough that Jesus has Rome in his sights. When Peter scolds Jesus, his words make sense if he is disturbed by what he judges to be a fool's errand against invincible power. The results of the First and Second Jewish Revolts against Rome make it clear that, if this is Peter's view, he has reason to be concerned.

If Peter had hoped to open Jesus' eyes to the dangers of militant messiahship, he does not succeed. Jesus scolds him, and then goes on to drag a cross (the symbol of Roman oppression) into a rant triggered by the thought that anyone could be ashamed of Jesus and his program. "You? Ashamed of me?" asks Jesus. Peter's reaction is not recorded. Jesus takes two other occasions to repeat his aim to court death, once in chapter 9 and once in chapter 10. On each occasion the detail increases. Peter no longer responds in Mark's story.

On the one hand, these three promises of the events at the end of the story increase the reliability of Mark's storyteller. Such a structure allows an audience to feel stable and in control of their hearing of the story. On the other hand, however, if the audience, listening as they are after the crushing of the First Jewish Revolt, shares Peter's view of the wisdom of courting death in Roman hands, these three promises of death increase the audience's uneasiness and concern.

A responsible interpreter must consider at least this many possibilities.

Inter-Text: The World We Think We Live In

To get a feeling of what is involved in the notion of "messiah," listen to the song "Shnirele Perele." The version I know is performed by the Klezmatics and appears on their CD *Rhythm and Jews.* Find the CD. Read the words. Feel the music. Track the flow of the performance. This Hasidic song, of course much later than Jesus' time, gives a feeling for what messiah will have meant through the years to Jewish faith.

The song makes it clear: no matter how messiah comes, the outcome is good. If messiah comes with evident military power in a chariot, the years will be good. If on horseback, still it is good times. Even if messiah has to walk, the outcome is good; in fact, it is the best of all: Jews will dwell in Israel. This is an image loaded with power and hope.

To get a feeling of what is involved with crucifixion in the ancient world, read the article on crucifixion in the Journal of the American Medical Association.[134] This article has become well-known in its twenty years of life. Students have been assigned to read it. Pastors have made it part of Holy Week services. Physicians have been asked to comment on it publicly. Most of this attention has, in my experience, used the article to show "how much he loved us to suffer this much for our sake." This use is driven by a specific theory of the Atonement, one that I do not share, one that I would argue leads to abuses of Christian theology. My experience is surely limited, but what I have heard is an emphasis on how far Jesus' suffering exceeds any other suffering. It is clear from the article that the word *excruciating* is well-derived, coming as it does from the Latin "excruciatus," or "out of the cross." Death by torture is a horrible thing. That is clear. What gets obscured in most such treatments is that Jesus is only one of millions of people who have died in the hands of torturers, in excruciating pain. This was surely true in the ancient world, where the Romans developed crucifixion as a way of reminding the colonials who was in charge, and who was not.

The practice, it appears, did not develop originally as a means of execution or even torture. It grew out of an entertainment developed by Roman soldiers with time on their hands. Soldiers need things to place bets on, so they nailed small animals to boards and made bets on how long it would take the animals to die. With time and creative innovation, the animals got larger. One day, someone wondered how long it would take a human being to die. Like car crashes and natural disasters, this horrified and fascinated the people who first heard the idea. They were horrified and surely felt that things had gone too far. They were fascinated enough that when a hapless and defenseless human was found for the experiment, they stayed informed about the progress of the activity. As things progressed they probably showed up to pity the poor man, and to look down on the brutes who had done this. The next time my guess is that they showed up earlier. And the next time earlier still. All the while they deplored the monstrous brutality of the act. Of course they did.

The problem, of course, was finding people whom you could safely crucify. There were, to be sure, logistical problems: a board was not big enough to hold a person, so a new structure needed to be developed, the size of the nails would be critical since they had to be stout enough to hold the increased body weight, and the placement of nails was also crucial since it would not do to have the nails rip out of the hands before the show was over and done. There will have been experiments and successes and failures. But the biggest problem remained finding subjects to crucify. If the person chosen had family or other defenders, the operation became more trouble than it was worth. Slaves and murderous bandits and other undefended (and indefensible) people were chosen, and this problem was solved. From there it was a fairly short step to using crucifixion as a means of social control. Initially it was the punishment of choice for heinous crimes against Empire, but as comes clear from any study of imperial policy in any age, the category of heinous crimes against

Empire tends to grow. The shock value increased the power of this new tool in pacifying a population. Listen to contemporary discussions of the necessity of using torture in military situations. You will hear someone say, and sooner rather than later, that to be effective you have to show that you are willing to go beyond all moral boundaries. If your captive believes that you will stop at an agreed-upon point, he will be able to resist you.[135] If your enemy is more brutal than you are, this line of thought argues, you will lose. Your enemy must believe that you are more brutal than they are. Of course, no one sees in this line of thought an ever-increasing spiral of brutality. Maybe I'm just missing something.

By the time Jesus was executed, Rome was using the original limitations on crucifixion to its own advantage. If originally no one could be crucified who had family to defend them, by the first century CE the Romans were using crucifixion to identify those people and movements that no family had better dare to defend. Thousands of people were crucified in response to occasions of rebellion, and they were crucified along main roads so that everyone would have their death cries carved into their souls.

It worked.

Crucifixion seems to have taken on a double meaning, as do so many things under imperial systems. On the one hand, it was the hated symbol of pagan domination and brutality. On the other hand, it did not become a rallying point for rebels. If anything, it became the opposite. If Paul in Galatians is quoting a Jewish voice critical of Jesus' courting of death when he quotes also Deuteronomy, "Cursed is anyone who hangs on a tree," then God has been enlisted in hammering home the Roman point. To be nailed to a cross makes you irretrievable.

Crucifixion was always obscenely brutal, but it became an Obscenity, an event that tarred both the crucifier and the crucified. This is a frightening development and grows out of the fearsome depths of pain involved in this form of public torture. When Paul calls "Christ crucified" scandalous and moronic (1 Corinthians), it is not hyperbole. He is giving evidence of the impact of the practice of crucifixion. It marked both the perpetrator and the victim as irretrievable.

To get a feeling of what is involved to link the notion of messiah to crucifixion, read Nils Dahl's essay "The Crucified Messiah." The first problem was that messiah simply does not die. Messiah does not fail and still merit the title "messiah." The hopes so long deferred demanded that when God acted to turn the world right-side-up, the act should be completed. The second problem is just as severe. To link God's "right-side-uping" of the world to a mode of execution used by the Romans to hold the world upside down is impossible. At the climax of the story, Jesus is shown to have been captured and slaughtered by the very forces he was sent to defeat. The third problem is the clincher. Even if Christians can find a way to solve the first two problems, they are still left with the insurmountable problem of being continually required to speak of an Obscenity, deep and vile. Their public language is forever marked with central speech that is simply not to be spoken. Any community that must learn this lesson is changed by it forever.

Provoking the Story

No matter what else you do with this scene, make sure that you explore the sayings at the end as a rant. Jesus' words about death and rejection and crucifixion deserve to be taken seriously. Part of taking them seriously is allowing them to be as wild as they sound.

After exploring this part of the scene, next explore the ways Jesus' words about his death could be said. The words could surely be sad. They could be determined. They could have the sound of overblown boasts. Young men in uniform sometimes use such words to impress civilians (especially young women). The words could be bitter and hopeless. Try as many options as you (and your ensemble) can manage. Honoring the text requires allowing the text to be what it is, even when it is offensive, especially at the heart of Christian faith.

Be sure as you develop your way of telling this story that you do not attempt to housebreak the crucifixion. The animal is wild and will not be tamed, much less housebroken. This would be the surest road to falsification you could find. Attempt to tell the truth.

31. Proper 20 (25) / Fifteenth Sunday after Pentecost Mark 9:30–37

(see translation, p. 296)

Ritual Text: The Life of the Worshiping Community

Be careful with the flow of this composite scene. It begins with stark words about Jesus' death by torture. It ends with a child. In between, grown men engage in a testosterone joust. Some things do not change. Be careful how you understand the progression of these scenes within the scene. The natural conclusion might be that the crucifixion and the child are both alike symbols of humility, and they are placed in this scene to bracket and shame the arrogance of the middle scene. Be careful with such an interpretive line. Ask yourself where you got the notion that the child is a picture of humility (or worse, humiliation) somehow comparable to the crucifixion. This is a typical reading of this scene, but it is troublesome. Children occupy a tenuous enough place in human communities without linking them imaginatively with an obscenity like crucifixion.

Could the operative flow in the passage be something more like from rejection to welcome? If the flow is sketched that way, the middle term, in which the disciples embarrass themselves yet again, becomes a picture of people too inattentive to catch the tragedy of the first moment, and too full of themselves to catch the last.

Intra-Text: The World of Mark's Story

This is the second of Jesus' promises of his death. However you played the last scene will influence the ways you can play this one. Explore several possibilities. The disciples perform badly in this scene. Interpreters sometimes link this performance with Peter's rebuke of Jesus, but this linkage is not necessary or obvious, except to Christians who have long ago made peace with the crucifixion.

Peter's reaction in Mark 9 is not recorded, and that may be significant for the way you play Mark's whole story. If Peter is the voice of reason in Mark's story, he may be expected to disapprove of the performance of both his colleagues and Jesus.

It is customary to read in this scene an injunction to humility. Such urgings are to be applauded, to be sure. It is a regular feature of interpretive work in any number of religions that they find occasions to urge humility and service and honesty and generosity, no matter what text is being read. But this practice, helpful as it is, is scarcely related to the text at hand. Crucifixion is a sign of Roman domination. The death penalty is the death penalty, but not even the most fervent opponents of the electric chair use it as a symbol of identification with the poor.

Inter-Text: The World We Think We Live In

This scene as constituted in the Revised Common Lectionary and as woven into Mark's story has its own odd inter-textual note. In the first third of the passage the focus is on a brutal execution by torture. In the last third of the passage, Jesus brings a child into the scene. There is here a deep and surprising impropriety. If adults who wish to become human and humane are well-advised to keep themselves away from contemplating crucifixion, why is it alright to bring a child into this scene? If even thinking about crucifixion coarsens and corrupts, what it the effect on a child who is made part of the story?

Provoking the Story

Aim to catch the sharp contrast between the three parts of this scene. Jesus' predictions can be played any number of ways, but the deep inappropriateness of the disciples' behavior needs to be highlighted. This is not an exercise in scolding them for not having an adequate theology of the cross. They could not possibly have such a thing until after the end of the story, and perhaps not even then. This is not an exercise in attacking their flawed notions of discipleship and contrasting them with our own potentially more adequate notions and practices. As Richard Horsley has pointed out, it is not clear that this is a story about discipleship in the first place,[136] and beyond that it is clear that it is unwise to take words that are applicable to situations of life-and-death combat and understand them as advice for daily living. Such a misuse of language misunderstands ordinary life and disrespects the disastrous experience of people who have lived and died in actual combat.

As I have told you, my father was in the 82nd Airborne during the Second World War. He was not in combat, but I have met his friends from those awful days who were. They came home and wanted to forget all the things that were necessary in those days, all the brutality, all the fear, all the things they had to do. No matter how many politicians want to ride on their coattails to political victory, no matter how many wannabes imagine themselves to be suited for combat, I hear them say over and over, "If you have seen such horrible things, all you know is that you never want to see them again." Christians should remember this for a solid year before casually talking about "cross-bearing" as a model for discipleship.

32. Proper 21 (26) / Sixteenth Sunday after Pentecost Mark 9:38–50

(see translation, p. 297)

Ritual Text: The Life of the Worshiping Community

Us and them.

This scene starts out with a ritual fortification of the boundary between Jesus' followers and another character, an outsider. Jesus rejects such extremism.

And then he turns around and launches into an extreme tirade that seems scarcely motivated and strangely out of control.

All theatre (including storytelling) is about transformation. That is what links theatre to ritual most tightly and inescapably. All performance of texts with real power must attend, therefore, to discovering and enacting the moments of ritual transformation in the scene at hand.

What transforms Jesus in this scene? He begins by speaking with a voice of reason when the disciples reveal that they intend to defend the border between Us and Them violently. Jesus' argument is deeply theological and deeply Jewish. He is not simply telling the disciples to pick their fights more carefully, though that would always be good advice along the border between Us and Them. His argument is rooted in a deep understanding of the implications of ethical monotheism. If God who is God is truly One, and only One, then God must be God of all creation and cannot ever finally be the possession of any group to the exclusion of others.[137] That means in the end that God approaches all of creation simultaneously from every angle and out of every history, and that all of creation encounters God in all of the various cultural forms and practices that grow naturally out of the ground that God, the God who is One, created and called good. That does not preclude revelation or depreciate the value of doing Torah (for instance), but it does inculcate humility before God in all things.

A Jewish colleague, a longtime teacher and friend of mine, tells a story about a Gentile Christian. My colleague asked this man, a professor and a confessing Lutheran theologian, to imagine that he had found himself inside the pearly gates and that once inside God had taken him aside and told him that he had been wrong all these years. The Muslims, it turns out, had been correct and the Lutherans had been wrong. What would he say then, my friend asked. The man, a careful thinker with a good imagination, pondered the situation. "It's God who takes me aside?" he asked, "and this happens inside the pearly gates?" Those were indeed the terms of this thought experiment. "Then," he said, "this would prove that Martin Luther had it right from the beginning: it is all grace and nothing but God's grace."

I love this story and find it illuminating from every angle that I have approached it. It is a story about humility. At the end, the joyful notion that Luther had it right is not an ideological trumping of the cards on the table, it is a confession that faith assumes its own incorrectness at every point if it is truly faithful. It fascinates me that this thought experiment is set up for a Gentile Christian by a Jew, with one of the terms of engagement being that the Muslims had it right all along, and no one else.

Intra-Text: The World of Mark's Story

This scene starts out with the disciples disgracing themselves. It ends with Jesus completely off the deep end. Up to this point the scenes have been balanced with one party or the other speaking with a reasonable voice. This time there is no such balance.

Jesus' words at the end of the scene are extreme. Though they are typically dismissed as "Oriental hyperbole," this misses the way they fit into a regular pattern of excessive demand in Mark's story. This pattern requires attention. How can Jesus adopt two such divergent positions in a single story? He speaks words that can be quoted by the most humane advocates of tolerance and diversity, and he speaks words that cut off all but the most fanatical of followers. It could be possible to develop a picture of a Jesus who is fanatical about tolerance, but that finally is only a clever dodge. Throughout Mark's whole story, Jesus does not agree with Jesus, at least not if you look closely. An interpreter could go hide behind old notions of a clumsy redactor who was not master of his scissors-and-paste trade. "Poor clumsy Mark," we could say with interpreters since Papias (at least), "he cannot tell a story with a properly unified plot."[138] Such dodging, such hiding is not honorable, neither is it particularly productive. Better we should begin with an assumption of the potential coherence and cogency of the story as it is handed to us. Better we should take it as our task to honor the disjunctions, expecting that the tensions will make for more structural soundness in the whole story.

Inter-Text: The World We Think We Live In

Calls for self-mutilation appear in many religious traditions. For the most part, religious communities are aware of, and appalled by, the calls for mutilation that can be found in other communities. Thus it is that Christians collect instances of extremism out of Islam, and Muslims point out excesses in Judaism, and Jews remember the abuses committed by Christians, who in their turn indict Jews who indict Muslims who indict Christians. The circle goes around and around. What is important for Christian readers (and performers) of this scene from Mark's story is that they honor the integrity of this scene. Performers must somehow embody the violence of this language. One way to do that is to watch and listen to the indictments lodged against extremists in other traditions. Pay attention to the moments that are selected out of the life and practice of the indicted community, noting especially the emotional tone and flavor of those moments. If radical Muslims are shown ranting and mutilating themselves, Jesus should embody that same dangerous violence in this scene. If Jews are portrayed as rigid and uncompromising, so should Jesus be portrayed in this scene. If Christians are shown as blood-thirsty Crusaders, so should Jesus be. This will yield a picture of Jesus in this scene that will be deeply disturbing. Honor the text.

Another way to honor the text is to examine carefully how these moments of extremism erupt in the story. The pattern is complex, and may not simplify to a single cause, but notice that there is a similar eruption tied to the first mention of crucifixion (Mark 8). Does mention of the crucifixion spark such violent eruptions in general? If so, this would be something that an interpreter would want to know. Watch how Christian groups use the image of the cross. You will see many things, a wide variety. Look especially for instances in which the cross is figured as a weapon. This will be something to worry over, the way a dog worries over a bone. Is there something about the way Christians understand Messiah and crucifixion that leads to violence? Remember the name of the white supremacist group: The Cross, The Sword, and the Arm of the Lord.

Provoking the Story

One way to explore this scene is to assign an actor to each side of the disjunction between Jesus and Jesus. This will seem strange in the beginning. It is worth working through the strangeness. It requires enormous energy to make sense. Welding a text together is a difficult task. This does not mean that sense and integrity are impossible. Quite to the contrary, it means that making sense is such an important activity that human communities invest exorbitant efforts in the task. One way to appreciate the importance of this effort is to play the fragments of Jesus against each other. Such an exercise helps to clarify the terms required for the text to make sense. Such an exercise points out the shape of the problem that must be solved. Such an exercise puts you and your ensemble inside the effort to make sense, which is a good place for a storyteller to be.

Play the scene with two Jesuses, one representing the voice of reason and one representing the voice of extremism. Do not divide the lines ahead of time for this exercise. Instead, send both actors up on stage to explore the scene. Let them fight it out to see who gets which lines. And then send them up to do it again. And again. And again. There is no predicting what all will happen out of this exploration. Maybe nothing will come that you can use, at least not yet. But maybe you will discover something about the tension between these two glimpses of Jesus, these two voices that speak out of his scenes.

33. Proper 22 (27) / Seventeenth Sunday after Pentecost
Mark 10:2–16

(see translation, p. 299)

Ritual Text: The Life of the Worshiping Community

Roman Catholic Christians understand marriage to be a sacrament. This basic ritual of intimacy and support is figured as a field on which we encounter God. This is an important understanding, especially because it takes place at the heart of human life. Encounters with God are often imagined as taking place on the edges of existence, in retreat from ordinary life. It matters for the understanding of this scene that a storyteller notice that encounter with God takes place, on this understanding, in the midst of the ordinary rituals of daily life. It is even more important that a storyteller notice that these rituals of relating explode with joy and despair and plain, dull boredom, and that many intimate relationships end in divorce. This would indicate that the ordinary encounter with God is similarly joyful and painful and complicated. If we replicate the image of God in intimacy, then the image of God involves tension, fear, and joy. A question to ask: what are the children doing as part of this scene?

Intra-Text: The World of Mark's Story

Jesus' Torah observance is spotty and unpredictable. He ignores basic practices and seems to favor loose interpretation of strictly detailed practices, and then suddenly he is advocating the strictest and most restrictive readings possible. He will cause unending trouble for his ideological readers no matter what their ideology. Contemporary "liberals" who find him narrow and restrictive, and contemporary "conservatives" who understand the meanings and implications in his daily practice, both of them will choke on his patterns of behavior. Interpreters will have a continuing task to figure out what Jesus is up to in his practice of Torah observance. Sometimes it almost works to imagine that he is making a distinction between ritual and ethical Torah. Such distinctions almost work because Jesus lives and acts out of a deeply Jewish faith, and Judaism will always be more interested in what you do than in what you say you are doing. In such a faith, the more intense the actual human doing, the more intense the theological attention.

But the problem is that the ritual/reality distinction is a modern invention and misunderstands the ancient world, a world that was thick in real ritual. Whatever contemporary modernists think about ancient Jewish faith, it needed no distinction between real and ritual.[139] And whatever contemporary pragmatists think about their solid practicality, the ritual practices that Jesus disregards are simple and are tied directly into extremely practical matters of survival. The dietary laws that he breaks are directly drawn from active Jewish resistance against Antiochus IV and the oppressors of his time. These simple practices allow practical Jewish families to train their children to resist those forces that would make them into something else.

Inter-Text: The World We Think We Live In

When God created humanity in Genesis 1, God created male and female simultaneously, and called the resulting intimate pair "the image of God." This is a piece that deserves thorough investigation. In Genesis 2, God creates humanity by dividing female from male and then giving them back to each other to unite in intimacy, to "cleave to each other" in the words of older translations.

The rabbis who read this text hard saw in these two stories a single story about the division of an original single androgynous being. This means that woman and man are each a "side" of the original being, and as such are permanent allies one of the other, since "having your side" in Hebrew body imagery means roughly what it means on the police force when your partner says, "I've got your back." This means, also, that sexual intimacy is created, in this story, as a revelation of the image of God.

Provoking the Story

Any audience for whom you play this scene will include people who are divorced, and people whose parents are divorced. Any audience will include people for whom divorce came about as a result of violation of vows of fidelity. Any audience will include people whose lives have been saved because divorce separated them from a dangerous spouse. Any audience will include people for whom remarriage was a gift from God.

To take matters further: any audience for whom you play this scene will include people who are lazily casual about sexual intimacy. This will be true no matter how old or young your audience might be. There was a saying among the older members in the congregation I served in the rural Midwest: The second child takes nine months to arrive, the first one is often born prematurely. An examination of old church records will prove this to be true. Any audience for whom you perform this scene will include people who are aware of the problems involved in casual sexual intimacy, most of them from their own experience. From fraternity house parties to high school memories of drive-in movies to the voyeuristic realities of movies and music videos, any audience will know (often without admitting it) that there are rocks in the waters of human sexuality that have made it hard for them to sail into adulthood.

And one step further: any audience for whom you perform this scene will have long ago mastered the art of displacing their moral fervor regarding sexuality so that the disapproving eye falls on someone else's poor practice and not their own. This is true especially for those Christian moralists who begin their self-pleasuring harangue by pronouncing themselves to have been the "chief of all sinners" in sexual terms. Thank goodness for gays and lesbians. They have provided American heterosexuals an easy escape that allows us to avoid dealing with our own falseness.

34. Proper 23 (28) / Eighteenth Sunday after Pentecost Mark 10:17–31

(see translation, p. 300)

Ritual Text: The Life of the Worshiping Community

How does one go into the dominion of God? The word implies a place and a rule, a fortified boundary. Jewish hopes from the ancient world are littered with notions of a final and culminative rule of God over creation. One hears in contemporary Judaism reflections on the messianic age.[140] These images mix temporal notions with spatial notions, and all of them recognize a qualitative disjunction between God's dominion/rule/age and the world of space and time in which we live. But this disjunction causes trouble. "Going into" is an act that requires space and the time to accomplish the act. But how does one go into a place that is disjunct from any place one could ever go? It is to answer such questions that rituals exist, but it is characteristic of human communities to be far better at seeing the rituals of other cultures than those of their own culture.[141] What ritual of entry does the young man in this scene presuppose? What rituals does Jesus presuppose? What rituals do you presuppose? Why do you disagree with Jesus?

Intra-Text: The World of Mark's Story

At the beginning of the story, Jesus calls people to follow him, and they leave family and home and responsibilities. Now Peter speaks for himself and the other disciples and reminds Jesus of all they have neglected. This link to the earlier story is important. On the one hand, it functions as another instance of a promise kept. The hollow spot left by the departure of otherwise dutiful sons is filled by a promise of balance in the age to come.

But on the other hand this scene calls to mind the scenes in which Jesus has asked too much of his followers. Even more it calls to mind Jesus' attack on those people who fail to do their duty to their parents and families because they have made a vow to God. The difference between the practice that Jesus condemns and the practice to which he calls his followers is invisible, especially from the point of view of the parents and families involved. If the disciples have left their parents to follow Jesus, they have not fulfilled their responsibilities, they have not honored the commandment.

This will be a painful reflection for Christians.

Inter-Text: The World We Think We Live In

What does the young man mean when he says that he has kept the commandments since early adulthood? Christian interpreters often get theological at this point and fault him for being self-righteous and foolish because "no one can be righteous before God." They misunderstand him completely. He is not claiming to be perfect. He is claiming to have fulfilled his responsibilities as a Jewish adult.

From his bar mitzvah on he has been a faithful "son of the commandment" (which is what "bar mitzvah" means). He has done what he is responsible to do, including making restitution for his failings along the way. Find a Jewish friend and ask about the meaning of her bat mitzvah (or bar mitzvah, if your friend is male). Listen for the ways this event has shaped her life. You will hear a wide variety of things, especially if you ask people whose observance varies widely. But you will meet several people who sound like the young man in the scene. Remember that Jesus is pleased with him.

While you are digging around in this scene about giving everything away, you might listen in on discussions about levels of taxation in the United States. Sometimes those who oppose taxes argue that taxes are too high because there is corruption in the federal government. There surely is such corruption, but it exists in equal measure in the corporate world, or in any world you would choose to specify. But the argument against taxation gets interesting, at least in terms of this scene in Mark's story, when the argument for lowering taxes swings to the notion that "it's your money." Which side of this argument would the young man find himself on? Why?

Provoking the Story

Is the command to give all away a serious command or a test? Is Jesus justified in placing such a weight on one whom he loves, a person who has shown real seriousness?

Jesus tells the young man to give everything away. Thus is born, at least for Christian preachers, the ethic of self-denial, even self-abnegation. Thus is born, at least for Christian community, the model of the hero of faith who surrenders all for the sake of the dominion of God. This model has been marvelously productive. We have the picture of Dietrich Bonhoeffer, who wrote, "When Christ calls a man, he calls him to come and die." The image we see of Bonhoeffer has him standing naked at the gallows saying, "This is the end — but for me, the beginning — of life." We have the picture of Mother Teresa, who gave her life to pick up dying people off the streets. We see the image of all of these heroes in the art of giving away.

These heroes mark a real contribution made by Christianity to the moral life of the world. The contributions made by people who found themselves free to give everything have been signs of God's favor for creation, signs of God's loving promise of life.

But we misunderstand this scene about giving everything away if we forget that we do not, not for a minute, believe that the young man should give everything away, at least not if the young man were our own son. Watch interpreters carefully. When faced with a passage like this one, they valorize self-denial mightily. They urge similar self-denial on the part of the audience. And then they go home and plan for their retirement, or for their child's career. I teach American undergraduates. They are a good lot, devoted to lives of service. I also talk to their parents with some frequency. Their parents are also a good lot, concerned for the well-being of their offspring. Parents sing a regular refrain in these conversations. It begins something like this: "But what can you do with a major in . . . ?" It does not matter what word comes next. If the major field in question is biology/pre-med, no one asks. But any other field can be a cause for concern. I teach religion. You can imagine the questions I get asked. So far no parent has said, "I hope my daughter picks up dying people off the street for no pay." Why not?

It's fine to be Mother Teresa once you are indeed MOTHER TERESA, clearly important, clearly a candidate for future sainthood. It's quite another thing to be some poor fool who picks up dying people, but never picks up the Nobel Peace Prize. Unless you recognize that none of us, neither performers, interpreters, nor audience, believes that our child should give everything away, you will misunderstand, misinterpret, and misrepresent this scene from beginning to end. This is a real challenge for any performer.

35. Proper 24 (29) / Nineteenth Sunday after Pentecost Mark 10:35–45

(see translation, p. 303)

Ritual Text: The Life of the Worshiping Community

This scene is loaded with ritual references: rituals of drinking, rituals of washing, rituals of entry into glory. The rituals of drinking and washing sound as if Jesus expects them to be danced out in time and space to which we have access. The disciples appear to be far more interested in the rituals of entry into glory and sitting on Jesus' right and left. James and John demand places of honor in a place discontinuous with any place we can go. The other disciples are angry because they share the same naïve view of this place. It would be worth asking whether and to what extent religious wrath is rooted in naïve notions of rituals of entry into places no one can go to.

Intra-Text: The World of Mark's Story

This scene immediately follows the third prediction of the death of Jesus. As with the previous courting of death, this occasion is also followed by a scene in which the disciples disgrace themselves. The last time the disciples in general were arguing about who was the greatest. It is not reported how serious this argument might have been. It might have been no more than the usual testosterone jousting that goes on when people have too little to do. I am starting to think, however, that what they show by their jousting over who is greatest is the behavior seen among green soldiers who are contemplating future battles in which they will earn glory.[142] Perhaps they are to be faulted not for paying too little attention to Jesus' words about the coming disaster, but for joining in too eagerly and ignorantly. If so, James and John are already imagining the battle done and over. They imagine that they will survive. They imagine that they will distinguish themselves. They imagine that they would properly belong on whatever ruling junta is put in place after the messianic war.

Jesus' words in response can be read different ways. He might be rejecting their whole military metaphor with its notions of an army of occupation and of a ruling junta. Or he might be explicitly sharing those notions but rebuking their immaturity, their greenness. It is not clear that Jesus can be counted as battle-hardened in any sense, since his experiences are roughly the same as those of his followers. So maybe his reaction is just another rookie's reaction: some prefer to contemplate silently, others pick fights, and others talk trash on the eve of battle. A paratrooper from my father's regiment in World War II told me that the way you could distinguish the men who had jumped into battle from the rookies who had not was that the combat veterans were first in line to use the latrines before the jump into Holland. There is a painful realism here that I do not see in anyone in the scene from Mark's story. No matter what Jesus meant to convey by his words, the disciples do not do well when the battle comes. The last view we will have of them is of their backs as they run away and vanish from the story. My friend who was a drill instructor would have called that a failure of training.

Inter-Text: The World We Think We Live In

Interpreters ought to be clear that Jesus' words about waiting table and disowning power, serving rather than being served, need to be heard in historical context. Such language frequently attends revolutionary movements and has not (in that context) done much to diminish the level of violence, the program of resentment and revenge. From the French Revolution (which beheaded statues that might represent royalty) to the purge in Cambodia (which reeducated the elite through manual labor and torture), the demand that the high and mighty become lowly is a regular theme. It is often the funeral march for the revolution. Does that mean the Jesus is the head of a movement that will become a repressive dictatorship? No. But interpreters will do well to remember that these words have been used by leaders of movements that most definitely did become dictatorships. Further, interpreters will do well to point out those moments when these words have been used by Christians to justify acts of brutality. Read again the documents out of the Crusades, the Inquisition, and the Holocaust. You will hear these good words twisted into something evil and unrecognizable. It is easier than you might imagine.

This is also a story about ransom. This single verse in Mark's story is used to make the whole story into a reflection on the substitutionary, sacrificial death of Jesus that brings about the forgiveness of sins. In order to make sense of the word "ransom" (λυτρον) in this passage, you must begin by noticing that this word does not bring with it any of the paraphernalia appropriate to the practice of animal sacrifice. The word, instead, plays on the field of the holding of hostages. Read this scene with an eye to ransom practice, not the practice of animal sacrifice, and you will see a stronger and richer scene to play.

Provoking the Story

This is a scene of contests. First there is the contest between James and John and Jesus. James and John have an objective, and they approach Jesus (who is both the keeper of the objective and the obstacle in their way). The pull and push of the scene is interesting. James and John seek to win their objective without having to state it. They try to manipulate Jesus into a position from which he cannot say no. Watch the dance Jesus does to avoid being cornered. As you begin to explore this scene you might want to stage a tug-of-war (always a useful tool for clarifying the clash of a scene). After clarifying the clash, play the scene in space to get a look at the evasive dance Jesus follows as he escapes their clumsy attempt at entrapment.

When the ten enter the scene, the conflict becomes more complex. James and John are opposed by the ten. This clash lasts (on paper) less than a verse. Onstage the clash would last considerably longer. Play the scene repeatedly to discover the extent of the conflict. The ten will have pushed at James and John at least up through the words about the "Great Ones." It might have gone on longer. At the same time, however, Jesus is doing his own pushing and pulling in this scene. He morphs from being an obstacle to James and John to being an obstacle for all the disciples. But what happens when you have a three-way tension in a scene? Explore this carefully. The final words in this scene are hard to figure. If all they are is a Christian maxim that acts as a moral to the story, then they are easy to play. But even this simplest of readings has its complications. How might the disciples react to the moral? Given Peter's reaction to Jesus' announcement of his fool's errand against Rome, how will he respond to this language about giving a life as a ransom? Be careful to honor those who oppose the foolish wasting of life, even if that life belongs to Jesus.

36. Proper 25 (30) / Twentieth Sunday after Pentecost Mark 10:46–52

(see translation, p. 305)

Ritual Text: The Life of the Worshiping Community

This scene traces the arc of a disruption of ritual. The man who is blind sits, as usual, by the road. He hears people, as usual, as they pass by. He surely has a regular pattern of words and gestures that draw people into engaging him and giving to him as he begs. All this is regular, follows a pattern, and the pattern serves to smooth the interactions between Bartimaeus and the people from whom he begs for support. Rituals are especially important in such matters because they create patterns that allow the exchange of support that is basic to creation. Of course, the existence of beggars and of the rituals of begging is evidence of a blockage in the created flow of support, and from recognition of this blockage comes the discomfort that attends all such rituals.

And then Bartimaeus hears the Son of David passing by. He seems to expect that this Son of David affords something that will break him out of his established patterns of begging and blindness. One wonders why Jesus has to ask him what he wants.

Intra-Text: The World of Mark's Story

Jesus has healed one other blind man in his entire career, at least according to Mark. That one didn't go terrifically well (see Mark 8:22–26). In this second attempt at healing, things go much better. It is worth asking whether Jesus' surprising question about what the blind man wants might be related to his memory of the first attempt that required two tries before he succeeded.

Inter-Text: The World We Think We Live In

Read the discussion of the word "netzer" on page 95. This translation hears in the blind man's identification of Jesus a perception that goes to the heart of his character in Mark's story. Jesus is the shoot of the stump of Jesse, the father of David. When Bartimaeus adds "son of David" to his naming of Jesus, you get the impression that he sees quite a lot for a blind man. Maybe "netzer" is exactly the right translation here.

Provoking the Story

How could you play this scene? In a story that spends a great deal of time talking about hearing, this is a scene about seeing. The two scenes that focus on seeing and on blindness bracket Jesus' long approach to Jerusalem and the end of the story. Somehow the transformation from blindness to sightedness needs to be physically real for the audience. But how?

Some suggestions. If you have people in your group of readers/performers who are not sighted, ask them for help. Their daily experience gives them an advantage in understanding this scene. Listen carefully to what they say; it may surprise you. Perhaps a nonsighted person would play the role of Jesus in the scene. Perhaps Bartimaeus would finish the scene nonsighted as well. He has plenty of insight before he can see, and perhaps this way of playing would emphasize that. Perhaps you could play the scene with all the characters affecting blindness. That would make Bartimaeus the most capable character onstage, since he would be accustomed to not seeing. I remember a movie with a scene like that: a killer was stalking a blind person, who leveled the playing field by shutting off the power so that both prey and predator would be blind. That might have an interesting effect here.

An even stranger idea: play the scene in the dark. This will require you to be able to cut the lights and achieve a total blackout at the beginning of the scene. Not every space will accommodate such a requirement, but it would be worth trying. That would put the audience in the same predicament as the players onstage. You would have to decide when to bring the lights back up, and why. Perhaps they stay off longer than anyone expects.

37. Bonus Scene Mark 12:1–12

(see translation, p. 310)

Ritual Text: The Life of the Worshiping Community

At the bottom this strange little story involves another ritual of exchange and support. The world of the story and of the audience has in it owners and tenants, and both live in God's fruitful creation. In this creation people dance together to owe and to pay, to take and to share. This makes it sound so simple.

The rabbis tell a story of a man who asked to see a vision of hell. The angel who attended to him took him to a room filled with everything needed for a banquet. This did not appear to be particularly hellish and the man said so. The angel then showed him the people who were ushered in. They all sat down at places especially for them. The food smelled wonderful, everyone's mouth watered, and none of this looked like hell.

"Just wait," said the angel.

The people reached for their food and suddenly discovered that they had no elbows. No one could eat. This was hellish, indeed.

Then the man asked the angel to show him a vision of heaven. The angel took him to another room, identical to the first. It, too, was set for a banquet with delicious food everywhere. Again people were ushered in, again they were seated at places prepared especially for them.

"Now I understand," said the man, "the difference between heaven and hell all comes down to the elbow. A banquet is not a banquet unless you can feed yourself."

"Be quiet and watch," said the angel.

The people sat down, they picked up their silverware. They had no elbows.

Now the man was really confused. "There has been a mistake," he said. "This is just like hell."

"Watch," said the angel.

All the people picked up the food on their plates and smoothly and gladly reached across the table to feed the person sitting opposite them. They didn't even notice that they didn't have elbows because they didn't need them.

In the parable of the Vineyard, both owner and tenants depend on the same earth. Owner and tenant are tied to each other in a dance of give and take. It is to be noted that there is no implication that this relationship is either just or unjust, and owner/tenant relationships can be both. It is also worth noting that the owner/tenant relationship presupposes that Jubilee has not been practiced in this narrative world, or there would be no landless tenants who must yield produce to an owner. Still, this is an entirely ordinary dance, and the ritual of giving and receiving is well-established. And then the tenants break the ritual. A storyteller working with this scene will have to find a way to establish the ritual and then to break it so that the audience can feel the way breaking the ritual escalates the tension in the parable.

Intra-Text: The World of Mark's Story

Read the exploration of the function of this parable in chapter 2. This parable sets up an opposing flow in the story to that established by the parable of the Sower. The Sower expects a good outcome, no matter what the obstacle. The parable of the Vineyard sees disaster erupt out of disaster as things go from improbably bad to inexplicably worse. The Sower appears early in the story, when things are going relatively well. There is opposition, and even the beginning of a death plot, but still things are relatively sunny (though Jesus' behavior is often less sunny than the reaction he occasions). Now here near the end of the story we get the contrasting paradigm: things will get far worse than you'd ever expect.

These two streams flow against each other throughout the story. At the outset, the Sower inclines the audience to expect the eruption of a good outcome, and the continuing troubles complicate that expectation. Now finally the audience is given a flow that explains the insistent problems encountered in the story, both in Jesus and in the people who oppose him. How does the story flow from here? Even that is not clear.

Inter-Text: The World We Think We Live In

The vineyard is an image for a beloved and productive Israel back through the prophets. These images are troublesome when Gentile Christians pick them up. It is one thing for a prophet to speak to his own people and charge them with being unproductive. It is quite another for a collection of foreigners to imagine that we can, at this distance in history, geography, and culture, agree or disagree productively with the parable Jesus told so long ago. Was Israel of his time guilty of treating messengers shamefully? It is not up to us to say. We can, however, notice profitably that the business of trading charge and countercharge has currency in the period in which this story was written in the form we now have. Jerusalem had been destroyed by the Romans, and with it the hopes that had led to the First Revolt. The Temple had been destroyed as well. Memory of such an act will have led to recriminations. Who was responsible for the wanton destruction? Rome, to be sure, but who triggered Rome's attack? Was it dangerous revolutionaries? Or was it the accommodationists? Was the assault brought on by the people who tended the Temple (whom Rome had chosen to be the organs of liaison between the Jewish people and the Roman Empire), or was it brought on by the groups that fractured the Jewish body politic, especially the Christians who seemed bent on stirring Gentiles into the community of faith and creating unstable mixes? In such situations, everybody accuses everybody, and the accusations run hot and angry. The parable of the Vineyard provides a paradigm to use in making sense of Mark's story, but it also provides a glimpse of the dangerous tensions that twisted the world of the Jewish community in the years between the two Jewish revolts. Read Justin Martyr's *Dialogue with Trypho the Jew* to see what happened to this tension after the crushing of the Second Jewish Revolt.

Provoking the Story

Since this parable and the parable of the Sower provide the two trajectories that the story might follow, you might try performing them competitively. Divide your company into two groups, and have them each tell their assigned parable over the top of the other. Let them figure out what it will take to get the audience to buy their construal of how the story is going. If this proves interesting, you might have each team ransack Mark's story looking for evidence to support its contention that one parable best explains the course of the action. Perhaps this evidence could also be woven into a final performance of this material.

38. Proper 26 (31) / Twenty-first Sunday after Pentecost, or All Saints Sunday Mark 12:28–34

(see translation, p. 313)

Ritual Text: The Life of the Worshiping Community

> Shema Yisroel, Adonai Elohenu, Adonai Echad.
> Hear, O Israel, the LORD our God, the LORD is One.

These words express the beating heart of Jewish faith, spoken every morning and every evening and in moments of danger. Jews on the brink of execution by Nazis spoke the Shema. The Rabbi Akiba (a near contemporary of Jesus), with his last breath as he was tortured to death by the Romans, spoke the Shema. And Jesus speaks it.

He speaks it in response to a question about the heart of Jewish faith and life. It is a good and faithful question, and a good and a faithful answer. A very Jewish answer. This ritual of speaking links Jesus to the scribe and to Rabbi Akiba and to every Jew of every century who remembered the Oneness of God in response to joy and danger. And this ritual of speaking separates Jesus from Christians for whom the ritual is not a regular practice, separates him from Christians who cooperated in the Holocaust, and before that in the pogroms that repeatedly swept Eastern Europe, and before that in the Crusades.

Intra-Text: The World of Mark's Story

This scene poses a problem for an interpreter. On the one hand, Jesus and the scribe meet in clear and simple agreement at the heart of their shared Jewish faith. This is a powerful and important moment. The scribe approaches, perhaps because Jesus has just trounced a Sadducean opponent. The scribe might be figured as a theological ally of Jesus against the Sadducees, who are opposed either because both Jesus and the scribe judge them to be theologically too conservative or because both Jesus and the scribe (and probably also the audience) judge them to be too tightly tied to Rome to be trustworthy. But the scribe might also approach Jesus simply because he hears the preceding argument and is excited at the prospect of a good knock-down, drag-out argument. Either option is a good one, and both present a positive view of a character who is not presented as a follower of Jesus. Either option works as a reading of this scene, but I prefer the second option, if only because it opens the possibility of affirming argument as a positive and faithful activity.

On the other hand, this scene in which Jesus affirms the beating heart of Judaism in terms that a Jew of any century would approve stands in tense contrast to many other scenes in Mark's story. It is not a surprise that Jesus argues with other members of his community of faith. Jewish faith, the faith of Israel, honors argument as an act of faith. It is not surprising that Jesus disagrees with members of his community about what is *halakah* in various situations. Such disagreements are the substance of faithful Jewish life and practice. The surprise is that Jesus seems at other points in Mark's story to choose a practice that could scarcely be defended as *halakah* under any circumstances. Although he condemns those who "say Korban" to their parents, thus avoiding the respect and support they owe them, he also refuses to acknowledge his mother when she comes to speak with him. He routinely disregards the Sabbath, and even defends his disciples, who make a road through a grain field, picking and threshing and eating on Sabbath. On another occasion when he heals on the Sabbath, the rest of the community waits for the end of the Sabbath to bring other people to him for healing, thus guarding Torah observance more carefully than does Jesus.

How do these two snapshots of Jesus fit together? Interpreters ought to be careful of solving the problem by making Jesus into some sort of ancient rationalist who honors the abstract principle of Torah observance while discarding its "husk." Such interpretive moves are indeed common, but they miss the importance of the habit of observance. Abstract observance, observance of the spirit of Torah, is made possible by the honoring of the letter of Torah. In a world that is solidly concrete, concrete acts have more weight than do thoughts and intentions. Ask Jesus' mother whether she would prefer to be honored in thought or in deed. Ask her when she is standing outside overhearing Jesus' dismissive remarks. I wonder if Jesus wished he could have taken those words back.

The problem for interpreters is to remember, when exploring a text in which Jesus acts badly, that he is carefully observant in other scenes. The problem for interpreters is to remember, when exploring a scene in which Jesus reveals a deep and warm Jewish faith, that he also has moments that make him look careless, even heedless.

Inter-Text: The World We Think We Live In

Find the poem "Shema" by Primo Levi. This poem, written shortly after Levi was released from Auschwitz, uses the model of the Shema to point readers to a new mandatory reflection for faithful humanity. "Consider whether this is a man," he directs. "Consider whether this is a woman." And then he directs our eyes to the reality of life in the camps, where human beings were driven down into the mud, and women were left with "Eyes empty and womb cold / As a frog in winter." This, says Levi, must be a matter of daily reflection for all of humanity, because this was reality. These things really happened, as impossible as that may seem to comfortable human beings.

Find also Elie Wiesel's testimony, *Night*. Find especially his memory of his first night in camp. He remembers the smoke. He remembers the flames. He remembers the little children's faces on their way to the flames. He remembers the silence. He vows to remember, even if he is "condemned to live as long as God himself." He hands us the task of remembering, as well.

If the Shema is to be remembered and repeated daily, in times of ease and times of extremity, Levi and Wiesel (and millions of others) require that we also remember the people who were crushed in the camps.[143]

Provoking the Story

Weave the inter-texts from Levi and Wiesel into this scene to see what happens. What if when the scribe asks for Jesus' response, Jesus were to respond with the words of Elie Wiesel about the horrors of the camps and crematoria? What if he were to answer back with Levi's poem? The point of such an experiment would be to provide an answer about the heart of the Jewish faith out of the twentieth century. While this is an entirely artificial act, remember that Christians are accustomed to speak of Jesus not in the past tense, but always in the present tense. For Christians, Jesus is a permanent contemporary, and should always be expected to speak to the world of the present moment. This leads to mischief, to be sure, as Albert Schweitzer demonstrated in *The Quest of the Historical Jesus*. But it also leads to a powerful sense of the presence of God in every situation of human life. Because this is true, interpreters ought to explore the possible dimensions of Jesus' answer to the scribe's question.

39. Proper 27 (32) / Twenty-second Sunday after Pentecost Mark 12:38–44

(see translation, p. 314)

Ritual Text: The Life of the Worshiping Community

The widow in this scene acts as a parable. Her action is excessive. If the two coins do indeed represent all that she has, she now has nothing. So it seems when the scene is viewed from a point of view that expects that a person is responsible first to gather for oneself, and only secondarily to share. But remember the ritual of sharing and the rabbinic story on page 238. At base, Jewish faith understands that God's creation is sufficiently rich to provide enough for all of creation to flourish. If there is poverty, it is because some in the creation have filled their pockets first. The widow is poor, and the causes of her poverty are understood in Jewish faith (and explicitly by Jesus) in theological terms that have social consequences. But notice that the widow does not act as if she were poor. She gives all that she has because she has the opportunity to give. In the terms handed us by the rabbinic story, she is a woman who needs no elbows.

Intra-Text: The World of Mark's Story

What is the relationship between Jesus' words about the houses of widows being eaten up and the picture of a poor widow immediately following? Such a conjunction of scenes might imply that the widow is an example of a person who has been driven into poverty by the villains Jesus has just described. Or it might imply that Jesus is drawing a distinction between widows who are driven into poverty by others and widows who impoverish themselves voluntarily. Or it could imply that Jesus like so many others is quite willing to commend the "deserving poor," to see virtue in actions that he does not understand. Or it could imply that Jesus misses a connection that he ought to have caught. What if he attacks the scribes' alleged practice because he has the scribes in his sights, and the widow is simply a rhetorical image that he found ready to hand, serviceable for a generic political attack on an opponent? Somehow in election years everyone is the friend of the deserving poor. Even politicians whose policies in every other year are corrosive to the connections that hold rich and poor together in bonds of mutual responsibility, even such politicians can demonstrate, in an election year, how electing their opponent will be bad for the poor. That is because the poor have no real standing in such wrangles. They are just there as a figure of speech. When real policy-making demands real attention to the causes and effects of poverty, it will generally emerge that figures of speech do not vote or make campaign contributions or lobby effectively. Or, as in the scene at hand, they show up as stock figures that can be used to illustrate something else entirely.

What if Jesus were revealed in this scene as such a politician? Christian expectations will surely militate against such tellings of this story. Jesus is, and has long been, the right answer to every question, the solution to every problem, without ever having to demonstrate any effectiveness whatsoever. Before you decide how to read this scene, soak in it for a long time. Remember, it is possible that Mark is telling a story that carries an embedded criticism of Jesus. That may not be an expected practice, but that does not mean that this old script does not preserve something that is foreign to the contemporary world, something strong and surprising, something that may turn out to be a key to other locked problems in the text.

Inter-Text: The World We Think We Live In

When people made guesses about the identity and character of Jesus, they guessed that he might be one of the prophets of old now returned. There are many prophets to choose from. Amos has words that would have spoken to the scene at hand.

Amos 2:6–8 NRSV

6This is what the LORD says:

"For three transgressions of Israel,
and for four, I will not revoke the punishment;
because they sell the righteous for silver,
and the needy for a pair of sandals—
7they who trample the head of the poor
into the dust of the earth,
and push the afflicted out of the way;
father and son go in to the same girl,
so that my holy name is profaned;
8they lay themselves down beside every altar
on garments taken in pledge;
and in the house of their God
they drink wine bought with fines they imposed."

Amos 5:11–15 NRSV

11Therefore because you trample on the poor
and take from them levies of grain.
you have built houses of hewn stone,
but you shall not live in them;
you have planted pleasant vineyards,
but you shall not drink their wine.

12For I know how many are your transgressions
and how great your sins —

You who afflict the righteous, who take a bribe
and push aside the needy in the gate.
13Therefore the prudent will keep silent in such a time,
for it is an evil time.

14Seek good, not evil,
that you may live;
so that the LORD, the God of hosts, will be with you,
just as you have said.
15Hate evil and love good,
and establish justice in the gates.
It may be that the LORD, the God of hosts,
will be gracious
to the remnant of Joseph.

Provoking the Story

How might you play this scene? The most obvious, and the one presupposed by the section exploring a possible inter-text for this scene taken from Amos the prophet, is to play Jesus as offering a pointed critique of the society on the basis of its treatment of the poor. More on that shortly.

Before taking the obvious road, it would be worth attempting to play Jesus as an out-of-towner who feels out of step with the bustle and busy-ness of urban life. Visitors to New York City often comment on the gap between rich and poor in Manhattan. The gap is surely there, but the same gap exists at home for every visitor. It is simply easier to see these gaps in a city that is disconcertingly big and busy. Perhaps Jesus is such a visitor.

Or perhaps Jesus is in fact offering a pointed critique of the social and economic structures that had led to the actions of both the poor widow and the rich people. It will be unsettling for many Christians to reflect that Jesus' prophetic critique, in this case, sounds vaguely Marxist.

40. Proper 28 (33) / Twenty-third Sunday after Pentecost Mark 13:1–8

(see translation, p. 316)

Ritual Text: The Life of the Worshiping Community

The Temple was the stable center of the world. It surrounded the Holy of Holies, the quiet, still place where the finger of God held the world still. In a chaotic and dangerous world, this one place was still and safe, and around it the Temple was stable and safe, and around it Jerusalem, and around it, Israel.[144] This made the Temple the physical embodiment of Torah observance. Torah observance is how a Jewish community aims its whole life so that everything it says, does, wears, and hopes for will add up to a witness to the stable and orderly love of God. The Temple represents the same witness, the same sign of hope and stability.

In the First Jewish Revolt against Rome, Jewish resistance was utterly crushed. Jerusalem was a ruin, and the Temple was destroyed. This scene from Mark's story looks forward to that destruction. It also looks back to it. Mark's story, in the judgment of most scholars, reached written form after the year 70 CE, after the destruction of the Temple. That makes this little scene a ritual of mourning for the physical embodiment of Torah, the gift from God for the healing of the world.

Intra-Text: The World of Mark's Story

By this time in the story, the audience has heard three times explicit promises of what to expect at the end of Mark's story. Jesus will be handed over, he will be rejected, he will die, he will rise. These promises, as noted in chapter 2, are all fulfilled in the course of the plotted narrative. The narrative proves itself reliable yet again.

In the scene at hand, we have promises that extend out beyond the end of the plotted narrative. How far? That is not altogether clear. Apocalyptic Christians hear in these promises a picture of the "end-times." This is not inappropriate, but it is not clear which "end-times" these might be. Generation after generation has seen in its own time the wars and earthquakes and famines. After all these centuries you begin to suspect that this set of promises describes the continuing experience of God's creation, the continuing cry for an act from God that will end the bloodshed and turn the world right-side-up. This seems a worthy reading of this scene.

There is, however, another angle that must be examined. The destruction of the Temple anchors these promises in the aftermath of the First Jewish Revolt. The betrayals and flight that are promised in 13:9–20 might also properly drop anchor there. The storm of those years nearly sank the Jewish people and finally split family from family, sometimes over the matter of allegiance to the character Jesus. These verses function like a prediction of the suffering of the Jewish people, analogous to the way the predictions of Jesus' sufferings (in Mark 8, 9, and 10) function for Jesus. If Jesus' suffering foreshadows the suffering that is coming for the whole Jewish people, then Jesus' cry of dereliction at the moment of his death will be echoed by many other members of his family before too very long.

In passing, it is intriguing to note that the advice given in 13:21 would be very like the advice given by members of Jesus' family who did not see him as Messiah:

> 21And whenever anyone should say to you:
> Look!
> The messiah.
> Look there!
> Do not trust it.

These words will pick up new echoes in the years between the two Jewish revolts, and the echoes will be painful for all who hear them.

Inter-Text: The World We Think We Live In

The Temple was the center of the world.

And it was a building whose form and beauty owed almost everything to the work of Herod the Great, that king of the Jews whom the rabbis judged not to be Jewish at all. This tense relationship to the

Temple must also be heard in this scene. Faithful Jews could not look at the Temple without seeing both the center of the world and clear evidence of the way Rome could corrupt even the holiest place on earth.

Dissatisfaction with practice in the Temple had led the Dead Sea Scrolls community to withdraw from Jerusalem years before. A powerful intention to make Temple-holiness available everywhere led to the Pharisaic practice of living as if all of life took place in the Temple confines. This way of shaping life led to the survival of the Pharisees after the destruction of the Temple by the Romans. But it also led to the survival of the Pharisees when the Temple was administered by the Sadducees. These two groups did not offer physical threat to each other, but their disagreements will have contributed to the Pharisees' desire to make the Temple a pervasive reality, not a territory controlled by the priests who were also controlled by Rome.

Christianity also, in its turn, developed as a kind of Jewish faith in a world without a Temple. This survival, however, was not an unmixed blessing. There developed in Christian writings a disturbing tendency to celebrate the destruction of the Temple as retribution against the Jewish people for "rejecting Jesus." For a painful reminder of what lurks in our theology, hear this from Justin Martyr's *Dialogue with Trypho the Jew*:

> We too would observe your circumcision of the flesh, your Sabbath days, and in a word, all your festivals, if we were not aware of the reason why they were imposed upon you, namely, because of your sins and the hardness of heart.
>
> The custom of circumcising the flesh, handed down from Abraham, was given to you as a distinguishing mark, to set you off from other nations and from us Christians. The purpose of this was that you and only you might suffer the afflictions that are now justly yours; that only your land be desolated, and your cities ruined by fire, that the fruits of your land be eaten by strangers before your very eyes; that not one of you be permitted to enter your city of Jerusalem. Your circumcision

> of the flesh is the only mark by which you can certainly be distinguished from other men. . . . As I stated before it was by reason of your sins and the sins of your fathers that, among other precepts, God imposed upon you the observance of the Sabbath as a mark.

To the extent that Justin's words represent Christian understandings of the Temple and of Jewish faith, we have much to repent.

Provoking the Story

Near the end of the first century CE, 2 Baruch was composed. This apocalypse presents itself as the work of Jeremiah's assistant, Baruch, and purports to describe the destruction of Jerusalem and the Temple by the Babylonians in the sixth century BCE. As is clear from its time of composition, however, it presents a reflection on the destruction of the Temple by the Romans during the crushing of the First Jewish Revolt in 70 CE. Its date of composition also makes it a close contemporary of the four canonical gospels (and of the Revelation to John, for that matter). Each of these works comes out of a segment within the Jewish population, and each reflects painfully on the destruction of the center of the Jewish world. You will understand Mark's reflection on this event more thoroughly if you reflect on what Baruch (his compositional contemporary) wrote about the same event.

2 Baruch 6–9

> 6:1 And it came to pass on the morrow that, lo! the army of the
> Chaldees surrounded the city, and at the time of the evening, I,
> Baruch, left the people, and I went forth and stood by the 2 oak.
> And I was grieving over Zion, and lamenting over the captivity
> which had come upon 3 the people. And lo! suddenly a strong
> spirit raised me, and bore me aloft over the wall of 4 Jerusalem.
> And I beheld, and lo! four angels standing at the four corners of
> the city, each of 5 them holding a torch of fire in his hands. And
> another angel began to descend from heaven, 6 and said unto

them: "Hold your lamps, and do not light them till I tell you. For I am first sent to speak a word to the earth, and to place in it what the Lord the Most High has commanded me." And I saw him descend into the Holy of holies, and take from thence the veil, and the holy ark, and the mercy-seat, and the two tables, and the holy raiment of the priests, and the altar of incense, and the forty-eight precious stones, wherewith the priest was adorned and all the holy [8]vessels of the tabernacle. And he spake to the earth with a loud voice: "Earth, earth, earth, hear the word of the mighty God, And receive what I commit to thee, And guard them until the last times, So that, when thou art ordered, thou mayst restore them, So that strangers may not get possession of them. [9]For the time comes when Jerusalem also will be delivered for a time, Until it is said, that it is again restored for ever." [10]And the earth opened its mouth and swallowed them up.

[7:1]And after these things I heard that angel saying unto those angels who held the lamps: "Destroy, therefore, and overthrow its wall to its foundations, lest the enemy should boast and say: 'We have overthrown the wall of Zion, And we have burnt the place of the mighty God.' " [2]And ye have seized the place where I had been standing before.

[8:1]Now the angels did as he had commanded them, and when they had broken up the corners of the walls, a voice was heard from the interior of the temple, after the wall had fallen, [2]"Enter, ye enemies, And come, ye adversaries; For he who kept the house has forsaken (it)." [3, 4]And I, Baruch, departed. And it came to pass after these things that the army of the Chaldees [5]entered and seized the house, and all that was around it. And they led the people away captive, and slew some of them, and bound Zedekiah the king, and sent him to the king of Babylon.

[9:1]And I, Baruch, came, and Jeremiah, whose heart was found pure from sins, who had not been [2]captured in the seizure of the city. And we rent our garments, we wept, and mourned, and fasted seven days.

THE GOSPEL OF MARK TRANSLATED

Chapter One

1Beginning of the good news of Jesus messiah, son of God:
2Just as it stands written in Isaiah the prophet:
Look! I am sending my messenger before your face,
who will prepare your road.
3A voice is bellowing in the wilderness:
Prepare the road of the LORD,
make straight his paths.
4John appeared,
John the Baptist,
appeared in the wilderness,
proclaiming a baptism of repentance
aiming at forgiveness of sins.
5All the region of Judea was going out to him,
all that region
and every person living in Jerusalem.
They were being baptized by him in the Jordan river,
baptized while they confessed their sins.
6John was clothed in camel hair.
He had a leather belt around his waist.
He ate locusts and wild honey.
7John proclaimed,
he said:

He is coming,
  the one who is stronger than I,
he is coming after me.
I am not worthy to stoop down to untie the thong of his sandals.
8I baptized you with water.
  He, however, will baptize you in holy spirit.
9It happened in those days:
Jesus came from Nazareth of Galilee
  and was baptized in the Jordan by John.
10He is coming up out of the water
  and BANG[145] he sees the heavens being torn apart
    and the spirit,
      like a pigeon,
  coming down into him.
11A voice came out of the heavens:
  You are my son, the beloved.
    With you I am well-pleased.
12Then BANG the spirit threw him out into the wilderness.
  13He was in the wilderness forty days,
    being tested by the satan.
    He was with the wild animals.
      Angels deaconed to him.
14After John was handed over,
  Jesus came into Galilee,
  proclaiming the good news of God, saying:
    15The right time stands ready,
    the dominion[146] of God is so close.
    Keep on repenting and keep on believing in the good news.
16As he walked along the Sea of Galilee,
he saw Simon and Andrew his brother
  double-throwing their net into the sea.
    They fished for a living.
17Jesus said to them:
  Come after me.
  I will make you fish for people.

18BANG they left their net and followed him.
19He went a little further
and saw James the son of Zebedee and John, his brother,
saw them in the boat mending their net.
20BANG he called them.
They left their father, Zebedee, in the boat with the hired help
and went off after him.
21They went into Capernaum.
BANG on the Sabbath,
into the synagogue he goes and teaches.
22They were driven out of their minds by his teaching:
he taught them as if he had authority,
not like the scribes.
23BANG a man was in their synagogue,
a man in an unclean spirit.
He screamed:
24What is all this to you and to me, Jesus Netzer?[147]
You came to destroy us?
I know you,
I know who you are: the Holy one of God.
25Jesus scolded him,
he said:
Be quiet and come out of him.
26After the unclean spirit convulsed him
and cried out in a great voice,
he came out of him.
27Everyone was so astounded that they kept on asking each other:
What is this?
A new teaching!
With authority
even to the unclean spirits he gives orders,
and they obey him!
28His fame went out,
BANG, everywhere,
into the whole surrounding region of Galilee.

29BANG out of the synagogue he went.
He went into the house of Simon and Andrew
with James and John.
30The mother-in-law of Simon was lying down because she had a fever.
BANG they speak to him about her.
31He came toward her
he raised her,
grasping her hand.
The fever left her and she deaconed to them.
32When it was evening,
when the sun was going down
they were carrying to him
all those who were sick
and those possessed by demons.
33The whole city gathered to the gate.
34He healed many who were sick with various diseases
and he cast out many demons.
He wasn't letting the demons speak
because they knew him.
35Early,
still in the night,
he got up,
He went out and went away to a wilderness place.
He was praying.
36They tracked him down,
Simon and the others.
37They found him
and they say to him:
Everyone is looking for you.
38He says to them:
Let us go elsewhere
into the neighboring villages,
so that also there I might proclaim.
To this end, indeed, I came out.

39And he went proclaiming,
into their synagogues,
into the whole Galilee
and he went casting out demons.
40And there comes to him
a leper,
begging him
and falling on his knees
and saying to him:
If you choose you are able to cleanse me.
41Jesus was moved,[148]
he extended his hand,
he touched him,
he says to him:
I choose, be cleansed.
42BANG away from him went the leprosy
He was cleansed.
43Jesus snorted at him indignantly
BANG he cast him out.
44He says to him:
See that you say nothing,
Not to anyone.
But go show yourself to the priest
and offer for your cleansing what Moses commanded,
as a witness to them.
45The man went out and began to proclaim many things
and to fame the word about,
so that Jesus was no longer able to go openly into a city,
but outside,
in wilderness places he was,
and they kept on coming to him from everywhere.

Chapter Two

1After he went again into Capernaum for a few days,
it was heard:

He is in a house.
2Many gathered,
there was no longer any room,
even near the door.
He was speaking to them.
He was speaking the word.
3They are coming,
they are carrying to him
a paralyzed man.
Four people are carrying him.
4Since they couldn't carry the man to him
because of the crowd,
they broke through the roof where Jesus was.
So they dug it out,
then they lower the pallet
on which the paralyzed man was lying.
5When Jesus saw their faithfulness,
he says to the paralyzed man:
Child, your sins are forgiven.
6But there were some of the scribes there,
sitting and arguing in their hearts:
7Why does this one speak like this?
It is blasphemy.
Who is able to forgive sin except one: God?
8BANG Jesus,
as soon as he knows in his spirit
that they were arguing in themselves like this,
he says to them:
Why are you arguing these things in your hearts?
9What is easier,
to say to the paralyzed man:
Your sins are forgiven,
or to say:
Rise,

pick up your pallet,
walk?
10But so that you see that the son of adam[149]
has authority to forgive sins on earth,
(he says to the paralyzed man)
11to you I say:
Rise,
pick up your pallet,
go home.
12He got up,
BANG picked up the pallet.
He went out
right in front of everybody,
Everybody was ecstasied[150]
and glorified God by saying:
We have never seen anything like this.
13He went out again by the sea;
the whole crowd was coming to him.
He was teaching them.
14And as he was going along
he saw Levi,
son of Alphaeus
sitting by the taxbooth
He says to him:
Follow me.
He got up and he followed him.
15It happened.
He sat to eat in his house.
Many tax traitors and sinful men
sat down to eat with Jesus and his disciples
(there were many of them
and they were following him).
16And the scribes of the Pharisees,
when they saw,
(he eats with sinners and tax traitors!)

were saying to his disciples:
So now he eats with tax traitors and sinners?
17 And after Jesus heard,
he says to them:
No need do they have,
the strong ones,
of a healer.
It is sick people who need a healer.
I did not come to call righteous but sinners.
18 John's disciples
and those of the Pharisees were fasting,
and they come
and they say to him:
Why is it?
The disciples of John?
They're fasting.
And the disciples of the Pharisees?
They're fasting.
But your disciples?
They're not fasting.
19 Jesus said to them:
The wedding party can't fast,
not when the groom is with them,
can they?
Of course not.
As long as the groom is with them,
they can't fast.
20 Days are coming
when the bridegroom
will be taken away from them.
Then, on that day, they will fast.
21 No one sews a patch of new cloth
on an old garment.
If they did, it's just a matter of time
until the new lifts up from the old

and a worse tear is made.
22And no one dumps new wine into old wineskins.
If they did,
it rips the skins,
the wine does.
The wine is lost
and the skins, too.
New wine goes into new skins.
23On the Sabbath,
he passed by through a planted field
and his disciples began to make a road through the field
by picking the heads of grain.
24The Pharisees tried to say to him:
Look, they do this on the Sabbath, and it is not allowed.
25He says to them:
So you've never read what David did?
He was in need,
he was hungry
and so were those with him,
26You've never read
how he went into the house of God
when Abiathar was high priest
and he ate the loaves of offering,
which it is not allowed for anyone to eat
(anyone except a priest, that is)
He not only ate the bread,
but he also gave it to those with him?
27And he kept saying to them:
The Sabbath came through humans,
and not humans through the Sabbath.
28So that the son of adam is lord also of the Sabbath.

Chapter Three

1He went again into the synagogue.
There, in the synagogue, was a man with a withered hand.

2 They were watching him
to see if he would heal him on the Sabbath
so that they might accuse him.
3 So he says to the man with the withered hand:
Come forward.
4 And he says to them:
Is it allowed on the Sabbath
to do good or to do evil?
To save a life or to kill?
But they kept silent.
5 He looked around at them with anger,
sympathizing with them because of their hard hearts.
He says to the man:
Reach out your hand.
He was reaching it out
and his hand was restored.
6 The Pharisees went out,
BANG with the Herodians,
and conspired against him in order to kill him.
7 Jesus departed with his disciples to the sea
and a great crowd from Galilee followed them
a great crowd,
from Galilee, from Judea,
8 from Jerusalem, from Idumea,
from the region of the Jordan,
from Tyre and Sidon:
a great crowd
and when they heard the sort of things he was doing,
they came to him.
9 He told his disciples to have a boat ready for him
because of the crowd,
so that it wouldn't crush him:
10 because he had healed so many people,
they pressed upon him
so that those with diseases

could touch him
[11]and unclean spirits,
whenever they saw him,
fell down before him
and screamed:
You are the son of God.
[12]He commanded them repeatedly not to make him visible.
[13]And he goes up into the hills.
He calls to him those whom he wished,
and they went away to him.
[14]He appointed twelve
(whom he named apostles)
in order that they should be with him
and in order that he might send them out
to proclaim
[15]and to have authority
to throw out demons,
[16]He appointed the twelve.
He gave to Simon the name Rock,
[17]and James the son of Zebedee
and John the brother of James,
to them he gave the name Boanerges
(sons of thunder),
[18]and Andrew and Philip,
and Bartholomew and Matthew
and Thomas and James, son of Alphaeus,
and Thaddeus and Simon the Cananaean,
[19]and Judas Iscariot,
who also handed him over.
[20]And he comes home and the crowd comes together again,
so that they are not able to eat bread.
[21]When his family heard this, they came to seize him.
They said:
He's out of his mind.
[22]Scribes who came down from Jerusalem were saying:

He has Beelzebul.
and,
By the authority of demons he casts out demons.
[23]After calling them to him,
he was saying (in parables) to them:
How is the satan able to cast out the satan?
[24]and,
If a dominion is divided against itself,
that dominion will not be able to stand.
[25]and,
If a house is divided against itself,
that house will not be able to stand.
[26]and,
If the satan has risen up against himself,
and is divided,
he will not be able to stand,
but is as good as dead.
[27]Think about it:
you can't go into a strong man's house,
and plunder his property
unless you tie the strong man up first.
Tie the strong man up,
then you can plunder his house.
[28]I am telling you the truth:
All things will be forgiven to human beings,
all sins
and whatever blasphemies you utter,
[29]but whoever blasphemes
against the holy spirit is not forgiven,
not even into the messianic age.
That is an eternal sin.
[30]They had been saying:
He has an unclean spirit.
[31]Then his mother and his brothers came.
When they had stationed themselves outside,

they sent to him,
calling him.
32Now there was seated around him a crowd.
They say to him:
Look,
your mother
and your brothers
and your sisters
are outside looking for you.
33And he answered them,
he says:
Who is my mother?
Who are my brothers?
34And looking around at those sitting circled around him,
he says:
Look!
My mother and my brothers!
35Whoever does the will of God,
that person is my brother
and my sister,
and my mother.

Chapter Four

1Again he began to teach beside the sea,
and there came to him an enormous crowd,
so that he got into a boat on the sea and sat there;
all the crowd was right at the edge of the sea
on the land.
2He was teaching them many things in parables,
and was saying to them in his teaching:
3Listen:
Look:
There went out
a sower.
He went out to sow,

4 and it happened while he was sowing,
that some fell along the road,
and the birds came and gobbled it up,
5 and another portion fell on the rocks
where it did not have much soil,
and BANG it sprang up
because it did not have deep soil.
6 And when the sun rose,
it was scorched.
Because it didn't have roots,
it withered.
7 And another portion fell into the thorns,
and the thorns came up and choked it,
and it bore no fruit.
8 But other seeds fell into beautiful soil
and kept bearing fruit,
growing up and increasing
bearing and bearing,
thirty,
sixty,
one hundred fold.
9 And he was saying:
The person who has ears to hear should hear.
10 When they were alone,
those around him with the twelve asked him about the parables.
11 He was saying to them:
To you the mystery has been given,
the mystery of the dominion of God.
To those outside, however,
everything happens in parables,
12 so that:
Looking they should look
and not see
and hearing they should hear
and not understand

lest they should turn
and it be forgiven to them.
13 He says to them:
You don't understand this parable?!
So how will you know all the parables?
14 The sower sows the word.
15 These are the ones that fall along the road
when the word is sown:
whenever they hear,
BANG the satan comes
and snatches the word sown in them.
16 And these are like those sown on the rocks:
who whenever they hear the word,
BANG with joy they receive it.
17 They do not have root in themselves
but are premature.
When pressure or persecution come
because of the word,
BANG they are scandalized.
18 And others are those sown into the thorns:
these are the ones who hear the word
19 and the cares of this era
and the lure of wealth
and the desire for all the rest
comes in and chokes the word,
and it becomes fruitless.
20 And those are the ones sown on beautiful soil:
these hear the word
and take it in,
and bear fruit,
thirty,
sixty,
one hundred fold.
21 And he was saying to them:
The lamp does not come in

(does it?)
in order to be placed under a basket
or under the bed.
Does it not rather come in
in order to be placed upon the lampstand?
22There is no thing hidden,
except in order to be revealed.
Neither does it happen secretly,
except in order that it should come into visibility.
23Anyone who has ears to hear should hear.
24And he was saying to them:
Look what you hear.
In the measure which you measure,
it will be measured out to you,
and it will be added beyond that.
25To the one who has,
it will be given,
and whoever does not have,
even what that one has will be taken away.
26And he was saying:
Thus is the dominion of God:
Suppose a person should dump seed on the ground,
27and then sleep and get up,
night after night
day after day.
The seed sprouts and grows,
who knows how?
28The soil produces automatically,
first the shoot,
then the stalk,
then full grain in the head.
29But when the grain is ripe,
BANG he sends the sickle,
because the harvest is standing ready.
30And he was saying:

How shall we compare the dominion of God,
or in what parable shall we put it?
31It is as a seed of mustard, which,
whenever it is sown upon the soil,
is smaller than all the seeds sown on earth,
32and whenever it is sown,
it goes up and becomes bigger than all shrubs,
and makes great branches,
so that under its shade
the birds of heaven can make nests.
33And in many parables of this sort he was speaking to them the word,
just as they were able to hear.
34Apart from parables he said nothing to them,
but alone with his own disciples he explained everything.
35On that day when it was evening, he says to them:
Let's go across to the other side.
36So they leave the crowd and take him,
since he was already in the boat.
Other boats were with him.
37A great windstorm arises;
the waves beat into the boat,
the boat is being swamped.
38He was in the stern,
his head on the pillow,
sound asleep.
They wake him up and say to him:
Teacher, don't you care that we are dying?
39He woke up;
he rebuked the wind
and he said to the sea:
Silence. Be still.
The wind stopped. There was a dead calm.
40He said to them:
Why are you afraid like this?

How do you not have faith?
41And they feared a great fear,
and they were saying to each other:
Who then is this? Even the wind and the sea obey him.

Chapter Five

1He came to the shore of the sea in the region of the Gerasenes.
2And as he came out of the boat,
BANG there met him out of the tombs
a man,
in an unclean spirit,
3a man who had lived in the tombs,
and nobody was able to restrain him any longer,
even with a chain.
4He had often been bound with shackles and chains.
The chains he wrenched apart
and the shackles he shivered to atoms.
No one had the strength to subdue him.
5All night and every day,
in the tombs and in the hills,
he was screaming
and beating himself with stones.
6When he saw Jesus from a distance,
he was running
and fell down before him
7and screaming in a great voice
he says:
What's all this to me and to you,
Jesus, son of God the most high?
I adjure you by God, do not torment me.
8For Jesus was saying to him:
Come out, unclean spirit,
come out of the man.
9Jesus replied to him:
What is your name?

He says to him:
Legion is my name,
because we are many.
10He begs him many times
that he not send him out of the area.
11But there on the hillside,
there was a great herd of pigs grazing.
12And they begged him saying:
Send us into the pigs,
that we go into them.
13And he gave them permission.
When the unclean spirits went into the pigs,
the herd rushed down the steep bank into the sea,
two thousand of them there were,
and they were drowned in the sea.
14And those feeding them were fleeing.
They brought the news
into the city
and into the fields
and people came to see what had happened.
15They come toward Jesus.
They see the demoniac,
sitting, clothed and having judgment,
They see the one who had had the legion
and they were afraid.
16The eyewitnesses described in detail to them
how it happened to the demoniac
and about the pigs.
17They began to ask him to go away from their area.
18After he got into the boat,
the demoniac asked to be with him.
19He did not allow him,
but he says to him:
Go to your own home.
Go to your own people.

Bring news to them
how many things the LORD has done for you
and pitied you.
20And he went away and began to proclaim in the Decapolis
how many things Jesus did for him and all were being amazed.
21When Jesus departed in the boat back to the other shore,
there came a huge crowd,
it came together upon him.
He was by the sea.
22There came a person,
one of the leaders of the synagogue,
(by name: Jairus).
When he saw Jesus,
he fell at his feet;
23he begs him desperately,
he says:
My daughter is at the point of death.
Come and lay your hands upon her
that she be rescued and live.
24Jesus went with him.
A crowd followed him,
a crowd so large that it crushed him.
25A woman came,
a woman twelve years in a river of blood,
26twelve years having suffered many things
under many healers,
a woman who had exhausted all her property,
all her substance,
after twelve years she had improved not at all,
in fact, her condition had grown worse.
A woman came into the area,
27came because she had heard about Jesus.
This woman came into the crowd behind Jesus
and touched his cloak.
28She was saying:

even if I only touch the hem of his garment,
I will be rescued.
29BANG the spring of her blood was dried up
and she knew in her body
that she was healed from her scourge.
30BANG Jesus knew in himself
that power had gone out from him.
Turning and turning, around in the crowd,
he kept saying:
Who touched my clothing?
31His disciples were saying to him:
You can see the crowd crushing you
and you say: Who touched me?
32He kept looking around
to find the woman who had done this.
33The woman,
afraid and trembling,
knew what had happened to her.
The woman came and fell down before him.
She told him the whole truth.
34He said to her:
Daughter, your faithfulness has rescued you.
Depart in peace
and be healed from your scourge.
35While he was still speaking
they came to him from the leader of the synagogue,
they said:
Your daughter has died,
why bother the teacher any longer?
36Jesus overheard what they were saying.
He says to the leader of the synagogue:
Do not fear, only be faithful.
37He would not allow anyone to be with him,
no one except Peter, James, and John
(the brother of James).

38 They come into the house of the leader of the synagogue.
He sees an uproar:
everywhere wild wailing,
everywhere shrieking,
everywhere howling.
39 He goes in and says to them:
Why are you wailing?
Why the uproar?
The child has not died, she's only asleep.
40 They laughed at him bitterly.
He throws everyone out.
He takes the father of the child,
the father and the mother,
and those with him.
He goes into where the child was.
41 He grasps the hand of the child.
He says to her:
Talitha cum
(translated: Little girl, I say to you, get up).
42 BANG the little girl rose and walked around
(she was, after all, twelve years old).
BANG: ecstasy beyond ecstasy.
43 He strictly ordered them
that no one should ever find out what had happened.
He told them to give her something to eat.

Chapter Six

1 And he left that place.
He comes into his hometown.
His disciples follow him.
2 When it was Sabbath,
he began to teach in the synagogue.
Many who heard him were driven crazy.
They said:
Where did this guy get this?

And:
What is this wisdom that is given to him
so that even such deeds of power are done at his hand?
3 Isn't this the carpenter,
the son of Mary
and brother of James
and Justus
and Judah
and Simon?
Aren't his sisters here before us?
And they were scandalized by him.
4 And Jesus kept saying to them:
Never is a prophet without honor
(except, of course, in his hometown,
and among his own kin,
and in his own house).
5 And he was not able there to do anything powerful,
except a few sick people
upon whom he laid his hands and healed them.
6 And he was amazed because of their unfaithfulness.
And he was going around the villages in a circle, teaching.
7 He calls the twelve.
He began to send them two by two.
He was giving to them authority over unclean spirits
8 and he instructed them
that they take nothing into the road except one staff,
no bread,
no pouch,
no money in their belts,
9 but to put on sandals,
and not put on two tunics.
10 And he was saying to them:
Wherever you go into a house,
remain there until you go out from there,
11 and whatever place does not receive you

and doesn't listen to you,
as you go out from there
shake off the dust clinging to your feet
to serve as a witness to them.
12 When they went out they proclaimed
that people should repent
13 and they were casting out many demons,
and they were anointing with oil many who were sick
and they were healing them.
14 And Herod the king heard,
for his name was becoming visible,
he was saying:
John the Baptizer has been raised out of death
and on account of this the deeds of power are being worked
in him.
15 But others were saying:
Elijah it is.
Others were saying:
a prophet as one of the prophets.
16 But after Herod heard, he was saying:
The one whom I beheaded
(John, wasn't it?),
that one has been raised.
17 For the same Herod sent
and arrested John
and imprisoned him in a guardhouse
on account of Herodias the wife of Phillip,
his brother,
because he married her.
18 For John kept saying to Herod:
It is not allowed for you to have the wife of your brother.
19 But Herodias had it in for him
and wanted to kill him,
and she was not able.
20 For Herod feared John

because he knew him to be a righteous and holy man.
He protected him;
he listened to him many times;
he was very much at a loss.
He did listen to him gladly.
21 An opportune day came when Herod
   for his birthday
made a feast for his courtiers
   and the commanders of the cohorts
   and the leading citizens of Galilee.
22 His daughter came in
   (the daughter of Herodias),
she danced and it was pleasing
   to Herod
   and to the dinner guests.
The king said to the little girl:
   Ask me whatever you wish and I will give it to you.
23 He swore to her:
   Whatever you ask me,
   I will give to you,
      up to half of my dominion.
24 She went out;
she said to her mother:
   What shall I ask?
She said:
   The head of John the Baptizer.
25 After she went in
   BANG with haste
to the king
   she asked,
      she says to him:
         I want . . . ,
            at once . . . ,
         I want you to give to me . . . ,
            upon a plate . . . ,

the head of John the Baptizer.
26 The king became very sad
on account of the oaths and the dinner guests
he did not want to put her off.
27 BANG the king sent a guard
he commanded him to bring the head to him.
After he went out he beheaded him in the guardhouse
28 and brought his head upon a plate
and gave it to the little girl
and the little girl gave it to her mother.
29 And after his disciples heard
they came and picked up his corpse
and placed it in a grave.
30 And the apostles gathered to Jesus
and reported to him all the things that they did
and the things that they taught.
31 And he says to them:
You yourselves come alone into a wilderness place and rest a little,
for those coming and those going were many
and they did not even have time to eat.
32 And they went away in the boat into a wilderness place
alone.
33 Many saw them going off
and knew them
and they ran together by foot from all the cities there.
They came there ahead of them.
34 After he got out,
he saw a great crowd.
He was moved[151] for them:
they were as sheep that did not have a shepherd.
He began to teach them many things.
35 It was already mostly evening
his disciples
after coming to him

were saying:
It is a wilderness,
this place,
and it is already mostly evening.
36Release them
so that they go in to the circling fields and villages
and buy for themselves something
and eat.
37But he answers,
he said to them:
Give to them,
yourselves,
something to eat.
They say to him:
Should we go and buy eight months' wages' worth of bread
and will we then give to them to eat?
38He says to them:
How many loaves do you have?
Go see.
And when they knew they say:
Five,
and two fish.
39And he commanded to them to sit down,
all of them,
banquet by banquet,
upon the green grass.
40They sat down,
row by row,
in hundreds and fifties.
41He took the five loaves and the two fish;
he looked into the heaven;
he blessed and broke the loaves.
He kept giving to his disciples
in order that they should set it before them
and the two fish he divided to all.

42They all ate and were stuffed.
43They picked up fragments
twelve baskets full,
also from the fish.
44Those who ate the bread were five thousand males.
45BANG
he forced his disciples to get into the boat
and to go ahead into the region by Bethsaida,
until he releases the crowd.
46After he ordered them off,
he went into the mountain to pray.
47When it was evening,
the boat was in the middle of the sea,
he was alone on the land,
48he saw them tortured in their rowing.
The wind was against them.
About the fourth watch of the night
he comes toward them,
walking upon the sea.
He wanted to go past them.
49But when they saw him
upon the sea
walking
they thought that he was a ghost.
They screamed.
50For they all saw him
and were thrown into chaos.
BANG he spoke with them
and says to them:
Be brave.
I AM.[152]
Stop being afraid.
51He got into the boat,
got in with them.
The wind stopped

and they were ecstasied[153] beyond all measure
52for they did not understand about the loaves.
Their hearts were calloused.
53After they crossed upon the land
they came into Gennesaret and dropped anchor.
54As they were getting out of the boat,
BANG they recognized him.
55The whole of that region ran around
and began to carry
upon pallets
those who were in a bad way.
They carried them around wherever they heard that he was.
56Wherever he went into a village,
or into a city,
or into a field,
in the fields they placed the weak.
They kept calling him
so that they touch even the fringe of
his garment.
As many as touched it were rescued.

Chapter Seven

1They gathered to him,
the Pharisees
and some of the scribes;
they came from Jerusalem.
2When they saw some of his disciples,
saw that with profane hands
(that is, unwashed)
they eat bread
3(The Pharisees,
and all Judeans,[154]
if they do not,
with a fist,

wash their hands
they do not eat.
They hold to the traditions of the elders.
4 From the market?
If they do not dip and wash,
they do not eat.
Many other things there are which they
received and hold onto:
dippings of cups
and pitchers
and copper kettles.)
5 And the Pharisees and the scribes ask him:
On account of what
do your disciples not walk according to the
traditions of the elders,
but with profane hands they eat bread?
6 He said to them:
Isaiah prophesied beautifully about you role-players,
as it stands written:
This people honors me with lips,
but their hearts they hold far from me.
7 To no purpose do they worship me,
for their teachings are human commandments.
8 Abandoning the commandment of God,
you hold fast human tradition.
9 He tried to say to them:
Beautifully do you set aside the commandment of God,
in order that you should establish your tradition.
10 For Moses said:
Honor your father and your mother,
And:
The one who insults father or mother,
let that one end in death.
11 But you say:

If a person should say to father
or mother:
Korban
(that is:
“It is Given, whatever I would have owed to you”),
12 you no longer allow him to give anything,
not to father or mother.
13 Thus you revoke the word of God
by your traditions which you pass on
and you do many other things just like this.
14 He called back the crowd,
he was saying to them:
Hear me, all of you, and get it:
15 There is nothing
outside of a person
which by going in
is able to make a person profane.
It is the things that come out of a person,
That’s what makes a person profane.
17 When he went into a house
away from the crowd,
his disciples asked him the parable.
18 He says to them:
So you also are ignorant?
You don’t know that everything that goes in,
from outside,
all the things that go in,
none of them can make you profane?
19 None of it goes into the heart.
It goes into the belly;
it goes into the latrine.
It goes away,
and this cleanses all foods.
20 He was saying:
What comes out of a person,

that is what makes a person profane.
21For from inside,
out of the human heart,[155]
ugly calculation goes out:
sexual immorality,
thefts,
murders,
22adulteries,
greeds,
worthlessness,
deceit,
shameless living,
evil eye,
blasphemy,
arrogance,
senselessness,
23all these worthless things from inside go out
and profane the person.
24He went up from there,
away into the region of Tyre.
He went into a house,
he wanted no one to know.
There was no hiding him.
25BANG A woman heard about him,
a woman whose daughter had an unclean spirit.
She came.
She fell at his feet.
26The woman was a Gentile,
Syrophoenician by birth.
She asked him to cast the demon out of her daughter.
27He tried to say to her:
Let the children be stuffed first,
for it is not good to take the children's bread
and throw it to the dogs.
28But she answered,

says to him, she does:
Sir, even the dogs under the table eat the children's bread crumbs.
29 And he said to her:
Because of this word, go,
the demon has come out of your daughter.
30 And after she went into her house,
she found the child thrown upon the bed,
the demon gone.
31 Again going out of the region of Tyre
he went through Sidon
to the Sea of Galilee
up into the middle of the region of the Decapolis.
32 They are bringing to him a man who could not hear;
he also could not speak.
They ask him that he place upon him
his hand.
33 He took him away from the crowd by himself.
He stuck his fingers into his ears.
He spat.
He touched his tongue.
34 He looked up into heaven.
He groaned.
He says to him:
Ephphatha,
which is: Be opened.
35 His ears were opened;
the shackle of his tongue let loose;
he was speaking correctly.
36 He commanded them that
to no one
should they speak:
but as much as he kept on commanding to them,
that much more they were proclaiming.
37 They were driven completely out of their minds.

They were saying:
He has done all things beautifully.
And:
He makes the deaf to hear
and the mute to speak.

Chapter Eight

1 In those days again
a large crowd there was
and nothing to eat,
He called together his disciples,
he says to them:
2 I am moved[156] by the crowd:
already three days they stay with me
and they have nothing to eat.
3 If I release them
hungry
into their home,
they will faint in the road
and some of them have come from far off.
4 They answered to him
his disciples did:
How would anyone be able
(this crowd!)
to stuff them with bread,
and in a wilderness, no less?
5 He asked them:
How many loaves do you have?
They said:
Seven.
6 He tells the crowd to fall upon the earth.
He takes the seven loaves.
He gives thanks.
He broke
And kept giving to his disciples,

that they should place before,
and they placed before the crowd.
[7]They also had a few fish.
He blessed the fish,
he spoke to the disciples.
The fish also were placed before the crowd.
[8]And they ate
and they were stuffed
and they picked up leftover fragments
seven baskets.
[9]They were about four thousand.
He left them.
[10]BANG
after he embarked into the boat with his disciples
he went into the region of Dalmanoutha.
[11]The Pharisees went out and began to try to figure things out with him.
They were seeking from him a sign from heaven;
They were testing him.
[12]Jesus groaned deeply;
he says:
What does this generation seek as a sign?
I tell you the truth:
Will this generation be given a sign?
[13]He left them,
got back into the boat.
He went away to the other shore.
[14]They had forgot to bring bread.
They had only one loaf with them in the boat.
[15]Jesus was commanding them:
Watch out.
Beware of the leaven of the Pharisees
and the leaven of Herod.
[16]They were saying to each other:
It's because we don't have any bread.

17When he realized what they were doing,
he says to them:
What are you saying?
You don't have any bread?
Don't you get it?
Do you really not understand?
How thick are your skulls, anyway?
18Eyes you have, but you can't see?
Ears you have, but you can't hear?
Nobody remembers?
19When I broke five loaves for five thousand people,
how many baskets of leftovers did you pick up?
They say to him:
Twelve.
20And the seven loaves for the four thousand?
How many baskets of leftovers did you pick up?
They say:
Seven.
21He kept saying to them:
You don't get it, do you?
22They went into Bethsaida.
They brought to him a blind man
and asked him to touch him.
23He took the blind man by the hand
and brought him out of the village.
He spat into his eyes.
He placed his hands upon him,
and then he asked him:
Do you see anything?
24The man looked carefully and tried to say:
I see people,
because I see them like trees that are walking.
25Then Jesus placed his hands on his eyes again,
and the man looked hard,
and his sight was restored,

he saw everything clearly.
26 Jesus sent him into his house and said:
Don't even go into the village.
27 Jesus went out,
his disciples with him,
into the village, Caesarea Philippi,
and while they were on the road,
he asked his disciples,
saying to them:
What do people say that I am?
28 They said to him:
John the Baptist,
others Elijah,
others one of the prophets.
29 And he asked them:
But you,
what are you saying that I am?
Peter answers,
he says to him:
You are the Messiah.
30 And he scolded them to speak to no one about him.
31 And he began to teach them
that it is necessary
that the son of adam
suffer many things
and be rejected
by the elders
and the high priests
and the scribes
and be killed
and after three days rise.
32 He was speaking the matter plainly.
Peter took him aside and began to scold him.
33 But Jesus,
after he turned and saw his disciples,

scolded Peter.
He says:
Get out of my sight, you satan,
You don't judge things the way God does,
but the way people do.
34 He called the crowd to him,
along with his disciples,
he said to them:
You want to follow me?
Deny yourself,
take up your cross,
Then follow me.
35 You want to save your life?
You will always lose it.
But when any of you loses your life,
for my sake or for the sake of the gospel,
you will save it.
36 What is it worth
to gain the whole wonderful world
and lose your life?
37 What could you trade to get your life back?
38 Are you ashamed of me and my words?
Ashamed in the midst of this generation,
As adulterous and sinful as it is?
You're ashamed of me?
The son of adam will be ashamed also of you
when he comes in the glory of his father
with the holy angels.

Chapter Nine

1 And he was saying to them:
I am telling you the truth:
Some are standing here
who will not taste death
before they see that the dominion of God

has come in power.
2Six days later
Jesus takes Peter
and James
and John,
brings them into a high mountain all alone.
He was changed in form before them
3and his clothes became gleaming white,
white like no bleach on earth could make
them.
4There appeared to them Elijah and Moses,
and they were talking with Jesus.
5Peter answers
he says to Jesus:
Rabbi, it is a good thing we're here.
Let's make three tents:
for you, one,
for Moses, one,
and for Elijah, one.
6(He didn't really know what he was saying.
They were, after all, terrified.)
7A cloud appeared,
a cloud that overshadowed them.
A voice spoke out of the cloud:
This is my son,
the beloved,
hear him.
8Suddenly, when they looked around,
they saw absolutely nobody,
only Jesus was with them.
9As they were coming down out of the mountain,
he was commanding them
that they tell no one what they had seen,
at least not until the son of adam should have
risen from death.

10They held onto the word,
trying to figure out what "rising from death"
might mean.
11And they were asking him,
they said:
The scribes say:
It is necessary that Elijah come first.
12He said to them:
Elijah comes first,
Elijah restores everything.
Indeed.
So then how does it stand written in the case of the son of adam
that he should suffer many things
and be considered as nothing?
Is that your question?[157]
13Here's what I say:
Elijah has come
and they did to him as many things as they wished,
just as it stands written in his case.[158]
14After they came to the disciples,
they saw a great crowd around them
and scribes arguing with them.
15BANG the whole crowd,
when they saw him,
they were amazed.
They ran toward him;
They were greeting him.
16He asked them:
What are you investigating with them?
17He answered him,
one out of the crowd did:
Teacher, I brought my son to you,
because he has an unspeaking spirit.
18And wherever it seizes him,
it dances him,

and he foams
and grinds his teeth
and he withers.
I spoke to your disciples
that they cast it out,
and they were not able.
19He answered them,
says to them:
O generation with no faithfulness,
How long will I be with you?
How long will I endure you?
Bring him to me.
20They brought him to him,
and when he saw him
the spirit
BANG
tore him to pieces:
he fell upon the ground;
he was rolling and foaming.
21Jesus asked his father:
How long has this been happening to him?
He said:
Ever since he was a child.
22Many times even into fire it throws him
and into water
in order that it should kill him.
But since you are able,
Help us!
Pity us!
23Jesus said to him:
With reference to your
"Since you are able":
all things are possible to the one who is faithful.
24BANG the father of the child screams,
he tried to say:

I am faithful!
You help my unfaithfulness![159]
25When Jesus saw that a crowd was running together,
he scolded the unclean spirit,
he said to him:
You voiceless and deaf spirit,
I order you:
Come out of him!
No longer go into him!
He screamed;
he mangled him;
he went out;
26he became like a dead person,
so that many said:
He died.
27Jesus grabbed his hands;
he picked him up;
and he got up.
28And after he went into a house,
his disciples
when they were alone
kept asking him:
We,
WE were not able to cast it out.
29And he said to them:
This sort!
This sort is strong enough
that it goes out for nothing
except prayer.
30After they left,
they traveled through Galilee,
and he did not want anyone to know.
31He was, in fact, teaching his disciples.
He kept saying to them:
The son of adam is handed over into human hands.

They will kill him,
and when he is killed, after three days he will rise.
32But they didn't understand what he was talking about,
and they were afraid to ask him.
33They came into Capernaum.
When he went into his house,
he asked them:
What were you discussing on the road?
34They said nothing:
they had been discussing who was the greatest.
35After he sat down,
he called the twelve
and says to them:
If you want to be first,
go be last of all,
go wait table for everyone else.
36He took a child,
placed her[160] in the middle of the group,
and hugged her.
He said to them:
37whoever welcomes a child like this one,
whoever welcomes her in my name,
welcomes me.
And whoever welcomes me,
welcomes not only me,
but the one who sent me.
38John said to him:
Teacher,
we saw someone
(in your name!)
casting out demons
and we tried to stop him.
because he was not following with us.
39Jesus said:
Stop hindering him,

for there is no one who will do a deed of power in my name
who will be able
quickly
to speak evil of me
40 for who is not against us, is for us.
41 For whoever should give a cup of water to you
in a name
because of Christ you are,
I tell you the truth:
that one will not lose his wage.
42 and whoever should scandalize one of these little ones who are faithful
better and more beautiful it is for him
if a millstone were placed around his neck
and he were thrown into the sea.
43 And if ever your hand scandalize you,
cut it off.
beautiful it is that you go
crippled
into life
than
having two hands
to go off into Gehenna,
into the unquenchable fire.
45 And if ever your foot scandalize you,
cut it off
beautiful it is that you go into life
lame
than
having two feet
be thrown into Gehenna.
47 And if ever your eye scandalize you,
throw it out.
beautiful it is that you
one-eyed

enter into the dominion of God
than having two eyes be thrown into Gehenna,
48where their worm does not come to an end
and the fire is not quenched.
49Everyone will be salted with fire.
50Salt is good.
If salt becomes unsalty,
How will you contrive it?
Have salt among you,
and be at peace with each other.

Chapter Ten

1He got up from there;
he comes into the territory of Judea across the Jordan,
Again a crowd comes together;
again it comes to him.
As he had been accustomed,
again he was teaching them.
2When Pharisees came to him,
they kept asking:
Since it is allowed to a husband
to release his wife . . .
(They were testing him.)
3He answered,
he said to them:
What to you did Moses command?
4They said:
Moses permitted that we write a book of separation
and that we release.
5Jesus said to them:
with an eye to your hardened hearts he wrote you this commandment.
6But from the beginning of creation:
"male and female he made them. . . . "
7"On account of this a person leaves his father and mother . . . "

[8]and:
"the two will be one flesh . . . ,"
so that there is no longer two,
but one body.
[9]Therefore that which God yokes together
let no one separate.
[10]Back in his house,
the disciples kept asking him about this.
[11]He says to them:
Whoever would release his wife
and marry another
commits adultery against her.
[12]And if ever a woman should release her husband
in order to marry another
she commits adultery.
[13]They kept bringing to him children
in order that he would touch them,
but the disciples scolded them
[14]But when Jesus saw he was angry.
He said to them:
Permit the children to come to me,
Stop hindering them.
Indeed of such as these is the dominion of God.
[15]I tell you the truth:
Whoever should not receive the dominion of God
the way a child does
will surely not go into it.
[16]And hugging them,
he kept blessing them,
placing his hands upon them.
[17]When he went out on a journey,
one man ran up,
fell on his knees.
He asked him:
Noble teacher,

What ought I do so that I inherit life of the messianic age?
18Jesus said to him:
Why are you saying that I am noble?
No one is noble except one,
God.
19You know the commandments:
do not kill,
do not commit adultery,
do not steal,
do not witness falsely,
do not refuse to return deposits,
honor your father and mother.
20The man said to him:
Teacher,
all these things I guarded from early adulthood.
21Jesus looked at him;
he was pleased with him.
He said to him:
One thing alone is lacking for you:
Go
whatever you have
sell
and give to the poor
and you will have treasure in heaven
and come follow me.
22He became sad because of the word.
He went away full of sorrow:
He used to have many possessions.
23Jesus looked around,
he says to his disciples:
How peevishly those who have what they need go into the dominion of God.
24The disciples were amazed because of his words,
so Jesus again answered,
he says to them:

Children,
how unpleasant it is to go into the dominion of God.
25Easier it is that a camel go through the eye of a needle
than that a rich man go into the dominion of God.
26Those standing by were driven out of their minds.
They said to themselves:
So who is able to be rescued?
27He looked at them,
Jesus says:
By humans:
can't be done.
but not by God.
Indeed by God all things can be done.
28Peter began to say to him:
Look,
We,
WE left everything.
WE have followed you.
29Jesus said:
I tell you the truth:
There is no one who left a house
or brothers
or sisters
or mother
or father
or children
or fields
on account of me
and on account of the good news,
30if they should not receive a hundredfold now
in this, the right time
houses
and brothers
and sisters
and mothers

and children
and fields
with persecutions,
and in the messianic age coming,
the life of the messianic age.
31Many will be first who are last,
and last first.
32They were on the road,
they were going up to Jerusalem.
Jesus was leading them.
They were amazed.
Those who followed were afraid.
He took the twelve aside;
he began to tell them the things that were about to happen.
33Look,
he said,
we are going up to Jerusalem.
The son of adam will be handed over
to the high priests
and the scribes,
They will condemn him to death,
and they will hand him over to the Gentiles.
34The Gentiles will mock him
and spit on him
and flog him
and kill him.
After three days he will rise.
35Then James and John walked up to him
(they're the two sons of Zebedee),
they walked up and said:
Teacher? Okay: whatever we ask, you have to do it, okay?
36He said to them:
What do you want me to do for you?
37They said to him:
Okay:

Give us this:
in your glory
one of us sits on your right,
one of us on your left,
okay?
38Jesus said to them:
You don't know what you are asking.
Are you able to drink the cup that I drink?
Or the baptism I undergo, are you able to take that, too?
39They said to him:
We can do that, no problem.
Jesus said to them:
The cup I drink, you will drink.
The baptism I undergo, you will undergo.
40But sitting at my right or my left?[161]
That isn't mine to give.
It belongs to those for which it was prepared.
41When the ten heard about this,
they began to be angry with James and John.
42Jesus called them,
he says to them:
You know
that the ones who seem to rule over the Gentiles
lord it over them.
You know
that their "Great Ones" push them around.
43It is not to be that way with you.
On the contrary:
You want to be great?
Wait tables.
44You want to be in first place?
Become everyone's slave.
45The son of adam, after all,
did not come to be served,
but to serve,

and to give his life, a ransom worth many people.
46And they came into Jericho.
As he was leaving Jericho,
his disciples with him along with a crowd of some considerable size,
the son of Timaeus, Bartimaeus,
blind,
a beggar,
was sitting,
as usual,
beside the road.
47After he heard that Jesus was the Netzer,[162]
he began to scream and to say:
Son of David,
Jesus,
Pity me.
48Many were scolding him, telling him to be silent.
But he screamed all the more:
Son of David, pity me.
49Jesus stopped and said:
Call him.
They called the blind man:
Have courage.
Get up, he is calling you.
50The man threw off his cloak,
jumped up,
and came toward Jesus.
51Jesus responded to him,
he said:
What do you want that I should do for you?
The blind man said to him:
My rabbi, that I should see.
52Jesus said to him:
Go, your faithfulness has rescued you.
BANG he could see and began following Jesus in the road.

Chapter Eleven

[1]When they were on the edge of Jerusalem
of Bethphage
and of Bethany,
near the Mount of Olives,
he sends two of his disciples
[2]and he says to them:
Go into the village opposite you
BANG as you are going into the village,
you will find a colt tied,
a colt upon which no person has sat.
Loose it and bring it.
[3]And if anyone should say to you:
What are you doing?
Say this:
The LORD has need of it.
BANG he will send it back here.
[4]They went off and found the colt tied near the gate
outside on the street.
They are untying it.
[5]Some people who had been standing there were saying to them:
What are you doing loosing the colt?
[6]They said to them exactly as Jesus told them
and they let them take it.
[7]They bring the colt to Jesus
and they throw their coats upon it,
and he sat upon it.
[8]Many spread their coats into the road;
others, leafy branches which they cut out of the fields.
[9]Those who led and those who followed screamed:
Hosanna.
Blessed by the one who is coming in the Name of the LORD.
[10]Blessed be the coming dominion of our father David.
Hosanna in the highest.

11He went into Jerusalem
into the Temple
and after looking around at everything,
since it was already evening
he went out into Bethany with the twelve.
12The next morning, after they went out from Bethany
he was hungry.
13He saw a fig tree from a distance
A fig tree that had leaves coming.
He went up to the tree to see if he could find some figs on it,
but all he found was leaves.
(It was not the season for figs.)
14He said to the tree:
Never,
not even in the messianic age,
Never will anyone eat fruit from you.
His disciples heard him.
15They went into Jerusalem.
After he went into the Temple,
he began to cast out
those who were selling
and those who were buying
in the Temple.
The tables of the moneychangers
and the chairs of those who sold doves,
those he overturned.
16And he would not permit it
that anyone should carry anything through the Temple.
17He was teaching and saying to them:
Does it not stand written:
My house
MY house:
let it be called a house of prayer
for all the Gentiles?
You have made it a hideout for bandits.

18The high priests and the scribes heard.
They started looking for ways to kill him.
They were afraid of him
because the whole crowd was driven out of their minds by his teaching.
19And when evening came, they went out of the city.
20When they came back early the next morning,
they saw the fig tree withered from its roots.
21Peter remembered,
he says to him:
Rabbi, look, the fig tree,
the one that you cursed,
it has completely withered.
22Jesus answers,
he says to them:
There you have the faithfulness of God.[163]
23I tell you the truth:
Whoever should say to this mountain:
Be lifted up and be thrown into the sea,
and not doubt in his heart
but trust that what he says happens,
he will have it.
24On account of this I say to you:
All
whatever you pray and ask,
trust that you are receiving it,
and it will be yours.
25And whenever you stand praying,
forgive
(since you have something against someone),
in order that also your father,
your father in the heavens,
should forgive to you your sins.
27They came again into Jerusalem,
and when he was in the Temple walking around

they came to him,
the chief priests
and the scribes
and the elders
28 and they kept saying to him:
In what authority are you doing these things?
Or
Who gave you this authority that you do these things?
29 Jesus said to them:
I will ask you one word,
and you answer to me
and I will say to you in what authority I am doing these things:
30 The baptism,
that baptism of John,
out of heaven was it
or out of humanity?
Answer me.
31 And they were discussing to themselves;
they said:
If we should say:
"Out of heaven."
he will say:
"Why did you not believe him?"
32 But if we should say:
"Out of humanity, . . . "
They were afraid of the crowd,
for everyone held John to be a prophet.
33 They answered,
they say to Jesus:
We don't know.
And Jesus says to them:
neither will I say to you in what authority I am doing these things.

Chapter Twelve

1 And he began to speak to them in parables:
A vineyard
a person planted.
He placed a wall around it
and he dug a trench
and built a tower
and let it out to tenant farmers
and went away on a trip.
2 He sent to the tenant farmers,
at the right time,
a slave,
in order that
from the tenant farmers
he should receive some of the fruit of the vineyard.
3 They took him;
they beat him;
they sent him away empty.
4 Again he sent to them
another slave,
and that one they hit on the head
and dishonored.
5 And another he sent:
this one they killed,
and many others,
some they beat,
some they killed
6 Still one he had:
a son,
beloved:
he sent him at last to them.
He said:
They will respect my son.
7 Those tenant farmers,

to themselves they said:
This is the inheritor:
come let us kill him,
and the inheritance will be ours.
8They seized him;
they killed him;
they cast out him out of the vineyard.
9What will the lord of the vineyard do?
He will come and destroy the tenant farmers
and will give the vineyard to other farmers.
10You don't know this Scripture?
A stone which the builders rejected
this one was changed into the head of the corner.
11by the LORD this happened,
and it is wonderful in our eyes.
12They kept seeking him to seize him.
They feared the crowd
for they knew that against them he spoke the parable.
They left him;
they went away.
13They sent to him some of the Pharisees
and of the Herodians
in order that they should trap him in words.
14After they came,
they say to him:
Teacher,
We know that you are true
and it is not a concern to you regarding anyone:
for you do not look into the face of people
but based on the truth the way of God you teach.
It is allowed to give poll tax tribute to Caesar...
or isn't it?
Should we give or should we not?
15But he saw their role-playing,
he said to them:

Why are you testing me?
Bring me a denarius in order that I should see.
16They brought,
and he says to them:
Of whom is this image and the epigraph?
They said to him:
Caesar.
17Jesus said to them:
The things of Caesar,
give to Caesar
and the things of God,
to God.
And they were amazed by him.
18And they came
Sadducees
toward him,
(those who say there is no resurrection),
and they kept asking him;
they said:
19Teacher,
Moses wrote to us:
If someone's brother should die
and leave a wife
and should not discharge a child,
his brother should take the wife
and raise seed to his brother.
20Seven brothers there were.
And the first took a wife.
He died;
he did not discharge seed.
21And the second took her,
and died without leaving seed,
and the third the same way
22None of the seven discharged seed.
Last of all, also the woman died.

23 In the resurrection
(whenever it is that they would rise)
of which of them will she be wife?
for the seven had the same wife.
24 Jesus said to them:
Isn't it on account of this you are deceived:
you know neither the Scripture nor the power of God?
25 For "whenever it is that they would rise" out of death
neither will they marry or be given in marriage.
But they are like angels in the heavens.
26 Concerning the dead,
that they are raised,
don't you read in the book of Moses
(the part about the bush)
how God said to him:
I AM the God of Abraham
and the God of Isaac
and the God of Jacob?
27 God is not God of the dead but of the living.
You are very much deceived.
28 One of the scribes approached.
He heard them arguing;
he saw how beautifully he answered them;
he asked him:
Which is the commandment,
the first of all?
29 Jesus answered:
First is:
Hear Israel,
The LORD your God is One LORD,
30 and you will love the LORD your God
out of the whole of your heart
and out of the whole of your life
and out of the whole of your mind,
and out of the whole of your strength.

31 Second, this:
You will love your neighbor as yourself.
There can exist no commandment greater than these.
32 He said to him
the scribe did:
Beautifully done, Teacher,
based on truth you spoke:
"One there is,
and there cannot be another
except God,"
33 and
"to love God
out of the whole of the heart
and out of the whole of the understanding
and out of the whole of the strength . . . "
and
"to love the neighbor as oneself . . . "
This exceeds all the whole burnt offerings and sacrifices.
34 Jesus,
seeing that he answered rationally,
said to him:
Not far you are,
not far from the dominion of God.
And no one any longer dared to question him.
35 And Jesus answered,
he kept saying while teaching in the Temple:
How do the scribes say that the messiah is son of David?
36 David himself said in the holy spirit:
The LORD said to my Lord:
Sit at my right hand
until I place your enemies under your feet.
37 David himself calls him Lord,
and how is he then his son?
The great crowd heard him gladly.
38 In his teaching he kept saying:

Beware of the scribes
who want
in garments of honor
to walk around
and want greetings in the marketplaces
39 and first seats in the synagogues
and first places in the feasts,
40 They eat up the houses of widows
and on a pretext pray long prayers:
these will receive a far greater judgment.
41 He sat opposite the treasury;
he was watching how the crowd threw coins into the treasury.
Many rich men threw in many things.
42 There came one woman,
a poor widow.
She came.
She threw two coins
(worth about a quarter of a cent).
43 He called to him his disciples;
he said to them:
I tell you the truth:
this widow,
this poor widow,
more than all the others she threw,
more than all those who threw into the treasury.
44 For all those,
out of their excess,
they threw.
She,
however,
out of her deficiency,
she threw all,
as much as she had.
She threw the whole of her life.

Chapter Thirteen

1When he went out of the Temple
he says to him,
one of his disciples does:
Teacher,
Look!
What stones and what buildings!
2and Jesus said to him:
you see these big buildings?
There will not be left here
stone on stone,
There will be nothing,
nothing not destroyed.
3When he was sitting on the Mount of Olives
opposite the Temple
Peter asked him alone
and James and John and Andrew:
4Tell us,
When will these things be?
and
What is the sign
that these things are about to come to an end?
5Jesus began to say to them:
Look out so no one deceives you.
6Many will come on the basis of my name saying:
I AM,
and they will deceive many.
7But whenever you should hear war and rumors of war,
do not raise an outcry.
It is necessary to happen,
but the end is not yet.
8For nation against nation will be raised,
and dominion against dominion,
there will be earthquakes,

place by place,
there will be famines.
These things are the beginning of the contractions of labor.
9 You all look yourselves.
They will hand you over to councils
and into synagogues
you will be beaten
and before rulers and kings you will be stood
on account of me
to be a witness to them.
10 And to all the Gentiles
first
it is necessary that the good news be proclaimed.
11 Whenever they lead you
to hand you over,
do not concern yourself ahead of time what you will say.
Rather, whatever is given to you in that hour
this you say.
For it is not you who speaks:
it is the holy spirit.
12 Brother will hand over brother to death,
and a father, his children,
and children will rise up against parents
and they will kill them.
13 You will be hated by all because of my name.
The one who endures into the end,
this one will be rescued.
14 When you see the detested maker-of-deserts[164]
having been set up where it ought not be,
(storyteller, know this)[165]
then,
people in Judea,
flee into the hills.
15 You on the roof,
do not come down.

Do not go in to pick up anything
out of the house.
16You in the field,
do not turn back to pick up your cloak.[166]
17Woe to those who are pregnant,
and to those nursing in those days.
18Pray that it not happen in winter.
19For those days will be:
"pressure such as has not happened
from the beginning of creation"
(which God created)
"up to now,"
Such tribulation should never be.
20If the LORD had not shortened the days,
no flesh would be saved.
But for the sake of the chosen people,
the Israel[167] God chose,
God shortened the days.
21And whenever anyone should say to you:
Look!
The messiah.
Look there!
Do not trust it.
22For there will be raised up false messiahs
and false prophets
and they will give signs and monstrosities
to lead astray,
if possible,
the chosen people.
23You look out:
I have said to you all things ahead of time.
24But in those days after that pressure:
"the sun will be darkened,
and the moon will not give its beams.
25and the stars will be falling out of the heaven

and the powers,
those in the heavens,
they will be shaken."
26 And then you see:
"the son of adam
coming in clouds"
with much power and glory
27 and then he will send the messengers
and he will gather together the chosen people
out of the four winds
from the end of earth
up to the end of heaven.
28 From the fig tree learn the parable:
whenever its branch is already become tender
and sprouts leaves,
you know that summer is very near.
29 Thus also you,
whenever you see these things happening,
you will know that it is very near,
at the gates.
30 I tell you the truth:
this generation will by no means pass by
before all these things happen.
31 The heaven and the earth?
They will pass by,
but my words will by no means pass by.
32 About those days, or those hours,
no one knows,
neither the messengers in heaven
nor the son,
only the father.
33 Look out,
chase sleep away,
you do not know when the right time is.
34 As a person away from home leaves his house

and gives to his slaves the authority,
to each his work,
and to the doorkeeper he orders
that he should watch.
35You watch, therefore.
for you do not know when the lord of the house is coming,
maybe evening?
maybe midnight?
maybe cockcrow?
maybe early morning?
36Let him not,
coming suddenly,
find you sleeping.
37What I say to you, I say to all:
watch.

Chapter Fourteen

1In two days it would be Passover, and the feast of Unleavened Bread
and the high priests and the scribes
were looking for a way to arrest and then kill Jesus.
2for they were saying:
Not during the feast,
lest there be an uprising among the people.
3And when he was in Bethany,
in the house of Simon the leper,
as he was sitting down to eat,
a woman came
a woman carrying an alabaster jar of perfume.
It was nard.
Pure,
very costly.
She broke the alabaster,
she anointed his head.
4There were some grumbling to each other:
Why waste good perfume?

5It could have been sold for more than three hundred denarii,
a year's wages!
The money could have been given to the poor!
They were snorting at her in anger.
6Jesus said:
Leave her alone.
Why cause her trouble?
She has performed a good service for me.
7Always the poor you will have with you.
Whenever you wish you could have done good for them.
Me, you will not always have.
8What she could do, she did.
She has anointed my body beforehand for burial.
9I tell you the truth:
wherever the good news is proclaimed
into all of the beautiful world,
what she did will be spoken as a memorial for her.
10And Judas Iscariot,
he, one of the twelve,
went off to the high priests in order to hand him over to them.
11Those who heard were very glad
and promised to give him money.
He began to look for a way to hand him over at the right time.
12On the first day of the feast of the Unleaveneds,
when the Passover lamb is killed,
they say to him, his disciples do:
Where do you want us to go and prepare,
so that you might eat the Passover?
13He sends two of his disciples,
he says to them:
Go into the city and a person carrying a jar of water will meet you.
Follow him,
14and wherever he goes in,
say to the master of the house:

The teacher says:
Where is my guest room
where I eat the Passover with my disciples?
15He will show to you a big upstairs room spread out and prepared.
There you prepare for us.
16The disciples went out and they came into the city.
They found things exactly as he told them,
and they prepared the Passover.
17When evening came he comes with the twelve.
18While Jesus and the twelve disciples were sitting and eating together,
Jesus said:
I tell you the truth:
One of you will hand me over, one who is now eating with me.
19The disciples began to be distressed, and one after another they said to Jesus:
Surely you don't mean me!
20Jesus said to them:
It is one of you twelve men,
one who is eating from this dish with me,
21The son of adam goes,
just as it stands written concerning him;
but it is going to be terrible for the one who
hands over the son of adam.[168]
That man would be better off if he had never been born.
22During the meal Jesus took some bread in his hands;
after he blessed the bread, he broke it.
Then he gave it to his disciples and said:
Take this. It is my body.
23Jesus picked up a cup of wine and gave thanks to God;
he gave it to his disciples.
They all drank some.
24Then he said:
This is my blood,

my blood of the covenant,
which is poured out for many people.
25I tell you the truth:
From now on I will not drink any wine,
until I drink new wine in God's dominion.
26After they had sung the hymn, they went out to the Mount of
Olives.
27He says to them, Jesus does:
You all will be scandalized,
for it stands written:
I will strike the shepherd
and the sheep will be scattered.
28But when I am raised,
I will go before you into Galilee.
29Peter said to him:
If everyone else is scandalized by you,
I will not be.
30Jesus says to him:
I tell you the truth:
You,
in this very night,
before the rooster crows twice,
three times you will deny me.
31Peter insisted vehemently:
Even if it be necessary that I suffer with you,
never will I deny you.
Everyone else was saying this sort of thing.
32They came into a place,
The name: Gethsemane.
He says to his disciples:
Sit here while I pray.
33He takes with him Peter and James and John,
he was in the grip of a shuddering horror.
He was in anguish.
34He says to them:

My whole life is surrounded by sorrow,
All the way up until death.
You three stay here
and keep awake.
35After going a little way forward
he fell upon the ground and prayed that,
if possible,
the hour should pass from him.
He was saying:
36Abba, Father, all things are possible to you.
Take this cup away from me.
But not what I want:
rather what you want.
37He comes and finds them sleeping.
He says to Peter:
Simon! You are sleeping!
Only one hour and you can't keep awake?
38Stay awake, pray, so that you might not come into testing.
Your spirit is willing,
your body is weak.
39He went away and prayed, saying the same words.
40Again when he came back,
he found them sleeping.
Their eyes, were, after all, weighed down.
They did not know what to answer to him.
41He came the third time.
He says to them:
Still sleeping are you? Still resting?
Enough of this.
The hour has come.
Look, the son of adam is handed over into the hands of sinners.
42Get up. Let's go.
Look: the one who hands me over is almost here.
43BANG while he was still speaking

Judas came up,
he, one of the twelve,
and with him a crowd with swords and clubs
from the high priests and the scribes and the elders.
44The one who handed him over had given a signal to them, saying:
The one that I kiss, he's the one.
Grab him and take him away safely.
45BANG, he comes up to Jesus and says:
Rabbi.
He kissed him.
46They grabbed him and arrested him.
47One of the bystanders,
having drawn his sword,
struck the slave of the high priest and cut off his ear.
48Jesus answered,
he said to them:
Am I a bandit that you came out with swords and clubs to seize me?
49Every day I was right by you in the Temple while I was teaching
and you didn't arrest me.
But let the Scriptures be fulfilled.
They abandoned him;
50they all fled.
51A young man was following him,
a young man who had wrapped a burial cloth around his naked body.
They grabbed him.
He ran away,
52leaving the burial cloth behind,
he ran away naked.
53They led Jesus away to the high priest.
All the high priests,
all the elders,
all the scribes,

all came together.
54Peter also,
from a distance,
followed him,
going as far as to enter the courtyard of the high priest.
He was sitting with the servants,
warming himself right near the fire.
55The high priests and the whole Council were examining[169]
testimony against Jesus
that would condemn him to death.
They weren't finding anything trustworthy.
56Many people were witnessing falsely against him, but their
testimony did not agree.
57Some stood up and tried to slander him by saying:
58We ourselves heard him say:
I will destroy this Temple
made by human hands
and in three days I will build another like it,
but not made with human hands.
59Even their testimony did not agree.
60The high priest stood up in the midst and asked Jesus:
You answer nothing?
Why are these people testifying against you?
61Jesus was silent.
He answered not at all.
Again the high priest questioned him,
says to him:
You are the Christ, the Son of the Blessed?
62Jesus said:
I AM.
You will see the son of adam sitting at the right
hand of Power,
coming with the clouds of heaven.
63The high priest tore his robe and says:
Why have we still any need of testimony?

64You heard his blasphemy.
How does this look to you?
All the others found him guilty, and condemned him to death.
65Some began to spit on him
and to blindfold him
and to beat him with their fists
and to say to him:
Prophesy.
The servants took him, and beat him.
66Now Peter was outside in the courtyard.
One of the maids of the high priest came up.
67When she saw Peter warming himself,
she looked him over and says:
You also were with the Netzer,[170] Jesus.
68Peter denied it,
he said:
I neither know nor understand what you are talking about.
He went out into the outer courtyard.
69When the maid saw him,
she began again to say to those who were standing around:
This guy is one of them!
70Peter again denied it.
After a little while, again those standing around were saying to Peter:
You are, in fact, one of them.
You are Galilean, after all.
71Peter began to call down curses on himself and to swear:
I do not know this man of whom you speak.
72BANG, the rooster crowed.
Peter remembered the word,
just the way Jesus said it to him:
Before the rooster crows twice,
three times you will deny that you ever heard of me.
He threw himself down and wept.

Chapter Fifteen

1BANG early in the morning,
after the high priests had consulted
with the elders
and the scribes
and the whole of the Council,
having bound Jesus
they took him away and handed him over to Pilate.
2Pilate asked him:
You are the king of the Jews?
Jesus answered him,
he says:
You yourself say so.
3The high priests accused him of many things.
4Pilate again asked him,
he said:
You're not answering?
See how many things they accuse you of.
5Jesus no longer answered, not at all.
Pilate was amazed.
6Every year at the feast Pilate used to release for them one prisoner,
whomever they asked for.
7(The one called Barabbas was in prison with the
insurrectionists.
He, in the insurrection, had committed murder.)
8The crowd rose up and began to ask that Pilate do what he
customarily did for them.
9Pilate answered them:
You wish that I release to you the king of the Jews?
10(He knew that it was because of jealousy that the high
priests
had handed him over.)
11The high priests stirred up the crowd
so that he should release Barabbas to them instead.

12Pilate again was saying to them:
Whatever will I do to the King of the Jews?
13They screamed again:
Crucify him.
14Pilate kept saying to them:
What evil did he do?
They screamed out of control:
Crucify him.
15Then Pilate,
because he wished to satisfy the crowd,
released to them Barabbas,
and after flogging him,
handed Jesus over to be crucified.
16The soldiers led him away into the courtyard,
which is the praetorium,
and they call together the whole cohort,
17and they clothe him in a purple robe
and after they wove a crown of thorns,
they place it around his head.
18They began to salute him:
Hail, king of the Jews.
19They were hitting him on the head with a reed;
they were spitting on him;
they bowed down and worshiped him.
20When they had finished mocking him,
they stripped the purple robe off him
and put his own clothes back on him.
They are leading him out to crucify him.
21They force a passerby,
Simon of Cyrene
who was coming in from the country,
Simon the father of Alexander and Rufus,
to carry his cross.
22They bring him to the place called Golgotha,
which means "Skull Place."

23They tried to give to him wine mixed with myrrh,
which he did not take.
24They are crucifying him and dividing his clothing,
throwing dice to see who would win them.
25It was the third hour and they crucified him.
26The inscription of the charge against him was written:
The king of the Jews.
27And with him they are crucifying two bandits,
one on his right
and one on his left.
29Those passing by were blaspheming him,
wagging their heads and saying:
Oo, the Destroyer of the Temple,
Build it again in three days!
30Save yourself.
Climb down from that cross.
31Likewise even the high priests mocked him to each other,
with the scribes, saying:
Others he saved.
Himself? He's not able.
32O Christ, O King of Israel,
Climb down now from the cross,
so that we can see and believe.
Those who were crucified with him also taunted him.
33When it came to be the sixth hour,
darkness came upon the whole earth until the ninth hour,
34and in the ninth hour Jesus bellowed in a great voice:
eloi eloi lema sabachthani
(translated: My God, my God,
why have you forsaken me?)
35Some of those standing by
when they heard him,
were saying:
Look!
He's calling Elijah.

36Someone ran and filled a sponge with sour wine,
put it on a reed,
and gave it to him to drink.
He said:
Wait,
let's see whether Elijah will come to take him down.
37Jesus let loose a loud cry
and breathed his last.
38And the curtain of the Temple was ripped in two,
from the top to the bottom.
39But when the centurion,
standing by opposite him,
saw that thus he breathed his last, he said:
No doubt: If ever there was a son of God, this guy was it.
40There were women at a distance,
Women who were watching.
Among whom were Mary Magdalene,
Mary the mother of James the younger and Joses,
and Salome.
41These women,
ever since he was in Galilee,
had followed him and deaconed to him.
There were many other women watching.
All of them had come up with him into Jerusalem.
42It was already evening,
the evening which is the preparation for the Sabbath,
43so Joseph came,
Joseph from Aramathea,
a respected member of the council,
he was himself watching expectantly for the dominion of God.
Joseph went boldly to Pilate
and asked for the body of Jesus.
44Pilate was amazed that he should be already dead, so,
after calling the centurion,

he asked if he had been dead a long time.
45When he learned from the centurion that Jesus was dead,
he presented the corpse to Joseph.
46Joseph bought a burial cloth,
took the corpse down,
wrapped it in the burial cloth,
and placed it in a tomb which was hewn from the rock.
He rolled a stone in front of the door of the tomb.
47Mary Magdalene
and Mary the mother of Joses
were watching where the corpse was laid.

Chapter Sixteen

1When the sabbath was over,
Mary Magdalene,
Mary the mother of James,
and Salome
bought spices so that they might go and anoint him.
2Very early on the first day of the week,
the sun was just coming up,
they come to the tomb.
3On their way they were asking one another
Who will roll away the stone for us from the entrance to
the tomb?
4But when they looked up,
they see that the stone has already been rolled away.
It was a huge stone.
5The women went into the tomb
and they saw a young man,
sitting on the right side,
dressed in a white robe.
They were alarmed.
6The man says:
Don't be alarmed.
You are looking for Jesus,

the Netzer,[171]
who was crucified.
He has been raised.
He isn't here.
Look, there is the place they laid him.
7But go, tell his disciples
and Peter
that he is going ahead of you to Galilee.
There you will see him, just as he told you.
8So they went out and fled from the tomb.
For terror and amazement had seized them.
And they said nothing.

Not a thing to anyone.

For they were afraid.

Appendix

THE REVISED COMMON LECTIONARY READINGS OF MARK IN STORY ORDER

NOTES

1. John D. Niles, *Homo Narrans* (Philadelphia: University of Pennsylvania Press, 1999), 52.

2. See Donald Juel, *A Master of Surprise: Mark Interpreted* (Minneapolis: Fortress Press, 1994). Ancients assumed Mark to be Peter's memoirs.

3. See Joanna Dewey, "The Survival of Mark's Gospel: A Good Story?" in *Journal of Biblical Literature* 123, no. 3 (Fall 2004).

4. Ibid., 504–7.

5. John Miles Foley, *How to Read an Oral Poem* (Urbana and Chicago: University of Illinois Press, 2002), 84.

6. Ibid., 82f.

7. Tim O'Brien, "The Magic Show," in *On Writing*, ed. Robert Pack and Jay Parini (Hanover, N.H., and London: Middlebury College Press, 1991).

8. Ibid., 176.

9. John Miles Foley refers to old oral stories that now exist only in written form as "Voices from the Past" in Foley, *How to Read an Oral Poem*, 45–50.

10. Aristotle, *Poetics* 1449b.25.

11. Perhaps 3 percent of the Jewish population would have been able to read, according to many estimates.

12. Foley, *How to Read an Oral Poem*, 45–50.

13. Note here the conclusions implicit in the common notion that "prompt book" texts omit material that a storyteller would be expected to perform. Does this mean that the broken end of Mark must be read simply as prompt for an improvised solo? If so, it will not be long before the interpreters' demand for narratives that are whole and rounded and uplifting will trump the inscribed scriptural text. How odd.

14. His actual words are somewhat less punchy, but still make the same point. See Hans-Georg Gadamer, *Truth and Method* (New York: Crossroad, 1990).

15. Note here the sign often included in the program for the performance of a melodrama: "Don't shoot the piano player. He's doing the best he can."

16. O'Brien, "The Magic Show," 176.

17. This echoes the argument offered by Gadamer in *Truth and Method.*

18. Pay attention to the twists of this simple question. For help, look again at the questions I ask in the introduction: What if the character Jesus in the stories emerges as looking different from the Jesus everyone meets in Sunday school? What if the story we are looking at does not confirm our own deeply held ideologies? What if the demands of playing these stories and honoring their physical integrity requires that we take risks that we would rather not take?

19. This is true, of course, for stories out of Jewish Scripture, but it is crucial for Christian interpreters to note that the tellers of the stories in the Christian Testament are also all of them Jewish. See the groundbreaking arguments of Jacob Jervell and Nils Dahl, and of their students Alan Segal and Donald Juel.

20. Gerson D. Cohen, in his essay "The Rabbinic Heritage," quoted by W. C. Smith in *What Is Scripture?* (Minneapolis: Fortress Press, 1993), 26. Note that "Aggadic Midrash" refers to the practice of interpreting Scripture by weaving stories around it. The point of the stories is to provoke the text into action and to provoke the audience into faithful wrestling, faithful living.

21. See Anna Johnston's article, "The Book Eaters: Textuality, Modernity, and the London Missionary Society," in *A Vanishing Mediator? The Presence/Absence of the Bible in Post-Colonialism*, Semeia 88 (Atlanta: Society of Biblical Literature, 2001): 13–40. While you are at it, listen to the ways that many "evangelism" programs mimic the language used by colonizers of an earlier generation. I haven't yet heard language about "the white man's burden" (quoting Kipling's famous poem), but that has more to do with squeamish political correctness than with anything else.

22. This will be another difficult notion for Gentile Christians to swallow. Wait a long time before you decide one way or the other on this matter. Read the midrash in which God rejoices, "My children have defeated me!" (Bava Mezia 59b). Reflect very slowly on the implications of telling this story to interpret life and faith lived before the God who alone is God.

23. Note here Richard Horsley's argument that we have falsely constrained our understanding of the gospel of Mark by working with a notion of where and how it was performed that is both "too narrow and too religious." *Hearing the Whole Story: The Politics of Plot in Mark's Gospel* (Louisville: Westminster John Knox, 2001), 65.

24. Tim O'Brien, "How to Tell a True War Story," in *The Things They Carried* (New York: Broadway Books, 1990), 67ff.

25. Ibid., 82.

26. Ibid.

27. Ibid., 77.

28. My favorite "unknown mechanism" is the speculation that Mark was finishing the gospel just as the Romans attacked to quell the First Jewish Revolt. He hurries to finish the story, he nearly makes it, and then, just as he is moving into the final scene, an arrow comes through the window and he falls dead at his writing desk. On this model, you would be able to identify the original manuscript by the bloodstains on the final page.

29. See my fuller discussion (page 122) of the significance of inclusion at table in a Jewish world that gave rise to the Pharisees, who treated every dining table as if it were the altar in the Temple.

30. The clearest unkept promises include the following:

1. 1:8 "He, however, will baptize you in holy spirit"
2. 8:38 "when he comes in the glory of his father with the holy angels"
3. 9:1 "some are standing here who will not taste death before they see that the dominion of God has come in power"
4. 10:39 "The cup I drink, you will drink. The baptism I undergo, you will undergo"
5. 13:2 "No stone will be left on top of a stone which is not destroyed"
6. 13:6 "Many will come on the basis of my name saying: I am, and they will deceive many"
7. 13:8 "For nation upon nation will be raised, and dominion upon dominion, there will be earthquakes, place by place, there will be famines"
8. 13:9 "They will hand you over to councils and into synagogues you will be beaten and before rulers and kings you will be stood on account of me to be a witness to them"
9. 13:12–13 "brother will hand over brother to death, and a father, his children, and children will rise up against parents and they will kill them and you will be hated by all because of my name. The one who endures into the end, this one will be rescued"
10. 13:19 "For those days will be tribulation such as has not happened from the beginning of creation which God created up to now, such tribulation should never be"
11. 13:24–27 "But in those days after the tribulation: the sun will be shadowed, and the moon will not give its beams, and the stars will be falling out of the heaven and the powers, those in the heavens, will be shaken and then you see the son of adam coming in clouds with much power and glory and then he will send the messengers

and he will gather together the chosen out of the four windstorms from the end of earth up to the end of heaven"

12. 13:30 "this generation will by no means pass by before all these things happen"
13. 14:25 "From now on I will not drink any wine, until I drink new wine in God's dominion"
14. 14:28 "But when I am raised, I will go before you into Galilee"
15. 14:62 "you will see the son of adam sitting at the right hand of Power, and coming with the clouds of heaven"
16. 16:7 "he is going ahead of you to Galilee. There you will see him, just as he told you"

31. C. E. B. Cranfield, *The Gospel According to Saint Mark: An Introduction and Commentary* (Cambridge: Cambridge University Press, 1959), 469.

32. Augustine Stock, *Call to Discipleship: A Literary Study of Mark's Gospel* (Wilmington, Del.: Michael Glazier, 1982), 203–7. See also Mary Ann Tolbert, *Sowing the Gospel: Mark's World in Literary-Historical Perspective* (Minneapolis: Fortress Press, 1989), 288–89; and J. Lee Magness, *Sense and Absence: Structure and Suspension in the Ending of Mark's Gospel* (Atlanta: Scholars Press, 1986), 125.

33. For a good appraisal of the dependence and independence of Mark 16:9–20, see Joseph Hug, *La finale de l'évangile de Marc* (Paris: J. Gabalda, 1978).

34. See, especially, ibid., 177–85, where he discusses the relationship between 16:9–20 (fMc, that is, "fin de Marc," or "the end of Mark") and the gospel. Hug notes especially the difference in fit between the conclusion of Matthew and Matthew as a whole and fMc and Mark. Hug's point must be kept in mind when considering the argument presented here, and it must be remembered that the argument here is not about the source of the material in the longer, or even about the tightness of its fit with the larger narrative. The argument is, rather, that the longer ending seems to recognize that more is lacking in the narrative than just some sort of resurrection appearance. What is lacking is the keeping of key promises that must be kept for the narrative to reach its apparent goal.

35. This matter has occasioned much discussion, and will probably continue to do so. For a recent, and thorough, discussion of the relationship of 16:9–20 to the rest of Mark, see ibid.

36. Magness, in his consideration of the ending of Mark, says, "The ability of the reader to fill in a few facts which have been carefully and consistently foreshadowed is hardly the mark of great literary sophistication and is an everyday reading skill which has not been sufficiently taken into account by

interpreters of Mark" (*Sense and Absence*, 8). Magness's discussion is solid and fascinating throughout, and his noting of Mark's foreshadowing is much to be appreciated, but it seems important to note that the ending of Mark is not simply suspended, but made impossible by the way the narrative ends. There is no road leading from 16:8 to either the future world of the narrative or the world of the reader. One must attend to this impossibility.

37. Tolbert, *Sowing the Gospel*, 122, 155.

38. John Drury, *The Parables in the Gospels: History and Allegory* (New York: Crossroad, 1985), 66.

39. Ibid., 51.

40. Tolbert, *Sowing the Gospel*, 105.

41. Ibid., 154.

42. Drury, *Parables*, 51.

43. It is, however, somewhat unclear what Tolbert means when she says that the use of oracles, or third-degree narrative, as a plot synopsis near the beginning of ancient novels is "fairly common" (*Sowing the Gospel*, 105), when she has noted that there are only five extant ancient novels of the type she is considering. In such a small sample, what does it take to be fairly common?

44. Tolbert, *Sowing the Gospel*, 105. Tolbert here uses the English translation of G. L. Schmeling, *Xenophon of Ephesus*, TWAS 613 (Boston: Twayne Publishers, 1980), 26–27.

45. Drury, *Parables*, 46.

46. John R. Donahue, *The Gospel in Parable: Metaphor, Narrative, and Theology in the Synoptic Gospels* (Philadelphia: Fortress Press, 1988).

47. James G. Williams, *Gospel against Parable: Mark's Language of Mystery*, Bible and Literature Series, no. 12 (Sheffield, England: JSOT Press, Almond Press, 1985).

48. Donahue, *Gospel in Parable*, 3.

49. Ibid., 4. This notion remains essentially static and quite misses the power of stories to project whole worlds. The parables are part of such a powerful story, and thus contribute to this projection of a world. To limit their work to opening a door on theology and Christology is to give them too little work to do.

50. Donahue, *Gospel in Parable*, 13.

51. Ibid., 19.

52. Ibid., 195.

53. Williams, *Gospel against Parable*, 178.

54. Ibid., 188.

55. Ibid., 189.

56. Ibid., 192, 193.

57. Ibid., 193.

58. Ibid., 196.

59. Yvàn Almeida, *L'Opérativité sémantique des récits-paraboles: Sémiotique narrative et textuelle, herméneutique du discours religieux* (Louvain, Belgium: Editions Peeters, and Paris: Editions du Cerf, 1978), 117. "...un récit raconté par un personnage d'un autre récit qui l'englobe."

60. Ibid., 287.

61. Ibid., 265. "...un micro-universe sémantique qui cristalliserait les principales categories du récit qui les englobe. De ce point de vue...on pourrait dire qu'ils constituent une espèce de miroir, plus schématique et donc plus frappant, de la structure narrative et sémantique de l'ensemble de Marc."

62. Paul Ricoeur, "La Bible et l'imagination," *Revue d'histoire et philosophie réligeuse* 62, no. 4 (October–December 1982): 345. "...qui marque déjà le dynamisme à l'oeuvre dans le récit, afin de comprendre comment ce dynamisme est transgressé par l'enchassement."

63. Ibid., 355. "Puis, deux paraboles prises ensemble — les Vignerons Meurtriers et le Semeur — créent un entrecroisement de second degré à l'intérieur cette fois du micro-universe des paraboles; cet entrecroisement entre le procès euphorique de la parole et le procès dysphorique de la marche du corps vers la mort prépare à son tour une intersection plus fondamentale encore, entre les deux paraboles prises ensemble et le récit qui les englobe et qui raconte l'histoire de celui qui raconte les paraboles."

64. Ibid., 356. Note that Ricoeur understands this process to aim beyond the level of the text to the reader, who is also to be made capable of recognizing Jesus.

65. Ibid., 357.

66. Ibid. "On voit ainsi surgir un certain parallélisme entre la structure narrative globale de l'Evangile et celle des deux paraboles prises ensemble. C'est ce parallélisme institué par le texte — par la texture du texte — qui donne lieu au procès de parabolisation mutuelle du récit englobant et des récits enchéssés."

67. See Almeida, *L'Opérativité*, 275, and Ricoeur, "La Bible et l'imagination," 356.

68. Most interpreters, indeed, tend to read it this way.

69. Donald Juel, *Mark*, Augsburg Commentary on the New Testament (Minneapolis: Augsburg Fortress Press, 1990), 227–28.

70. It is important to see that these three identifications (Son of the Blessed, King of the Jews, and Son of God) are equivalent. For the best discussion of this matter, see Juel, *Messianic Exegesis* (Philadelphia: Fortress Press, 1988).

71. See Almeida, *L'Opérativité*, 293–95, and Ricoeur, "La Bible et l'imagination," 356, n. 7.

72. O'Brien, "How to Tell a True War Story," 77.

73. Which is why, I think, the word for God's love used in Jewish Scripture is a cousin for the word for womb. See Phyllis Trible's probing discussion in *God and the Rhetoric of Sexuality* (Philadelphia: Fortress Press, 1978).

74. See Donald Juel, *A Master of Surprise: Mark Interpreted* (Minneapolis: Fortress Press, 1994).

75. See the full argument on page 74.

76. For a thorough presentation of the argument, see Juel's *Messianic Exegesis: Christological Interpretation of the Old Testament in Early Christianity* (Philadelphia: Fortress Press, 1988).

77. Emil Fackenheim, *The Jewish Bible after the Holocaust: A Re-Reading* (Bloomington: Indiana University Press, 1990).

78. Which may establish a connection not only to the baptism scenes in the other synoptics but also to the Pentecost scene in Acts.

79. See Alan Segal's analysis of the differences between the gospels and the writings of Paul, and of the ways those differences are rooted in the ruins of the Temple. *Rebecca's Children: Judaism and Christianity in the Roman World* (Cambridge, Mass.: Harvard University Press, 1986).

80. The commandment about honoring parents is, after all, aimed at adults who must care for their own parents, and the promise of long life for these adults hangs on having their children learn from their example. Honor your parents, says the commandment, and your children will learn to honor you in turn.

81. The reference is to C. S. Lewis, *The Screwtape Letters* (New York: Macmillan, 1944).

82. See Wendy Cotter, *Miracles in Greco-Roman Antiquity* (London: Routledge, 1999).

83. See Paula Fredriksen, *Jesus of Nazareth, King of the Jews: A Jewish Life and the Emergence of Christianity* (New York: Knopf, 1999), on John the Purifier.

84. See Fredriksen's discussion of the purification of an army.

85. "Charlie Brown," sung by the Coasters.

86. Jo-Ann A. Brant translates the question the same way when she reads John 2:4 in her essay, "Divine Birth and Apparent Parents: The Plot of the Fourth Gospel," in *Ancient Fiction and Early Christian Narrative*, ed. Ronald F. Hock, J. Bradley Chance, and Judith Perkins (Atlanta: Scholars Press, 1998), 205.

87. Elisabeth Moltmann-Wendel, *The Women around Jesus* (New York: Crossroad, 1982).

88. See Donald Juel's *Messiah and Temple: The Trial of Jesus in the Gospel of Mark* (Missoula, Mont.: Scholars Press, 1977) for an analysis of the way Mark's story is anchored by the Temple. Note that whatever one makes of Jesus' harsh action in the Temple at the end of Mark's story, it is clear that

the Temple has overwhelming ritual significance for him in Mark's telling of this story.

89. See Jacob Neusner, *The Idea of Purity in Ancient Judaism* (Leiden: Brill, 1973).

90. Nevus flammeus.

91. Some rabbinic texts pass the offense on to the victim after three requests for forgiveness, but not all do; definitely not all take this questionable leap. Compulsory forgiving is dangerous and potentially abusive.

92. Think here about George Steiner's *Language and Silence* (New Haven, Conn.: Yale University Press, 1998), which wonders, painfully, whether the murderous lies of the Holocaust have destroyed language.

93. Paula Fredriksen, in *Jesus of Nazareth, King of the Jews* (New York: Alfred A. Knopf, 2000), a resource quite unlike *Slaughterhouse Five.*

94. See the discussion of the *bat qol* on page 88.

95. See the book of Enoch, and compare the Sibylline Oracles.

96. See Jarl Fossum's *The Name of God and the Angel of the Lord: Samaritan and Jewish Concepts of Intermediation and the Origin of Gnosticism* (Tübingen: J. C. B. Mohr [Paul Siebeck], 1985).

97. Though, of course, there is narrative coding available for both Moses and Elijah.

98. See the discussion of this cry on page 74.

99. See Tim O'Brien, *The Things They Carried* (New York: Broadway Books, 1990), 78–80. Pay careful attention to the pointless obscenity of the death.

100. Fredriksen, *Jesus of Nazareth*, 42–50.

101. Ibid., 236–59. The heart of her exploration may be read in 250–59, but reading the longer passage allows the argument to ripen.

102. Ibid., 247.

103. See Donald Juel's *Messiah and Temple* for a thorough discussion of this matter.

104. See Segal, *Rebecca's Children.*

105. The fact that she is a woman who is in the scene because she is a mother means that the violence of the language is even more intense. She is being addressed as a female dog, a strong insult also in English.

106. Fredriksen, *Jesus of Nazareth*, 241.

107. Even the word "Seder" (which means "order") testifies to the importance of the orderliness of this traditional observance.

108. Many hundreds of thousands by some estimates.

109. See Stephen Einstein and Lydia Kukoff's very helpful book, *Every Person's Guide to Judaism* (New York: URJ Press, 1990).

110. Here see ibid.

111. See ibid.

112. See ibid.

113. Bernard Brandon Scott, *Hear Then the Parable* (Minneapolis: Fortress Press, 1989).

114. Martin Luther, *WA* 32.134.34–235.36, as cited by Santmire, *The Travail of Nature* (Philadelphia: Fortress Press, 1985).

115. For a thorough discussion of this matter, see Mark Nanos, *The Mystery of Romans: The Jewish Context of Paul's Letter* (Minneapolis: Fortress Press, 1996).

116. It is worth noting, in passing, that the emblem of the Legion that occupied this territory was a boar, so even the pigs are related to the Legion involved. See Donald Juel, *Master of Surprise.*

117. See Amy-Jill Levine's "Discharging Responsibility: Matthean Jesus, Biblical Law, and the Hemorrhaging Woman," in *A Feminist Companion to Matthew*, ed. Amy-Jill Levine (Sheffield: Sheffield Academic Press, 2001), 70–87.

118. The usual translation, "flow," is surely better. But it intrigues me that this word can also be translated as "river." I think there is something going on here, something about how this woman's life is swept along by a condition that persists for far too many years.

119. Levine, "Discharging Responsibility."

120. See page 31 in chapter 1.

121. Lamar Williamson, *Mark* (Atlanta: John Knox Press, 1983), 109.

122. See Horsley's discussion in *Hearing the Whole Story*, 90–97.

123. Warren Carter, *Matthew and the Margins* (Sheffield: Sheffield Academic Press, 2000).

124. For an exploration of the significance of place, ritually and otherwise, see Halvor Moxnes, *Putting Jesus in His Place: A Radical Vision of Household and Kingdom* (Louisville: Westminster John Knox, 2003).

125. See Sharon H. Ringe, "A Gentile Woman's Story Revisited: Re-reading Mark 7:24–31," in *A Feminist Companion to Mark*, ed. Amy-Jill Levine and Marianne Blickenstaff (Sheffield: Sheffield Academic Press, 2001), 79–80.

126. These sayings are quoted in *The Book of Legends*, ed. Hayim Nahman Bialik and Yehoshua Hana Ravnitzky (New York: Schocken, 1992), 557:201, 565–6:281, 592:170, 782:229.

127. The word "docetism" comes from the Greek word δοκεω, which means "I appear." Docetism is the name given to a heresy that holds that Jesus was not an actual human being, he was only God APPEARING to be a regular human being. Docetists emphasize the divinity of Jesus to the point that he cannot have any normal human experience, including that of changing his mind. Such notions were rightly rejected as heretical.

128. A. E. J. Rawlinson, *St. Mark: With Introduction, Commentary and Additional Notes* (London: Methuen, 1925).

129. The link to the time of Jezebel provides, of course, another point of entry to the story for John the Baptist, who is coded for Elijah.

130. See Amy-Jill Levine for a thorough discussion of this, in "Discharging Responsibility."

131. See Moltmann-Wendel, *The Women around Jesus.* See also my discussion of this matter on page 107.107.

132. This is, incidentally, the way Albert Schweitzer read Jesus' decision to go up to Jerusalem in *The Quest of the Historical Jesus: A Critical Study of Its Progress from Reimarus to Wrede* (New York: Macmillan, 1968).

133. Which would, technically, make it easier for Elijah to reenter the story than for John, who was observed to actually die.

134. W. D. Edwards, W. J. Gabel, and F. E. Hosmer, "On the Physical Death of Jesus Christ," *JAMA* 255 (1986): 1455–63.

135. Remember the discussions of how the Geneva Conventions hamper military interrogation during the invasion of Iraq.

136. Horsley, *Whole Story*, 81–86.

137. For a full development of this argument, see Nanos, *The Mystery of Romans.*

138. See Papias quoted in Eusebius. See Juel's discussion of this in *Master of Surprise*, 12–17.

139. This notion will be foreign to most American Christians.

140. See Einstein and Kukoff, *Every Person's Guide.*

141. See Kathryn Tanner, *Theories of Culture: A New Agenda for Theology* (Minneapolis: Fortress Press, 1997).

142. See the conversations reported in O'Brien's *The Things They Carried.*

143. The writings of Levi and Wiesel may easily be found in libraries. They are also widely available online. A simple search will suffice. For starters, these links work as I write today:

http://oldpoetry.com/poetry/24406
http://www.pbs.org/speaktruthtopower/elie.html
http://www.legacy-project.org/lit/display.html?ID=54

Links change and vanish; you may have to search further on your own.

144. See Segal's *Rebecca's Children.*

145. I am guessing that you are not accustomed to seeing this word in your Bible. It translates the Greek word ευθυς, a short, punchy word that usually comes into English as "immediately." "Immediately" is too long a word to mean "immediately." Besides, it does not catch the way Mark uses ευθυς to speed up and intensify the story. Sometimes he uses it to mark time. Sometimes there is no noticeable time reference at all. I have been told by my students that John Madden uses the word "BOOM" in a similar way when he explains football plays on television. Who knew that a former football coach would know about ευθυς?

146. The translation of βασιλεια του θεου ("kingdom of God") is, and will remain, thorny. Some leave it untranslated (basileia). Some opt for "reign" or "realm." The Scholar's Bible chooses "imperial rule" and "domain." Of these several options, the most promising seems to be "imperial rule." I have sometimes used "empire" as a translation, but have chosen "dominion" for this translation. It renders both the imperious power of this reign and the physical closeness that are to be felt in Mark's story.

147. The customary translation takes this word to be a geographical reference to Nazareth. The customary reading is probably correct. I translate it, following Donald Juel, as "netzer," a Hebrew word for the shoot that springs forth from the stump of Jesse in the prophet Isaiah.

148. This word is a particularly vigorous and physical word: σπλαγχνιζομαι. It makes explicit reference to the state of Jesus' bowels (σπλαγχνα), and catches the physical reality of being "moved." When the old King James Version made reference to the "bowels of mercy," this was the Greek word behind the image. What is interesting is that this word may, in fact, pick up something out of the Hebrew word *racham* (love), which echoes the word *rechem* (womb), and is used to express a love of God for creation that is motherly.

149. For this translation of υιος του ανθρωπου ("son of man"), see Daryl D. Schmidt's *The Gospel of Mark*, a volume in the Scholar's Bible series (Sonoma, Calif.: Polebridge, 1990).

150. This, of course, is not an English word. You could translate it as "ecstatic" and that would work well. But that loses the note of being driven out of one's mind that is in the Greek original. You could translate it, therefore, as "Everybody was driven out of their minds," but that loses the ecstatic joy. Mark uses this word with some frequency, so you will have many opportunities to find a better word than "ecstasied."

151. On "moved" in Mark 1:41 (page 259), see note 148 above.

152. This does not mean, "Be brave, I am brave." The usual translation is just fine: "Be brave, it is I," but my translation attempts to catch a possible allusion to the Divine Name ("I AM"). It is not clear that this is such an allusion, but the presence of Jesus walking on the surface of chaos and helping his people in time of danger makes it tempting to translate using the Name in which Jewish faith hears the "Mercy Attribute" of God.

153. On "ecstasied" in Mark 2:12 (page 261), see note 150 above.

154. Should this word (*Ioudaioi*) be translated as "Jews" or "Judeans"? Good question. Taking my lead from Paula Fredriksen's examination of the tension between Judeans and Galileans in her *Jesus of Nazareth, King of the Jews*, I translate it here as "Judeans." The problem is complex, however, as may be heard in Shaye Cohen's *The Beginnings of Jewishness: Boundaries, Varieties, Uncertainties* (Berkeley and London: University of California Press, 1999). Geography and religious practice and cultural background could often

be mapped onto each other in the ancient Near East. The hard thing to decide, now as always, is how this mapping is best and most responsibly accomplished.

155. In this case and in all others in Mark, the "heart" is the physical metaphor for the human power to choose, decide, and act.

156. On "moved" in Mark 1:41 (page 259), see note 148 above.

157. This sentence, not in the text in so many words, represents an attempt to render the flow and bite of the argument Jesus is exploring with his disciples. The argument goes something like this: If Elijah comes first, and if Elijah restores everything to its proper created state, then how can it still be the case that the son of adam (coming after the restoration of creation) could still suffer? This is a good question, and an old one. If the world is in such a dreadful state, why is it that Messiah does not come? And if Messiah has come, why is the world in such a dreadful state?

158. This finishes the argument: The world is so broken that even Elijah suffers. Then the question is: can the world hope to be restored?

159. It is tempting to translate here to reflect the rabbinic story told of a man who had lost his wife, his sons, and all other things. He turns to God and says: "God, you are certainly doing a lot to make me lose my faith. But know this, despite everything you try to do to me, I am a Jew and I will remain a Jew." Perhaps the father of the child in this story means to say: "I am faithful, but you are certainly doing a lot to help me to give up on faithfulness." The verb form is not right, but the tone is close to right.

160. There is no reason to suppose that this child is female. Neither is there any reason to suppose that the child is male.

161. Note, in passing, that Jesus uses the euphemism ευωνυμων ("good-omened") to refer to the ill-omened left hand. James and John do not. Is Jesus more superstitious than his followers?

162. On "netzer" in Mark 1:24 (page 257), see note 147 above.

163. The customary translation is still probably to be preferred: "Since you have faith in God . . . " The reason I choose "faithfulness of God" here is, first, because the word πιστις (often translated as "faith") will more often mean "faithfulness" in a Jewish text, translating the Hebrew word *enuma*. Second, the Greek reads "of God" rather than "in God." Though it is surely possible to read the genitive ("of God") as the object of belief, the other possibilities ought to be explored.

164. This could be a reference to Antiochus IV Epiphanes, who conducted pagan sacrifice in the Temple in order to spoil it for Jewish use. Its use in Daniel would suggest such a reference. It also calls to mind the statement by Suetonius concerning the Romans: They make a desert and they call it peace. In any case, the reference points to the incursions of foreign oppressors.

165. The usual translation, "reader," misleads contemporary audiences who assume a high rate of literacy in the general population. In the ancient

Near East, the one who could read would likely be also the one who would be telling the story, perhaps using a text as a prompt book. This bit of side-coaching may imply that this reference called for some particular physical emphasis in performance.

166. Does anyone else hear echoes of Lot's wife in this passage? I surely do.

167. The word "Israel" is not in the text, but the reference to chosen people makes this clear. Audiences need to hear this note.

168. Because the term "son of adam" is most likely and most often a form of self-reference, going back to an Aramaic phrase, this line might best be translated as "...the one who hands me over."

169. This translation takes seriously the legal context of this scene. The Greek word ζητεω can mean "I am seeking." This is the usual translation. It can also, and would normally in courtroom context, mean "I am examining." Since the usual reading assumes that nothing but foul motives drive Jesus' interrogators, this translation pushes the scene in a different direction.

170. On "netzer" in Mark 1:24 (page 257), see note 147 above.

171. On "netzer" in Mark 1:24 (page 257), see note 147 above.